S0-AAB-593

Published 2009 by SoHo Books

Made in the USA

ISBN 1441419209

How to Think Like a Computer Scientist

Java Version

How to Think Like a Computer Scientist

Java Version

Allen B. Downey

Version 4.1

April 23, 2008

The original form of this book is LaTeX source code. Compiling this LaTeX source has the effect of generating a device-independent representation of the book, which can be converted to other formats and printed.

The LaTeX source for this book is available from

    thinkapjava.com

This book was typeset using LaTeX. The illustrations were drawn in xfig. All of these are free, open-source programs.

Preface

"As we enjoy great Advantages from the Inventions of others, we should be glad of an Opportunity to serve others by any Invention of ours, and this we should do freely and generously."

—Benjamin Franklin, quoted in *Benjamin Franklin* by Edmund S. Morgan.

Why I wrote this book

This is the fourth edition of a book I started writing in 1999, when I was teaching at Colby College. I had taught an introductory computer science class using the Java programming language, but I had not found a textbook I was happy with. For one thing, they were all too big! There was no way my students would read 800 pages of dense, technical material, even if I wanted them to. And I didn't want them to. Most of the material was too specific—details about Java and its libraries that would be obsolete by the end of the semester, and that obscured the material I really wanted to get to.

The other problem I found was that the introduction to object oriented programming was too abrupt. Many students who were otherwise doing well just hit a wall when we got to objects, whether we did it at the beginning, middle or end.

So I started writing. I wrote a chapter a day for 13 days, and on the 14th day I edited. Then I sent it to be photocopied and bound. When I handed it out on the first day of class, I told the students that they would be expected to read one chapter a week. In other words, they would read it seven times slower than I wrote it.

The philosophy behind it

Here are some of the ideas that made the book the way it is:

- Vocabulary is important. Students need to be able to talk about programs and understand what I am saying. I tried to introduce the minimum number of terms, to define them carefully when they are first used, and to organize them in glossaries at the end of each chapter. In my class, I include vocabulary questions on quizzes and exams, and require students to use appropriate terms in short-answer responses.

- In order to write a program, students have to understand the algorithm, know the programming language, and they have to be able to debug. I think too many books neglect debugging. This book includes an appendix on debugging and an appendix on program development (which can help avoid debugging). I recommend that students read this material early and come back to it often.

- Some concepts take time to sink in. Some of the more difficult ideas in the book, like recursion, appear several times. By coming back to these ideas, I am trying to give students a chance to review and reinforce or, if they missed it the first time, a chance to catch up.

- I try to use the minimum amount of Java to get the maximum amount of programming power. The purpose of this book is to teach programming and some introductory ideas from computer science, not Java. I left out some language features, like the `switch` statement, that are unnecessary, and avoided most of the libraries, especially the ones like the AWT that have been changing quickly or are likely to be replaced.

The minimalism of my approach has some advantages. Each chapter is about ten pages, not including the exercises. In my classes I ask students to read each chapter before we discuss it, and I have found that they are willing to do that and their comprehension is good. Their preparation makes class time available for discussion of the more abstract material, in-class exercises, and additional topics that aren't in the book.

But minimalism has some disadvantages. There is not much here that is intrinsically fun. Most of my examples demonstrate the most basic use of a language feature, and many of the exercises involve string manipulation and mathematical ideas. I think some of them are fun, but many of the things that excite students about computer science, like graphics, sound and network applications, are given short shrift.

The problem is that many of the more exciting features involve lots of details and not much concept. Pedagogically, that means a lot of effort for not much payoff. So there is a tradeoff between the material that students enjoy and the material that is most intellectually rich. I leave it to individual teachers to find the balance that is best for their classes. To help, the book includes appendices that cover graphics, keyboard input and file input.

Object-oriented programming

Some books introduce objects immediately; others warm up with a more procedural style and develop object-oriented style more gradually. This book is probably the extreme of the "objects late" approach.

Many of Java's object-oriented features are motivated by problems with previous languages, and their implementations are influenced by this history. Some of these features are hard to explain if students aren't familiar with the problems they solve.

It wasn't my intention to postpone object-oriented programming. On the contrary, I got to it as quickly as I could, limited by my intention to introduce concepts one at a time, as clearly as possible, in a way that allows students to practice each idea in isolation before adding the next. It just happens that it takes 13 steps.

Data structures

In Fall 2000 I taught the second course in the introductory sequence, called Data Structures, and wrote additional chapters covering lists, stacks, queues, trees, and hashtables.

Each chapter presents the interface for a data structure, one or more algorithms that use it, and at least one implementation. In most cases there is also an implementation in the `java.utils` package, so teachers can decide on a case-by-case basis whether to discuss the implementation, and whether students will build an implementation as an exercise. For the most part I present data structures and interfaces that are consistent with the implementation in `java.utils`.

The Computer Science AP Exam

During Summer 2001 I worked with teachers at the Maine School of Science and Mathematics on a version of the book that would help students prepare for the Computer Science Advanced Placement Exam, which used C++ at the time. The translation went quickly because, as it turned out, the material I covered was almost identical to the AP Syllabus.

Naturally, when the College Board announced that the AP Exam would switch to Java, I made plans to update the Java version of the book. Looking at the proposed AP Syllabus, I saw that their subset of Java was all but identical to the subset I had chosen.

During January 2003, I worked on the Fourth Edition of the book, making these changes:

- I added a new chapter covering Huffman codes.

- I revised several sections that I had found problematic, including the transition to object-oriented programming and the discussion of heaps.

- I improved the appendices on debugging and program development.

- I added a few sections to improve coverage of the AP syllabus.

- I collected the exercises, quizzes, and exam questions I had used in my classes and put them at the end of the appropriate chapters. I also made up some problems that are intended to help with AP Exam preparation.

Free books!

Since the beginning, this book and its descendents have been available under the GNU Free Documentation License. Readers are free to download the book in a variety of formats and print it or read it on screen. Teachers are free to send the book to a short-run printer and make as many copies as they need. And, maybe most importantly, anyone is free to customize the book for their needs. You can download the LaTeX source code, and then add, remove, edit, or rearrange material, and make the book that is best for you or your class.

People have translated the book into other computer languages (including Python and Eiffel), and other natural languages (including Spanish, French and German). Many of these derivatives are also available under the GNU FDL.

This approach to publishing has a lot of advantages, but there is one drawback: my books have never been through a formal editing and proofreading process and, too often, it shows. Motivated by Open Source Software, I have adopted the philosophy of releasing the book early and updating it often. I do my best to minimize the number of errors, but I also depend on readers to help out.

The response has been great. I get messages almost every day from people who have read the book and liked it enough to take the trouble to send in a "bug report." Often I can correct an error and post an updated version almost immediately. I think of the book as a work in progress, improving a little whenever I have time to make a revision, or when readers take the time to send feedback.

Oh, the title

I get a lot of grief about the title of the book. Not everyone understands that it is—mostly—a joke. Reading this book will probably not make you think like a computer scientist. That takes time, experience, and probably a few more classes.

But there is a kernel of truth in the title: this book is not about Java, and it is only partly about programming. If it is successful, this book is about a way of thinking. Computer scientists have an approach to problem-solving, and a way of crafting solutions, that is unique, versatile and powerful. I hope that this book gives you a sense of what that approach is, and that at some point you will find yourself thinking like a computer scientist.

Allen Downey
Needham, Massachusetts
March 6, 2003

Contributors List

When I started writing free books, it didn't occur to me to keep a contributors list. When Jeff Elkner suggested it, it seemed so obvious that I am embarassed by the omission. This list starts with the 4th Edition, so it omits many people who contributed suggestions and corrections to earlier versions.

- Tania Passfield pointed out that the glossary of Chapter 4 has some left-over terms that no longer appear in the text.

- Elizabeth Wiethoff noticed that my series expansion of e^{-x^2} was wrong. She is also working on a Ruby version of the book!

- Matt Crawford sent in a whole patch file full of corrections!

Contents

Chapter 1

The way of the program

The goal of this book, and this class, is to teach you to think like a computer scientist. I like the way computer scientists think because they combine some of the best features of Mathematics, Engineering, and Natural Science. Like mathematicians, computer scientists use formal languages to denote ideas (specifically computations). Like engineers, they design things, assembling components into systems and evaluating tradeoffs among alternatives. Like scientists, they observe the behavior of complex systems, form hypotheses, and test predictions.

The single most important skill for a computer scientist is **problem-solving**. By that I mean the ability to formulate problems, think creatively about solutions, and express a solution clearly and accurately. As it turns out, the process of learning to program is an excellent opportunity to practice problem-solving skills. That's why this chapter is called "The way of the program."

On one level, you will be learning to program, which is a useful skill by itself. On another level you will use programming as a means to an end. As we go along, that end will become clearer.

1.1 What is a programming language?

The programming language you will be learning is Java, which is relatively new (Sun released the first version in May, 1995). Java is an example of a **high-level language**; other high-level languages you might have heard of are Pascal, C, C++ and FORTRAN.

As you might infer from the name "high-level language," there are also **low-level languages**, sometimes referred to as machine language or assembly language. Loosely-speaking, computers can only execute programs written in low-level languages. Thus, programs written in a high-level language have to be translated before they can run. This translation takes some time, which is a small disadvantage of high-level languages.

But the advantages are enormous. First, it is *much* easier to program in a high-level language; by "easier" I mean that the program takes less time to write, it's shorter and easier to read, and it's more likely to be correct. Secondly, high-level languages are **portable**, meaning that they can run on different kinds of computers with few or no modifications. Low-level programs can only run on one kind of computer, and have to be rewritten to run on another.

Due to these advantages, almost all programs are written in high-level languages. Low-level languages are only used for a few special applications.

There are two ways to translate a program; **interpreting** or **compiling**. An interpreter is a program that reads a high-level program and does what it says. In effect, it translates the program line-by-line, alternately reading lines and carrying out commands.

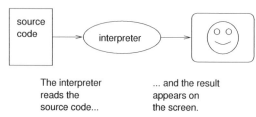

The interpreter   ... and the result
reads the   appears on
source code...   the screen.

A compiler is a program that reads a high-level program and translates it all at once, before executing any of the commands. Often you compile the program as a separate step, and then execute the compiled code later. In this case, the high-level program is called the **source code**, and the translated program is called the **object code** or the **executable**.

As an example, suppose you write a program in C. You might use a text editor to write the program (a text editor is a simple word processor). When the program is finished, you might save it in a file named program.c, where "program" is an arbitrary name you make up, and the suffix .c is a convention that indicates that the file contains C source code.

Then, depending on what your programming environment is like, you might leave the text editor and run the compiler. The compiler would read your source code, translate it, and create a new file named program.o to contain the object code, or program.exe to contain the executable.

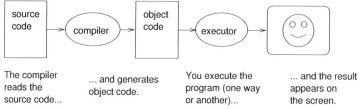

The compiler   ... and generates   You execute the   ... and the result
reads the   object code.   program (one way   appears on
source code...   or another)...   the screen.

The Java language is unusual because it is both compiled and interpreted. Instead of translating Java programs into machine language, the Java compiler generates Java byte code. Byte code is easy (and fast) to interpret, like machine language, but it is also portable, like a high-level language. Thus, it is possible to compile a Java program on one machine, transfer the byte code to another machine over a network, and then interpret the byte code on the other machine. This ability is one of the advantages of Java over many other high-level languages.

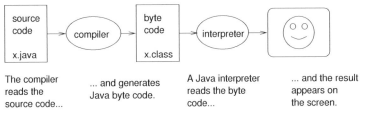

The compiler reads the source code...   ... and generates Java byte code.   A Java interpreter reads the byte code...   ... and the result appears on the screen.

Although this process may seem complicated, in most programming environments (sometimes called development environments), these steps are automated for you. Usually you will only have to write a program and press a button or type a single command to compile and run it. On the other hand, it is useful to know what the steps are that are happening in the background, so that if something goes wrong you can figure out what it is.

1.2   What is a program?

A program is a sequence of instructions that specifies how to perform a computation. The computation might be something mathematical, like solving a system of equations or finding the roots of a polynomial, but it can also be a symbolic computation, like searching and replacing text in a document or (strangely enough) compiling a program.

The instructions, which we will call **statements**, look different in different programming languages, but there are a few basic operations most languages can perform:

input: Get data from the keyboard, or a file, or some other device.

output: Display data on the screen or send data to a file or other device.

math: Perform basic mathematical operations like addition and multiplication.

testing: Check for certain conditions and execute the appropriate sequence of statements.

repetition: Perform some action repeatedly, usually with some variation.

That's pretty much all there is to it. Every program you've ever used, no matter how complicated, is made up of statements that perform these operations. Thus, one way to describe programming is the process of breaking a large, complex task up into smaller and smaller subtasks until eventually the subtasks are simple enough to be performed with one of these basic operations.

1.3   What is debugging?

Programming is a complex process, and since it is done by human beings, it often leads to errors. For whimsical reasons, programming errors are called **bugs** and the process of tracking them down and correcting them is called **debugging**.

There are a few different kinds of errors that can occur in a program, and it is useful to distinguish between them in order to track them down more quickly.

1.3.1   Compile-time errors

The compiler can only translate a program if the program is syntactically correct; otherwise, the compilation fails and you will not be able to run your program. **Syntax** refers to the structure of your program and the rules about that structure.

For example, in English, a sentence must begin with a capital letter and end with a period. this sentence contains a syntax error. So does this one

For most readers, a few syntax errors are not a significant problem, which is why we can read the poetry of e e cummings without spewing error messages.

Compilers are not so forgiving. If there is a single syntax error anywhere in your program, the compiler will print an error message and quit, and you will not be able to run your program.

To make matters worse, there are more syntax rules in Java than there are in English, and the error messages you get from the compiler are often not very helpful. During the first few weeks of your programming career, you will probably spend a lot of time tracking down syntax errors. As you gain experience, though, you will make fewer errors and find them faster.

1.3.2   Run-time errors

The second type of error is a run-time error, so-called because the error does not appear until you run the program. In Java, run-time errors occur when the interpreter is running the byte code and something goes wrong.

The good news for now is that Java tends to be a **safe** language, which means that run-time errors are rare, especially for the simple sorts of programs we will be writing for the next few weeks.

Later on in the semester, you will probably start to see more run-time errors, especially when we start talking about objects and references (Chapter 8).

In Java, run-time errors are called **exceptions**, and in most environments they appear as windows or dialog boxes that contain information about what happened and what the program was doing when it happened. This information is useful for debugging.

1.3.3   Logic errors and semantics

The third type of error is the **logical** or **semantic** error. If there is a logical error in your program, it will compile and run successfully, in the sense that the computer will not generate any error messages, but it will not do the right thing. It will do something else. Specifically, it will do what you told it to do.

The problem is that the program you wrote is not the program you wanted to write. The meaning of the program (its semantics) is wrong. Identifying logical errors can be tricky, since it requires you to work backwards by looking at the output of the program and trying to figure out what it is doing.

1.3.4   Experimental debugging

One of the most important skills you will acquire in this class is debugging. Although it can be frustrating, debugging is one of the most intellectually rich, challenging, and interesting parts of programming.

In some ways debugging is like detective work. You are confronted with clues and you have to infer the processes and events that lead to the results you see.

Debugging is also like an experimental science. Once you have an idea what is going wrong, you modify your program and try again. If your hypothesis was correct, then you can predict the result of the modification, and you take a step closer to a working program. If your hypothesis was wrong, you have to come up with a new one. As Sherlock Holmes pointed out, "When you have eliminated the impossible, whatever remains, however improbable, must be the truth." (from A. Conan Doyle's *The Sign of Four*).

For some people, programming and debugging are the same thing. That is, programming is the process of gradually debugging a program until it does what you want. The idea is that you should always start with a working program that does *something*, and make small modifications, debugging them as you go, so that you always have a working program.

For example, Linux is an operating system that contains thousands of lines of code, but it started out as a simple program Linus Torvalds used to explore the Intel 80386 chip. According to Larry Greenfield, "One of Linus's earlier projects was a program that would switch between printing AAAA and BBBB. This later evolved to Linux" (from *The Linux Users' Guide* Beta Version 1).

In later chapters I will make more suggestions about debugging and other programming practices.

1.4   Formal and natural languages

Natural languages are the languages that people speak, like English, Spanish, and French. They were not designed by people (although people try to impose some order on them); they evolved naturally.

Formal languages are languages that are designed by people for specific applications. For example, the notation that mathematicians use is a formal language that is particularly good at denoting relationships among numbers and symbols. Chemists use a formal language to represent the chemical structure of molecules. And most importantly:

> **Programming languages are formal languages that have been designed to express computations.**

As I mentioned before, formal languages tend to have strict rules about syntax. For example, $3 + 3 = 6$ is a syntactically correct mathematical statement, but $3 = +6\$$ is not. Also, H_2O is a syntactically correct chemical name, but $_2Zz$ is not.

Syntax rules come in two flavors, pertaining to tokens and structure. Tokens are the basic elements of the language, like words and numbers and chemical elements. One of the problems with 3=+6$ is that $ is not a legal token in mathematics (at least as far as I know). Similarly, $_2Zz$ is not legal because there is no element with the abbreviation Zz.

The second type of syntax rule pertains to the structure of a statement; that is, the way the tokens are arranged. The statement 3=+6$ is structurally illegal, because you can't have a plus sign immediately after an equals sign. Similarly, molecular formulas have to have subscripts after the element name, not before.

When you read a sentence in English or a statement in a formal language, you have to figure out what the structure of the sentence is (although in a natural language you do this unconsciously). This process is called **parsing**.

For example, when you hear the sentence, "The other shoe fell," you understand that "the other shoe" is the subject and "fell" is the verb. Once you have parsed a sentence, you can figure out what it means, that is, the semantics of the sentence. Assuming that you know what a shoe is, and what it means to fall, you will understand the general implication of this sentence.

Although formal and natural languages have many features in common—tokens, structure, syntax and semantics—there are many differences.

ambiguity: Natural languages are full of ambiguity, which people deal with by using contextual clues and other information. Formal languages are designed to be nearly or completely unambiguous, which means that any statement has exactly one meaning, regardless of context.

redundancy: In order to make up for ambiguity and reduce misunderstandings, natural languages employ lots of redundancy. As a result, they are often verbose. Formal languages are less redundant and more concise.

literalness: Natural languages are full of idiom and metaphor. If I say, "The other shoe fell," there is probably no shoe and nothing falling. Formal languages mean exactly what they say.

People who grow up speaking a natural language (everyone) often have a hard time adjusting to formal languages. In some ways the difference between formal and natural language is like the difference between poetry and prose, but more so:

Poetry: Words are used for their sounds as well as for their meaning, and the whole poem together creates an effect or emotional response. Ambiguity is not only common but often deliberate.

Prose: The literal meaning of words is more important and the structure contributes more meaning. Prose is more amenable to analysis than poetry, but still often ambiguous.

Programs: The meaning of a computer program is unambiguous and literal, and can be understood entirely by analysis of the tokens and structure.

Here are some suggestions for reading programs (and other formal languages). First, remember that formal languages are much more dense than natural languages, so it takes longer to read them. Also, the structure is very important, so it is usually not a good idea to read from top to bottom, left to right. Instead, learn to parse the program in your head, identifying the tokens and interpreting the structure. Finally, remember that the details matter. Little things like spelling errors and bad punctuation, which you can get away with in natural languages, can make a big difference in a formal language.

1.5 The first program

Traditionally the first program people write in a new language is called "Hello, World." because all it does is display the words "Hello, World." In Java, this program looks like this:

```
class Hello {

  // main: generate some simple output

  public static void main (String[] args) {
    System.out.println ("Hello, world.");
  }
}
```

Some people judge the quality of a programming language by the simplicity of the "Hello, World." program. By this standard, Java does not do very well. Even the simplest program contains a number of features that are hard to explain to beginning programmers. We are going to ignore a lot of them for now, but I will explain a few.

All programs are made up of `class` definitions, which have the form:

```
class CLASSNAME {

  public static void main (String[] args) {
    STATEMENTS
  }
}
```

Here `CLASSNAME` indicates an arbitrary name that you make up. The class name in the example is `Hello`.

In the second line, you should ignore the words `public static void` for now, but notice the word `main`. `main` is a special name that indicates the place in the program where execution begins. When the program runs, it starts by executing the first statement in `main` and it continues, in order, until it gets to the last statement, and then it quits.

There is no limit to the number of statements that can be in `main`, but the example contains only one. It is a **print statement**, meaning that it prints a message on the screen. It is a bit confusing that "print" sometimes means "display something on the screen," and sometimes means "send something to the printer." In this book I won't say much about sending things to the printer; we'll do all our printing on the screen.

The statement that prints things on the screen is `System.out.println`, and the thing between the parentheses is the thing that will get printed. At the end of the statement there is a semi-colon (;), which is required at the end of every statement.

There are a few other things you should notice about the syntax of this program. First, Java uses squiggly-braces ({ and }) to group things together. The outermost squiggly-braces (lines 1 and 8) contain the class definition, and the inner braces contain the definition of `main`.

Also, notice that line 3 begins with `//`. This indicates that this line contains a **comment**, which is a bit of English text that you can put in the middle of a program, usually to explain what the program does. When the compiler sees a `//`, it ignores everything from there until the end of the line.

1.6   Glossary

problem-solving: The process of formulating a problem, finding a solution, and expressing the solution.

high-level language: A programming language like Java that is designed to be easy for humans to read and write.

low-level language: A programming language that is designed to be easy for a computer to execute. Also called "machine language" or "assembly language."

formal language: Any of the languages people have designed for specific purposes, like representing mathematical ideas or computer programs. All programming languages are formal languages.

natural language: Any of the languages people speak that have evolved naturally.

portability: A property of a program that can run on more than one kind of computer.

interpret: To execute a program in a high-level language by translating it one line at a time.

compile: To translate a program in a high-level language into a low-level language, all at once, in preparation for later execution.

source code: A program in a high-level language, before being compiled.

object code: The output of the compiler, after translating the program.

executable: Another name for object code that is ready to be executed.

byte code: A special kind of object code used for Java programs. Byte code is similar to a low-level language, but it is portable, like a high-level language.

statement: A part of a program that specifies an action that will be performed when the program runs. A print statement causes output to be displayed on the screen.

comment: A part of a program that contains information about the program, but that has no effect when the program runs.

algorithm: A general process for solving a category of problems.

bug: An error in a program.

syntax: The structure of a program.

semantics: The meaning of a program.

parse: To examine a program and analyze the syntactic structure.

syntax error: An error in a program that makes it impossible to parse (and therefore impossible to compile).

exception: An error in a program that makes it fail at run-time. Also called a run-time error.

logical error: An error in a program that makes it do something other than what the programmer intended.

debugging: The process of finding and removing any of the three kinds of errors.

1.7   Exercises

Exercise 1.1

Computer scientists have the annoying habit of using common English words to mean something different from their common English meaning. For example, in English, a statement and a comment are pretty much the same thing, but when we are talking about a program, they are very different.

The glossary at the end of each chapter is intended to highlight words and phrases that have special meanings in computer science. When you see familiar words, don't assume that you know what they mean!

    a. In computer jargon, what's the difference between a statement and a comment?

    b. What does it mean to say that a program is portable?

    c. What is an executable?

Exercise 1.2

Before you do anything else, find out how to compile and run a Java program in your environment. Some environments provide sample programs similar to the example in Section 1.5.

    a. Type in the "Hello, world" program, then compile and run it.

    b. Add a second print statement that prints a second message after the "Hello, world!". Something witty like, "How are you?" Compile and run the program again.

    c. Add a comment line to the program (anywhere) and recompile it. Run the program again. The new comment should not affect the execution of the program.

This exercise may seem trivial, but it is the starting place for many of the programs we will work with. In order to debug with confidence, you have to have confidence in your programming environment. In some environments, it is easy to lose track of which program is executing, and you might find yourself trying to debug one program while you are accidentally executing another. Adding (and changing) print statements is a simple way to establish the connection between the program you are looking at and the output when the program runs.

Exercise 1.3

It is a good idea to commit as many errors as you can think of, so that you see what error messages the compiler produces. Sometimes the compiler will tell you exactly what is wrong, and all you have to do is fix it. Sometimes, though, the compiler will produce wildly misleading messages. You will develop a sense for when you can trust the compiler and when you have to figure things out yourself.

    a. Remove one of the open squiggly-braces.

    b. Remove one of the close squiggly-braces.

    c. Instead of `main`, write `mian`.

    d. Remove the word `static`.

    e. Remove the word `public`.

    f. Remove the word `System`.

    g. Replace `println` with `pintln`.

    h. Replace `println` with `print`. This one is tricky because it is a logical error, not a syntax error. The statement `System.out.print` is legal, but it may or may not do what you expect.

    i. Delete one of the parentheses. Add an extra one.

Chapter 2

Variables and types

2.1 More printing

As I mentioned in the last chapter, you can put as many statements as you want in main. For example, to print more than one line:

```
class Hello {

  // main: generate some simple output

  public static void main (String[] args) {
    System.out.println ("Hello, world.");      // print one line
    System.out.println ("How are you?");       // print another
  }
}
```

Also, as you can see, it is legal to put comments at the end of a line, as well as on a line by themselves.

The phrases that appear in quotation marks are called **strings**, because they are made up of a sequence (string) of letters. Actually, strings can contain any combination of letters, numbers, punctuation marks, and other special characters.

`println` is short for "print line," because after each line it adds a special character, called a **newline**, that causes the cursor to move to the next line of the display. The next time `println` is invoked, the new text appears on the next line.

Often it is useful to display the output from multiple print statements all on one line. You can do this with the `print` command:

```
class Hello {

  // main: generate some simple output
```

```
   public static void main (String[] args) {
     System.out.print ("Goodbye, ");
     System.out.println ("cruel world!");
   }
}
```

In this case the output appears on a single line as `Goodbye, cruel world!`. Notice that there is a space between the word "Goodbye" and the second quotation mark. This space appears in the output, so it affects the behavior of the program.

Spaces that appear outside of quotation marks generally do not affect the behavior of the program. For example, I could have written:

```
class Hello {
public static void main (String[] args) {
System.out.print ("Goodbye, ");
System.out.println ("cruel world!");
}
}
```

This program would compile and run just as well as the original. The breaks at the ends of lines (newlines) do not affect the program's behavior either, so I could have written:

```
class Hello { public static void main (String[] args) {
System.out.print ("Goodbye, "); System.out.println
("cruel world!");}}
```

That would work, too, although you have probably noticed that the program is getting harder and harder to read. Newlines and spaces are useful for organizing your program visually, making it easier to read the program and locate syntax errors.

2.2   Variables

One of the most powerful features of a programming language is the ability to manipulate **variables**. A variable is a named location that stores a **value**. Values are things that can be printed and stored and (as we'll see later) operated on. The strings we have been printing (`"Hello, World."`, `"Goodbye, "`, etc.) are values.

In order to store a value, you have to create a variable. Since the values we want to store are strings, we will declare that the new variable is a string:

```
   String fred;
```

This statement is a **declaration**, because it declares that the variable named `fred` has the type `String`. Each variable has a type that determines what kind of values it can store. For example, the `int` type can store integers, and it will probably come as no surprise that the `String` type can store strings.

You will notice that some types begin with a capital letter and some with lower-case. We will learn the significance of this distinction later, but for now you should take care to get it right. There is no such type as `Int` or `string`, and the compiler will object if you try to make one up.

To create an integer variable, the syntax is `int bob;`, where `bob` is the arbitrary name you made up for the variable. In general, you will want to make up variable names that indicate what you plan to do with the variable. For example, if you saw these variable declarations:

```
String firstName;
String lastName;
int hour, minute;
```

you could probably make a good guess at what values would be stored in them. This example also demonstrates the syntax for declaring multiple variables with the same type: `hour` and `second` are both integers (`int` type).

2.3   Assignment

Now that we have created some variables, we would like to store values in them. We do that with an **assignment statement**.

```
fred = "Hello.";      // give fred the value "Hello."
hour = 11;            // assign the value 11 to hour
minute = 59;          // set minute to 59
```

This example shows three assignments, and the comments show three different ways people sometimes talk about assignment statements. The vocabulary can be confusing here, but the idea is straightforward:

- When you declare a variable, you create a named storage location.

- When you make an assignment to a variable, you give it a value.

A common way to represent variables on paper is to draw a box with the name of the variable on the outside and the value of the variable on the inside. This figure shows the effect of the three assignment statements:

For each variable, the name of the variable appears outside the box and the value appears inside.

As a general rule, a variable has to have the same type as the value you assign it. You cannot store a `String` in `minute` or an integer in `fred`.

On the other hand, that rule can be confusing, because there are many ways that you can convert values from one type to another, and Java sometimes converts things automatically. So for now you should remember the general rule, and we'll talk about special cases later.

Another source of confusion is that some strings *look* like integers, but they are not. For example, fred can contain the string "123", which is made up of the characters 1, 2 and 3, but that is not the same thing as the *number* 123.

```
fred = "123";      // legal
fred = 123;        // not legal
```

2.4   Printing variables

You can print the value of a variable using the same commands we used to print Strings.

```
class Hello {
  public static void main (String[] args) {
    String firstLine;
    firstLine = "Hello, again!";
    System.out.println (firstLine);
  }
}
```

This program creates a variable named firstLine, assigns it the value "Hello, again!" and then prints that value. When we talk about "printing a variable," we mean printing the *value* of the variable. To print the *name* of a variable, you have to put it in quotes. For example: System.out.println ("firstLine");

If you want to get a little tricky, you could write

```
String firstLine;
firstLine = "Hello, again!";
System.out.print ("The value of firstLine is ");
System.out.println (firstLine);
```

The output of this program is

```
The value of firstLine is Hello, again!
```

I am pleased to report that the syntax for printing a variable is the same regardless of the variable's type.

```
int hour, minute;
hour = 11;
minute = 59;
System.out.print ("The current time is ");
System.out.print (hour);
System.out.print (":");
System.out.print (minute);
System.out.println (".");
```

The output of this program is The current time is 11:59.

WARNING: It is common practice to use several print commands followed by a println, in order to put multiple values on the same line. But you have to be careful to remember the `println` at the end. In many environments, the output from `print` is stored without being displayed until the `println` command is invoked, at which point the entire line is displayed at once. If you omit `println`, the program may terminate without ever displaying the stored output!

2.5   Keywords

A few sections ago, I said that you can make up any name you want for your variables, but that's not quite true. There are certain words that are reserved in Java because they are used by the compiler to parse the structure of your program, and if you use them as variable names, it will get confused. These words, called **keywords**, include `public`, `class`, `void`, `int`, and many more.

The complete list is available at

`http://java.sun.com/docs/books/jls/second_edition/html/lexical.doc.html`

This site, provided by Sun, includes Java documentation I will be referring to throughout the book.

Rather than memorize the list, I would suggest that you take advantage of a feature provided in many Java development environments: code highlighting. As you type, different parts of your program should appear in different colors. For example, keywords might be blue, strings red, and other code black. If you type a variable name and it turns blue, watch out! You might get some strange behavior from the compiler.

2.6   Operators

Operators are special symbols that are used to represent simple computations like addition and multiplication. Most of the operators in Java do exactly what you would expect them to do, because they are common mathematical symbols. For example, the operator for adding two integers is +.

The following are all legal Java expressions whose meaning is more or less obvious:

```
1+1        hour-1       hour*60 + minute      minute/60
```

Expressions can contain both variable names and numbers. In each case the name of the variable is replaced with its value before the computation is performed.

Addition, subtraction and multiplication all do what you expect, but you might be surprised by division. For example, the following program:

```
int hour, minute;
hour = 11;
minute = 59;
```

```
System.out.print ("Number of minutes since midnight: ");
System.out.println (hour*60 + minute);
System.out.print ("Fraction of the hour that has passed: ");
System.out.println (minute/60);
```

would generate the following output:

```
Number of minutes since midnight: 719
Fraction of the hour that has passed: 0
```

The first line is what we expected, but the second line is odd. The value of the variable `minute` is 59, and 59 divided by 60 is 0.98333, not 0. The reason for the discrepancy is that Java is performing **integer division**.

When both of the **operands** are integers (operands are the things operators operate on), the result must also be an integer, and by convention integer division always rounds *down*, even in cases like this where the next integer is so close.

A possible alternative in this case is to calculate a percentage rather than a fraction:

```
System.out.print ("Percentage of the hour that has passed: ");
System.out.println (minute*100/60);
```

The result is:

```
Percentage of the hour that has passed: 98
```

Again the result is rounded down, but at least now the answer is approximately correct. In order to get an even more accurate answer, we could use a different type of variable, called floating-point, that is capable of storing fractional values. We'll get to that in the next chapter.

2.7   Order of operations

When more than one operator appears in an expression the order of evaluation depends on the rules of **precedence**. A complete explanation of precedence can get complicated, but just to get you started:

- Multiplication and division take precedence (happen before) addition and subtraction. So 2*3-1 yields 5, not 4, and 2/3-1 yields -1, not 1 (remember that in integer division 2/3 is 0).

- If the operators have the same precedence they are evaluated from left to right. So in the expression `minute*100/60`, the multiplication happens first, yielding 5900/60, which in turn yields 98. If the operations had gone from right to left, the result would be 59*1 which is 59, which is wrong.

- Any time you want to override the rules of precedence (or you are not sure what they are) you can use parentheses. Expressions in parentheses are evaluated first, so 2 * (3-1) is 4. You can also use parentheses to make an expression easier to read, as in (minute * 100) / 60, even though it doesn't change the result.

2.8 Operators for Strings

In general you cannot perform mathematical operations on Strings, even if the strings look like numbers. The following are illegal (if we know that fred has type String)

```
fred - 1        "Hello"/123       fred * "Hello"
```

By the way, can you tell by looking at those expressions whether fred is an integer or a string? Nope. The only way to tell the type of a variable is to look at the place where it is declared.

Interestingly, the + operator *does* work with Strings, although it does not do exactly what you might expect. For Strings, the + operator represents **concatenation**, which means joining up the two operands by linking them end-to-end. So "Hello, " + "world." yields the string "Hello, world." and fred + "ism" adds the suffix *ism* to the end of whatever fred is, which is often handy for naming new forms of bigotry.

2.9 Composition

So far we have looked at the elements of a programming language—variables, expressions, and statements—in isolation, without talking about how to combine them.

One of the most useful features of programming languages is their ability to take small building blocks and **compose** them. For example, we know how to multiply numbers and we know how to print; it turns out we can do both at the same time:

```
System.out.println (17 * 3);
```

Actually, I shouldn't say "at the same time," since in reality the multiplication has to happen before the printing, but the point is that any expression, involving numbers, strings, and variables, can be used inside a print statement. We've already seen one example:

```
System.out.println (hour*60 + minute);
```

But you can also put arbitrary expressions on the right-hand side of an assignment statement:

```
int percentage;
percentage = (minute * 100) / 60;
```

This ability may not seem so impressive now, but we will see other examples where composition makes it possible to express complex computations neatly and concisely.

WARNING: There are limits on where you can use certain expressions; most notably, the left-hand side of an assignment statement has to be a *variable* name, not an expression. That's because the left side indicates the storage location where the result will go. Expressions do not represent storage locations, only values. So the following is illegal: minute+1 = hour;.

2.10   Glossary

variable: A named storage location for values. All variables have a type, which is declared when the variable is created.

value: A number or string (or other thing to be named later) that can be stored in a variable. Every value belongs to one type.

type: A set of values. The type of a variable determines which values can be stored there. So far, the types we have seen are integers (`int` in Java) and strings (`String` in Java).

keyword: A reserved word that is used by the compiler to parse programs. You cannot use keywords, like `public`, `class` and `void` as variable names.

statement: A line of code that represents a command or action. So far, the statements we have seen are declarations, assignments, and print statements.

declaration: A statement that creates a new variable and determines its type.

assignment: A statement that assigns a value to a variable.

expression: A combination of variables, operators and values that represents a single result value. Expressions also have types, as determined by their operators and operands.

operator: A special symbol that represents a simple computation like addition, multiplication or string concatenation.

operand: One of the values on which an operator operates.

precedence: The order in which operations are evaluated.

concatenate: To join two operands end-to-end.

composition: The ability to combine simple expressions and statements into compound statements and expressions in order to represent complex computations concisely.

2.11   Exercises

Exercise 2.1

a. Create a new program named `Date.java`. Copy or type in something like the "Hello, World" program and make sure you can compile and run it.

b. Following the example in Section 2.4, write a program that creates variables named `day`, `date`, `month` and `year`. `day` will contain the day of the week and `date` will contain the day of the month. What type is each variable? Assign values to those variables that represent today's date.

c. Print the value of each variable on a line by itself. This is an intermediate step that is useful for checking that everything is working so far.

    d. Modify the program so that it prints the date in standard American form:
Wednesday, February 17, 1999.

    e. Modify the program again so that the total output is:

American format:
Wednesday, February 17, 1999
European format:
Wednesday 17 February, 1999

The point of this exercise is to use string concatenation to display values with different types (int and String), and to practice developing programs gradually by adding a few statements at a time.

Exercise 2.2

    a. Create a new program called Time.java. From now on, I won't remind you to start with a small, working program, but you should.

    b. Following the example in Section 2.6, create variables named hour, minute and second, and assign them values that are roughly the current time. Use a 24-hour clock, so that at 2pm the value of hour is 14.

    c. Make the program calculate and print the number of seconds since midnight.

    d. Make the program calculate and print the number of seconds remaining in the day.

    e. Make the program calculate and print the percentage of the day that has passed.

    f. Change the values of hour, minute and second to reflect the current time (I assume that some time has elapsed), and check to make sure that the program works correctly with different values.

The point of this exercise is to use some of the arithmetic operations, and to start thinking about compound entities like the time of day that that are represented with multiple values. Also, you might run into problems computing percentages with ints, which is the motivation for floating point numbers in the next chapter.

HINT: you may want to use additional variables to hold values temporarily during the computation. Variables like this, that are used in a computation but never printed, are sometimes called intermediate or temporary variables.

Chapter 3

Methods

3.1 Floating-point

In the last chapter we had some problems dealing with numbers that were not integers. We worked around the problem by measuring percentages instead of fractions, but a more general solution is to use floating-point numbers, which can represent fractions as well as integers. In Java, the floating-point type is called `double`.

You can create floating-point variables and assign values to them using the same syntax we used for the other types. For example:

```
double pi;
pi = 3.14159;
```

It is also legal to declare a variable and assign a value to it at the same time:

```
int x = 1;
String empty = "";
double pi = 3.14159;
```

In fact, this syntax is quite common. A combined declaration and assignment is sometimes called an **initialization**.

Although floating-point numbers are useful, they are often a source of confusion because there seems to be an overlap between integers and floating-point numbers. For example, if you have the value 1, is that an integer, a floating-point number, or both?

Strictly speaking, Java distinguishes the integer value 1 from the floating-point value 1.0, even though they seem to be the same number. They belong to different types, and strictly speaking, you are not allowed to make assignments between types. For example, the following is illegal:

```
int x = 1.1;
```

because the variable on the left is an `int` and the value on the right is a `double`. But it is easy to forget this rule, especially because there are places where Java will automatically convert from one type to another. For example:

```
double y = 1;
```

should technically not be legal, but Java allows it by converting the `int` to a `double` automatically. This leniency is convenient, but it can cause problems; for example:

```
double y = 1 / 3;
```

You might expect the variable `y` to be given the value `0.333333`, which is a legal floating-point value, but in fact it will get the value `0.0`. The reason is that the expression on the right appears to be the ratio of two integers, so Java does *integer* division, which yields the integer value `0`. Converted to floating-point, the result is `0.0`.

One way to solve this problem (once you figure out what it is) is to make the right-hand side a floating-point expression:

```
double y = 1.0 / 3.0;
```

This sets `y` to `0.333333`, as expected.

All the operations we have seen so far—addition, subtraction, multiplication, and division—also work on floating-point values, although you might be interested to know that the underlying mechanism is completely different. In fact, most processors have special hardware just for performing floating-point operations.

3.2 Converting from `double` to `int`

As I mentioned, Java converts `int`s to `double`s automatically if necessary, because no information is lost in the translation. On the other hand, going from a `double` to an `int` requires rounding off. Java doesn't perform this operation automatically, in order to make sure that you, as the programmer, are aware of the loss of the fractional part of the number.

The simplest way to convert a floating-point value to an integer is to use a **typecast**. Typecasting is so called because it allows you to take a value that belongs to one type and "cast" it into another type (in the sense of molding or reforming, not throwing).

Unfortunately, the syntax for typecasting is ugly: you put the name of the type in parentheses and use it as an operator. For example,

```
int x = (int) Math.PI;
```

The `(int)` operator has the effect of converting what follows into an integer, so `x` gets the value 3.

Typecasting takes precedence over arithmetic operations, so in the following example, the value of `PI` gets converted to an integer first, and the result is 60, not 62.

```
int x = (int) Math.PI * 20.0;
```

Converting to an integer always rounds down, even if the fraction part is 0.99999999.

These two properties (precedence and rounding) can make typecasting awkward.

3.3   Math methods

In mathematics, you have probably seen functions like sin and log, and you have learned to evaluate expressions like $\sin(\pi/2)$ and $\log(1/x)$. First, you evaluate the expression in parentheses, which is called the **argument** of the function. For example, $\pi/2$ is approximately 1.571, and $1/x$ is 0.1 (assuming that x is 10).

Then you can evaluate the function itself, either by looking it up in a table or by performing various computations. The sin of 1.571 is 1, and the log of 0.1 is -1 (assuming that log indicates the logarithm base 10).

This process can be applied repeatedly to evaluate more complicated expressions like $\log(1/\sin(\pi/2))$. First we evaluate the argument of the innermost function, then evaluate the function, and so on.

Java provides a set of built-in functions that includes most of the mathematical operations you can think of. These functions are called **methods**. Most math methods operate on `doubles`.

The math methods are invoked using a syntax that is similar to the `print` commands we have already seen:

```
double root = Math.sqrt (17.0);
double angle = 1.5;
double height = Math.sin (angle);
```

The first example sets `root` to the square root of 17. The second example finds the sine of 1.5, which is the value of the variable `angle`. Java assumes that the values you use with `sin` and the other trigonometric functions (`cos`, `tan`) are in *radians*. To convert from degrees to radians, you can divide by 360 and multiply by 2π. Conveniently, Java provides π as a built-in value:

```
double degrees = 90;
double angle = degrees * 2 * Math.PI / 360.0;
```

Notice that `PI` is in all capital letters. Java does not recognize `Pi`, `pi`, or `pie`.

Another useful method in the `Math` class is `round`, which rounds a floating-point value off to the nearest integer and returns an `int`.

```
int x = Math.round (Math.PI * 20.0);
```

In this case the multiplication happens first, before the method is invoked. The result is 63 (rounded up from 62.8319).

3.4   Composition

Just as with mathematical functions, Java methods can be **composed**, meaning that you use one expression as part of another. For example, you can use any expression as an argument to a method:

```
double x = Math.cos (angle + Math.PI/2);
```

This statement takes the value Math.PI, divides it by two and adds the result to the value of the variable angle. The sum is then passed as an argument to the cos method. (Notice that PI is the name of a variable, not a method, so there are no arguments, not even the empty argument ()).

You can also take the result of one method and pass it as an argument to another:

```
double x = Math.exp (Math.log (10.0));
```

In Java, the log function always uses base e, so this statement finds the log base e of 10 and then raises e to that power. The result gets assigned to x; I hope you know what it is.

3.5   Adding new methods

So far we have only been using the methods that are built into Java, but it is also possible to add new methods. Actually, we have already seen one method definition: main. The method named main is special in that it indicates where the execution of the program begins, but the syntax for main is the same as for other method definitions:

```
public static void NAME ( LIST OF PARAMETERS ) {
  STATEMENTS
}
```

You can make up any name you want for your method, except that you can't call it main or any other Java keyword. The list of parameters specifies what information, if any, you have to provide in order to use (or **invoke**) the new function.

The single parameter for main is String[] args, which indicates that whoever invokes main has to provide an array of Strings (we'll get to arrays in Chapter 10). The first couple of methods we are going to write have no parameters, so the syntax looks like this:

```
public static void newLine () {
  System.out.println ("");
}
```

This method is named newLine, and the empty parentheses indicate that it takes no parameters. It contains only a single statement, which prints an empty String, indicated by "". Printing a String with no letters in it may not seem all that useful, except remember that println skips to the next line after it prints, so this statement has the effect of skipping to the next line.

In `main` we can invoke this new method using syntax that is similar to the way we invoke the built-in Java commands:

```
public static void main (String[] args) {
  System.out.println ("First line.");
  newLine ();
  System.out.println ("Second line.");
}
```

The output of this program is

```
First line.
```

```
Second line.
```

Notice the extra space between the two lines. What if we wanted more space between the lines? We could invoke the same method repeatedly:

```
public static void main (String[] args) {
  System.out.println ("First line.");
  newLine ();
  newLine ();
  newLine ();
  System.out.println ("Second line.");
}
```

Or we could write a new method, named `threeLine`, that prints three new lines:

```
public static void threeLine () {
  newLine ();  newLine ();  newLine ();
}
```

```
public static void main (String[] args) {
  System.out.println ("First line.");
  threeLine ();
  System.out.println ("Second line.");
}
```

You should notice a few things about this program:

- You can invoke the same procedure repeatedly. In fact, it is quite common and useful to do so.

- You can have one method invoke another method. In this case, `main` invokes `threeLine` and `threeLine` invokes `newLine`. Again, this is common and useful.

- In `threeLine` I wrote three statements all on the same line, which is syntactically legal (remember that spaces and new lines usually don't change the meaning of a program). On the other hand, it is usually a better idea to put each statement on a line by itself, to make your program easy to read. I sometimes break that rule in this book to save space.

So far, it may not be clear why it is worth the trouble to create all these new methods. Actually, there are a lot of reasons, but this example only demonstrates two:

1. Creating a new method gives you an opportunity to give a name to a group of statements. Methods can simplify a program by hiding a complex computation behind a single command, and by using English words in place of arcane code. Which is clearer, `newLine` or `System.out.println ("")`?

2. Creating a new method can make a program smaller by eliminating repetitive code. For example, how would you print nine consecutive new lines? You could just invoke `threeLine` three times.

3.6   Classes and methods

Pulling together all the code fragments from the previous section, the whole class definition looks like this:

```
class NewLine {

  public static void newLine () {
    System.out.println ("");
  }

  public static void threeLine () {
    newLine ();  newLine ();  newLine ();
  }

  public static void main (String[] args) {
    System.out.println ("First line.");
    threeLine ();
    System.out.println ("Second line.");
  }
}
```

The first line indicates that this is the class definition for a new class called `NewLine`. A class is a collection of related methods. In this case, the class named `NewLine` contains three methods, named `newLine`, `threeLine`, and `main`.

The other class we've seen is the `Math` class. It contains methods named `sqrt`, `sin`, and many others. When we invoke a mathematical function, we have to specify the name of the class (`Math`) and the name of the function. That's why the syntax is slightly different for built-in methods and the methods that we write:

```
Math.pow (2.0, 10.0);
newLine ();
```

The first statement invokes the `pow` method in the `Math class` (which raises the first argument to the power of the second argument). The second statement invokes the `newLine` method, which Java assumes (correctly) is in the `NewLine` class, which is what we are writing.

If you try to invoke a method from the wrong class, the compiler will generate an error. For example, if you type:

```
pow (2.0, 10.0);
```

The compiler will say something like, "Can't find a method named `pow` in class `NewLine`." If you have seen this message, you might have wondered why it was looking for `pow` in your class definition. Now you know.

3.7   Programs with multiple methods

When you look at a class definition that contains several methods, it is tempting to read it from top to bottom, but that is likely to be confusing, because that is not the **order of execution** of the program.

Execution always begins at the first statement of `main`, regardless of where it is in the program (in this case I deliberately put it at the bottom). Statements are executed one at a time, in order, until you reach a method invocation. Method invocations are like a detour in the flow of execution. Instead of going to the next statement, you go to the first line of the invoked method, execute all the statements there, and then come back and pick up again where you left off.

That sounds simple enough, except that you have to remember that one method can invoke another. Thus, while we are in the middle of `main`, we might have to go off and execute the statements in `threeLine`. But while we are executing `threeLine`, we get interrupted three times to go off and execute `newLine`.

For its part, `newLine` invokes the built-in method `println`, which causes yet another detour. Fortunately, Java is quite adept at keeping track of where it is, so when `println` completes, it picks up where it left off in `newLine`, and then gets back to `threeLine`, and then finally gets back to `main` so the program can terminate.

Actually, technically, the program does not terminate at the end of `main`. Instead, execution picks up where it left off in the program that invoked `main`, which is the Java interpreter. The Java interpreter takes care of things like deleting windows and general cleanup, and *then* the program terminates.

What's the moral of this sordid tale? When you read a program, don't read from top to bottom. Instead, follow the flow of execution.

3.8   Parameters and arguments

Some of the built-in methods we have used have **parameters**, which are values that you provide to let the method do its job. For example, if you want to find the sine of a number, you have to indicate what the number is. Thus, sin takes a double value as a parameter. To print a string, you have to provide the string, which is why println takes a String as a parameter.

Some methods take more than one parameter, like pow, which takes two doubles, the base and the exponent.

Notice that in each of these cases we have to specify not only how many parameters there are, but also what type they are. So it shouldn't surprise you that when you write a class definition, the parameter list indicates the type of each parameter. For example:

```
public static void printTwice (String phil) {
  System.out.println (phil);
  System.out.println (phil);
}
```

This method takes a single parameter, named phil, that has type String. Whatever that parameter is (and at this point we have no idea what it is), it gets printed twice. I chose the name phil to suggest that the name you give a parameter is up to you, but in general you want to choose something more illustrative than phil.

In order to invoke this method, we have to provide a String. For example, we might have a main method like this:

```
public static void main (String[] args) {
  printTwice ("Don't make me say this twice!");
}
```

The string you provide is called an **argument**, and we say that the argument is **passed** to the method. In this case we are creating a string value that contains the text "Don't make me say this twice!" and passing that string as an argument to printTwice where, contrary to its wishes, it will get printed twice.

Alternatively, if we had a String variable, we could use it as an argument instead:

```
public static void main (String[] args) {
  String argument = "Never say never.";
  printTwice (argument);
}
```

Notice something very important here: the name of the variable we pass as an argument (argument) has nothing to do with the name of the parameter (phil). Let me say that again:

> **The name of the variable we pass as an argument has nothing to do with the name of the parameter.**

They can be the same or they can be different, but it is important to realize that they are not the same thing, except that they happen to have the same value (in this case the string "Never say never.").

The value you provide as an argument must have the same type as the parameter of the method you invoke. This rule is very important, but it often gets complicated in Java for two reasons:

- There are some methods that can accept arguments with many different types. For example, you can send *any* type to `print` and `println`, and it will do the right thing no matter what. This sort of thing is an exception, though.

- If you violate this rule, the compiler often generates a confusing error message. Instead of saying something like, "You are passing the wrong kind of argument to this method," it will probably say something to the effect that it could not find a method with that name that would accept an argument with that type. Once you have seen this error message a few times, though, you will figure out how to interpret it.

3.9   Stack diagrams

Parameters and other variables only exist inside their own methods. Within the confines of `main`, there is no such thing as `phil`. If you try to use it, the compiler will complain. Similarly, inside `printTwice` there is no such thing as `argument`.

One way to keep track of where each variable is defined is with a **stack diagram**. The stack diagram for the previous example looks like this:

For each method there is a gray box called a **frame** that contains the methods parameters and local variables. The name of the method appears outside the frame. As usual, the value of each variable is drawn inside a box with the name of the variable beside it.

3.10   Methods with multiple parameters

The syntax for declaring and invoking methods with multiple parameters is a common source of errors. First, remember that you have to declare the type of every parameter. For example

```
public static void printTime (int hour, int minute) {
  System.out.print (hour);
```

```
    System.out.print (":");
    System.out.println (minute);
  }
```

It might be tempting to write `int hour, minute`, but that format is only legal for variable declarations, not for parameters.

Another common source of confusion is that you do not have to declare the types of arguments. The following is wrong!

```
    int hour = 11;
    int minute = 59;
    printTime (int hour, int minute);    // WRONG!
```

In this case, Java can tell the type of `hour` and `minute` by looking at their declarations. It is unnecessary and illegal to include the type when you pass them as arguments. The correct syntax is `printTime (hour, minute)`.

Exercise 3.1   Draw a stack frame that shows the state of the program when `main` invokes `printTime` with the arguments 11 and 59.

3.11   Methods with results

You might have noticed by now that some of the methods we are using, like the `Math` methods, yield results. Other methods, like `println` and `newLine`, perform some action but they don't return a value. That raises some questions:

- What happens if you invoke a method and you don't do anything with the result (i.e. you don't assign it to a variable or use it as part of a larger expression)?

- What happens if you use a `print` method as part of an expression, like `System.out.println ("boo!") + 7`?

- Can we write methods that yield results, or are we stuck with things like `newLine` and `printTwice`?

The answer to the third question is "yes, you can write methods that return values," and we'll do it in a couple of chapters. I will leave it up to you to answer the other two questions by trying them out. In fact, any time you have a question about what is legal or illegal in Java, a good way to find out is to ask the compiler.

3.12   Glossary

floating-point: A type of variable (or value) that can contain fractions as well as integers. In Java this type is called `double`.

class: A named collection of methods. So far, we have used the `Math` class and the `System` class, and we have written classes named `Hello` and `NewLine`.

method: A named sequence of statements that performs some useful function. Methods may or may not take parameters, and may or may not produce a result.

parameter: A piece of information you provide in order to invoke a method. Parameters are like variables in the sense that they contain values and have types.

argument: A value that you provide when you invoke a method. This value must have the same type as the corresponding parameter.

invoke: Cause a method to be executed.

3.13   Exercises

Exercise 3.2

The point of this exercise is to practice reading code and to make sure that you understand the flow of execution through a program with multiple methods.

a. What is the output of the following program? Be precise about where there are spaces and where there are newlines.

   HINT: Start by describing in words what `ping` and `baffle` do when they are invoked.

b. Draw a stack diagram that shows the state of the program the first time `ping` is invoked.

```
public static void zoop () {
  baffle ();
  System.out.print ("You wugga ");
  baffle ();
}

public static void main (String[] args) {
  System.out.print ("No, I ");
  zoop ();
  System.out.print ("I ");
  baffle ();
}

public static void baffle () {
  System.out.print ("wug");
  ping ();
}

public static void ping () {
  System.out.println (".");
}
```

Exercise 3.3   The point of this exercise is to make sure you understand how to write and invoke methods that take parameters.

a. Write the first line of a method named `zool` that takes three parameters: an `int` and two `Strings`.

b. Write a line of code that invokes `zool`, passing as arguments the value 11, the name of your first pet, and the name of the street you grew up on.

Exercise 3.4

The purpose of this exercise is to take code from a previous exercise and encapsulate it in a method that takes parameters. You should start with a working solution to Exercise 2.1.

a. Write a method called `printAmerican` that takes the day, date, month and year as parameters and that prints them in American format.

b. Test your method by invoking it from `main` and passing appropriate arguments. The output should look something like this (except that the date might be different):

```
Wednesday, September 29, 1999
```

c. Once you have debugged `printAmerican`, write another method called `printEuropean` that prints the date in European format.

Exercise 3.5

Many computations can be expressed concisely using the "multadd" operation, which takes three operands and computes `a*b + c`. Some processors even provide a hardware implementation of this operation for floating-point numbers.

a. Create a new program called `Multadd.java`.

b. Write a method called `multadd` that takes three `doubles` as parameters and that prints their multadditionization.

c. Write a `main` method that tests `multadd` by invoking it with a few simple parameters, like `1.0`, `2.0`, `3.0`, and then prints the result, which should be `5.0`.

d. Also in `main`, use `multadd` to compute the following values:

$$\sin \frac{\pi}{4} + \frac{\cos \frac{\pi}{4}}{2}$$
$$\log 10 + \log 20$$

e. Write a method called `yikes` that takes a double as a parameter and that uses `multadd` to calculate and print

$$xe^{-x} + \sqrt{1 - e^{-x}}$$

HINT: the Math method for raising e to a power is `Math.exp`.

In the last part, you get a chance to write a method that invokes a method you wrote. Whenever you do that, it is a good idea to test the first method carefully before you start working on the second. Otherwise, you might find yourself debugging two methods at the same time, which can be very difficult.

One of the purposes of this exercise is to practice pattern-matching: the ability to recognize a specific problem as an instance of a general category of problems.

Chapter 4

Conditionals and recursion

4.1 The modulus operator

The modulus operator works on integers (and integer expressions) and yields
the *remainder* when the first operand is divided by the second. In Java, the
modulus operator is a percent sign, %. The syntax is exactly the same as for
other operators:

```
int quotient = 7 / 3;
int remainder = 7 % 3;
```

The first operator, integer division, yields 2. The second operator yields 1.
Thus, 7 divided by 3 is 2 with 1 left over.

The modulus operator turns out to be surprisingly useful. For example, you
can check whether one number is divisible by another: if x % y is zero, then x
is divisible by y.

Also, you can use the modulus operator to extract the rightmost digit or digits
from a number. For example, x % 10 yields the rightmost digit of x (in base
10). Similarly x % 100 yields the last two digits.

4.2 Conditional execution

In order to write useful programs, we almost always need the ability to check
certain conditions and change the behavior of the program accordingly. **Conditional statements** give us this ability. The simplest form is the if statement:

```
if (x > 0) {
  System.out.println ("x is positive");
}
```

The expression in parentheses is called the condition. If it is true, then the
statements in brackets get executed. If the condition is not true, nothing happens.

The condition can contain any of the comparison operators, sometimes called **relational operators**:

```
x == y              // x equals y
x != y              // x is not equal to y
x > y               // x is greater than y
x < y               // x is less than y
x >= y              // x is greater than or equal to y
x <= y              // x is less than or equal to y
```

Although these operations are probably familiar to you, the syntax Java uses is a little different from mathematical symbols like $=$, $\neq$ and $\leq$. A common error is to use a single = instead of a double ==. Remember that = is the assignment operator, and == is a comparison operator. Also, there is no such thing as =< or =>.

The two sides of a condition operator have to be the same type. You can only compare ints to ints and doubles to doubles. Unfortunately, at this point you can't compare Strings at all! There is a way to compare Strings, but we won't get to it for a couple of chapters.

4.3   Alternative execution

A second form of conditional execution is alternative execution, in which there are two possibilities, and the condition determines which one gets executed. The syntax looks like:

```
if (x%2 == 0) {
  System.out.println ("x is even");
} else {
  System.out.println ("x is odd");
}
```

If the remainder when x is divided by 2 is zero, then we know that x is even, and this code prints a message to that effect. If the condition is false, the second print statement is executed. Since the condition must be true or false, exactly one of the alternatives will be executed.

As an aside, if you think you might want to check the parity (evenness or oddness) of numbers often, you might want to "wrap" this code up in a method, as follows:

```
public static void printParity (int x) {
  if (x%2 == 0) {
    System.out.println ("x is even");
  } else {
    System.out.println ("x is odd");
  }
}
```

Now you have a method named `printParity` that will print an appropriate message for any integer you care to provide. In `main` you would invoke this method as follows:

```
printParity (17);
```

Always remember that when you *invoke* a method, you do not have to declare the types of the arguments you provide. Java can figure out what type they are. You should resist the temptation to write things like:

```
int number = 17;
printParity (int number);          // WRONG!!!
```

4.4 Chained conditionals

Sometimes you want to check for a number of related conditions and choose one of several actions. One way to do this is by **chaining** a series of `if`s and `else`s:

```
if (x > 0) {
  System.out.println ("x is positive");
} else if (x < 0) {
  System.out.println ("x is negative");
} else {
  System.out.println ("x is zero");
}
```

These chains can be as long as you want, although they can be difficult to read if they get out of hand. One way to make them easier to read is to use standard indentation, as demonstrated in these examples. If you keep all the statements and squiggly-brackets lined up, you are less likely to make syntax errors and you can find them more quickly if you do.

4.5 Nested conditionals

In addition to chaining, you can also nest one conditional within another. We could have written the previous example as:

```
if (x == 0) {
  System.out.println ("x is zero");
} else {
  if (x > 0) {
    System.out.println ("x is positive");
  } else {
    System.out.println ("x is negative");
  }
}
```

There is now an outer conditional that contains two branches. The first branch contains a simple `print` statement, but the second branch contains another conditional statement, which has two branches of its own. Fortunately, those two branches are both `print` statements, although they could have been conditional statements as well.

Notice again that indentation helps make the structure apparent, but nevertheless, nested conditionals get difficult to read very quickly. In general, it is a good idea to avoid them when you can.

On the other hand, this kind of **nested structure** is common, and we will see it again, so you better get used to it.

4.6   The return statement

The `return` statement allows you to terminate the execution of a method before you reach the end. One reason to use it is if you detect an error condition:

```
public static void printLogarithm (double x) {
  if (x <= 0.0) {
    System.out.println ("Positive numbers only, please.");
    return;
  }

  double result = Math.log (x);
  System.out.println ("The log of x is " + result);
}
```

This defines a method named `printLogarithm` that takes a `double` named x as a parameter. The first thing it does is check whether x is less than or equal to zero, in which case it prints an error message and then uses `return` to exit the method. The flow of execution immediately returns to the caller and the remaining lines of the method are not executed.

I used a floating-point value on the right side of the condition because there is a floating-point variable on the left.

4.7   Type conversion

You might wonder how you can get away with an expression like `"The log of x is " + result`, since one of the operands is a `String` and the other is a `double`. Well, in this case Java is being smart on our behalf, by automatically converting the `double` to a `String` before it does the string concatenation.

This kind of feature is an example of a common problem in designing a programming language, which is that there is a conflict between *formalism*, which is the requirement that formal languages should have simple rules with few exceptions, and *convenience*, which is the requirement that programming languages be easy to use in practice.

More often than not, convenience wins, which is usually good for expert programmers (who are spared from rigorous but unwieldy formalism), but bad for beginning programmers, who are often baffled by the complexity of the rules and the number of exceptions. In this book I have tried to simplify things by emphasizing the rules and omitting many of the exceptions.

Nevertheless, it is handy to know that whenever you try to "add" two expressions, if one of them is a `String`, then Java will convert the other to a `String` and then perform string concatenation. What do you think happens if you perform an operation between an integer and a floating-point value?

4.8 Recursion

I mentioned in the last chapter that it is legal for one method to call another, and we have seen several examples of that. I neglected to mention that it is also legal for a method to invoke itself. It may not be obvious why that is a good thing, but it turns out to be one of the most magical and interesting things a program can do.

For example, look at the following method:

```
public static void countdown (int n) {
  if (n == 0) {
    System.out.println ("Blastoff!");
  } else {
    System.out.println (n);
    countdown (n-1);
  }
}
```

The name of the method is `countdown` and it takes a single integer as a parameter. If the parameter is zero, it prints the word "Blastoff." Otherwise, it prints the number and then invokes a method named `countdown`—itself—passing n−1 as an argument.

What happens if we invoke this method, in `main`, like this:

```
countdown (3);
```

The execution of `countdown` begins with n=3, and since n is not zero, it prints the value 3, and then invokes itself...

> The execution of `countdown` begins with n=2, and since n is not zero, it prints the value 2, and then invokes itself...
>
> > The execution of `countdown` begins with n=1, and since n is not zero, it prints the value 1, and then invokes itself...
> >
> > > The execution of `countdown` begins with n=0, and since n is zero, it prints the word "Blastoff!" and then returns.
> >
> > The countdown that got n=1 returns.
>
> The countdown that got n=2 returns.

The countdown that got n=3 returns.

And then you're back in main (what a trip). So the total output looks like:

```
3
2
1
Blastoff!
```

As a second example, let's look again at the methods newLine and threeLine.

```
public static void newLine () {
  System.out.println ("");
}

public static void threeLine () {
  newLine ();  newLine ();  newLine ();
}
```

Although these work, they would not be much help if I wanted to print 2 new-lines, or 106. A better alternative would be

```
public static void nLines (int n) {
  if (n > 0) {
    System.out.println ("");
    nLines (n-1);
  }
}
```

This program is very similar; as long as n is greater than zero, it prints one newline, and then invokes itself to print n-1 additional newlines. Thus, the total number of newlines that get printed is 1 + (n-1), which usually comes out to roughly n.

The process of a method invoking itself is called **recursion**, and such methods are said to be **recursive**.

4.9 Stack diagrams for recursive methods

In the previous chapter we used a stack diagram to represent the state of a program during a method call. The same kind of diagram can make it easier to interpret a recursive method.

Remember that every time a method gets called it creates a new instance of the method that contains a new version of the method's local variables and parameters.

The following figure is a stack diagram for countdown, called with n = 3:

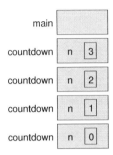

There is one instance of main and four instances of countdown, each with a different value for the parameter n. The bottom of the stack, countdown with n=0 is the base case. It does not make a recursive call, so there are no more instances of countdown.

The instance of main is empty because main does not have any parameters or local variables.

Exercise 4.1   Draw a stack diagram that shows the state of the program after main invokes nLines with the parameter n=4, just before the last instance of nLines returns.

4.10   Convention and divine law

In the last few sections, I used the phrase "by convention" several times to indicate design decisions that are arbitrary in the sense that there are no significant reasons to do things one way or another, but dictated by convention.

In these cases, it is to your advantage to be familiar with convention and use it, since it will make your programs easier for others to understand. At the same time, it is important to distinguish between (at least) three kinds of rules:

Divine law: This is my phrase to indicate a rule that is true because of some underlying principle of logic or mathematics, and that is true in any programming language (or other formal system). For example, there is no way to specify the location and size of a bounding box using fewer than four pieces of information. Another example is that adding integers is commutative. That's part of the definition of addition and has nothing to do with Java.

Rules of Java: These are the syntactic and semantic rules of Java that you cannot violate, because the resulting program will not compile or run. Some are arbitrary; for example, the fact that the + symbol represents addition *and* string concatenation. Others reflect underlying limitations of the compilation or execution process. For example, you have to specify the types of parameters, but not arguments.

Style and convention: There are a lot of rules that are not enforced by the compiler, but that are essential for writing programs that are correct, that you can debug and modify, and that others can read. Examples include indentation and the placement of squiggly braces, as well as conventions for naming variables, methods and classes.

As we go along, I will try to indicate which category various things fall into, but you might want to give it some thought from time to time.

While I am on the topic, you have probably figured out by now that the names of classes always begin with a capital letter, but variables and methods begin with lower case. If a name includes more than one word, you usually capitalize the first letter of each word, as in `newLine` and `printParity`. Which category are these rules in?

4.11   Glossary

modulus: An operator that works on integers and yields the remainder when one number is divided by another. In Java it is denoted with a percent sign (`%`).

conditional: A block of statements that may or may not be executed depending on some condition.

chaining: A way of joining several conditional statements in sequence.

nesting: Putting a conditional statement inside one or both branches of another conditional statement.

coordinate: A variable or value that specifies a location in a two-dimensional graphical window.

pixel: The unit in which coordinates are measured.

bounding box: A common way to specify the coordinates of a rectangular area.

typecast: An operator that converts from one type to another. In Java it appears as a type name in parentheses, like (`int`).

interface: A description of the parameters required by a method and their types.

prototype: A way of describing the interface to a method using Java-like syntax.

recursion: The process of invoking the same method you are currently executing.

infinite recursion: A method that invokes itself recursively without ever reaching the base case. The usual result is a StackOverflowException.

fractal: A kind of image that is defined recursively, so that each part of the image is a smaller version of the whole.

4.12   Exercises

Exercise 4.2   If you are given three sticks, you may or may not be able to arrange them in a triangle. For example, if one of the sticks is 12 inches long and the other two are one inch long, it is clear that you will not be able to get the short sticks to meet in the middle. For any three lengths, there is a simple test to see if it is possible to form a triangle:

> "If any of the three lengths is greater than the sum of the other two, then you cannot form a triangle. Otherwise, you can."

Write a method named `isTriangle` that it takes three integers as arguments, and that returns either `true` or `false`, depending on whether you can or cannot form a triangle from sticks with the given lengths.

The point of this exercise is to use conditional statements to write a method that returns a value.

Exercise 4.3   This exercise reviews the flow of execution through a program with multiple methods. Read the following code and answer the questions below.

```
public class Buzz {

    public static void baffle (String blimp) {
        System.out.println (blimp);
        zippo ("ping", -5);
    }

    public static void zippo (String quince, int flag) {
        if (flag < 0) {
            System.out.println (quince + " zoop");
        } else {
            System.out.println ("ik");
            baffle (quince);
            System.out.println ("boo-wa-ha-ha");
        }
    }

    public static void main (String[] args) {
        zippo ("rattle", 13);
    }
}
```

a. Write the number 1 next to the first *statement* of this program that will be executed. Be careful to distinguish things that are statements from things that are not.

b. Write the number 2 next to the second statement, and so on until the end of the program. If a statement is executed more than once, it might end up with more than one number next to it.

c. What is the value of the parameter `blimp` when `baffle` gets invoked?

d. What is the output of this program?

Exercise 4.4   The first verse of the song "99 Bottles of Beer" is:

> 99 bottles of beer on the wall, 99 bottles of beer, ya' take one down, ya'
> pass it around, 98 bottles of beer on the wall.

Subsequent verses are identical except that the number of bottles gets smaller by one
in each verse, until the last verse:

> No bottles of beer on the wall, no bottles of beer, ya' can't take one down,
> ya' can't pass it around, 'cause there are no more bottles of beer on the
> wall!

And then the song (finally) ends.

Write a program that prints the entire lyrics of "99 Bottles of Beer." Your program
should include a recursive method that does the hard part, but you also might want
to write additional methods to separate the major functions of the program.

As you are developing your code, you will probably want to test it with a small number
of verses, like "3 Bottles of Beer."

The purpose of this exercise is to take a problem and break it into smaller problems,
and to solve the smaller problems by writing simple, easily-debugged methods.

Exercise 4.5   What is the output of the following program?

```
public class Narf {

    public static void zoop (String fred, int bob) {
        System.out.println (fred);
        if (bob == 5) {
            ping ("not ");
        } else {
            System.out.println ("!");
        }
    }

    public static void main (String[] args) {
        int bizz = 5;
        int buzz = 2;
        zoop ("just for", bizz);
        clink (2*buzz);
    }

    public static void clink (int fork) {
        System.out.print ("It's ");
        zoop ("breakfast ", fork) ;
    }

    public static void ping (String strangStrung) {
```

```
        System.out.println ("any " + strangStrung + "more ");
    }
}
```

Exercise 4.6   Fermat's Last Theorem says that there are no integers a, b, and c such that

$$a^n + b^n = c^n$$

except in the case when $n = 2$.

Write a method named `checkFermat` that takes four integers as parameters—a, b, c and n—and that checks to see if Fermat's theorem holds. If n is greater than 2 and it turns out to be true that $a^n + b^n = c^n$, the program should print "Holy smokes, Fermat was wrong!" Otherwise the program should print "No, that doesn't work."

You should assume that there is a method named `raiseToPow` that takes two integers as arguments and that raises the first argument to the power of the second. For example:

```
    int x = raiseToPow (2, 3);
```

would assign the value 8 to x, because $2^3 = 8$.

Chapter 5

Fruitful methods

5.1 Return values

Some of the built-in methods we have used, like the Math functions, have produced results. That is, the effect of invoking the method is to generate a new value, which we usually assign to a variable or use as part of an expression. For example:

```
double e = Math.exp (1.0);
double height = radius * Math.sin (angle);
```

But so far all the methods we have written have been **void** methods; that is, methods that return no value. When you invoke a void method, it is typically on a line by itself, with no assignment:

```
nLines (3);
g.drawOval (0, 0, width, height);
```

In this chapter, we are going to write methods that return things, which I will refer to as **fruitful** methods, for want of a better name. The first example is area, which takes a double as a parameter, and returns the area of a circle with the given radius:

```
public static double area (double radius) {
   double area = Math.PI * radius * radius;
   return area;
}
```

The first thing you should notice is that the beginning of the method definition is different. Instead of public static void, which indicates a void method, we see public static double, which indicates that the return value from this method will have type double. I still haven't explained what public static means, but be patient.

Also, notice that the last line is an alternative form of the return statement that includes a return value. This statement means, "return immediately from this method and use the following expression as a return value." The expression you provide can be arbitrarily complicated, so we could have written this method more concisely:

```
public static double area (double radius) {
  return Math.PI * radius * radius;
}
```

On the other hand, **temporary** variables like area often make debugging easier. In either case, the type of the expression in the return statement must match the return type of the method. In other words, when you declare that the return type is double, you are making a promise that this method will eventually produce a double. If you try to return with no expression, or an expression with the wrong type, the compiler will take you to task.

Sometimes it is useful to have multiple return statements, one in each branch of a conditional:

```
public static double absoluteValue (double x) {
  if (x < 0) {
    return -x;
  } else {
    return x;
  }
}
```

Since these return statements are in an alternative conditional, only one will be executed. Although it is legal to have more than one return statement in a method, you should keep in mind that as soon as one is executed, the method terminates without executing any subsequent statements.

Code that appears after a return statement, or any place else where it can never be executed, is called **dead code**. Some compilers warn you if part of your code is dead.

If you put return statements inside a conditional, then you have to guarantee that *every possible path* through the program hits a return statement. For example:

```
public static double absoluteValue (double x) {
  if (x < 0) {
    return -x;
  } else if (x > 0) {
    return x;
  }                              // WRONG!!
}
```

This program is not legal because if x happens to be 0, then neither condition will be true and the method will end without hitting a return statement. A typical compiler message would be "return statement required in absoluteValue," which is a confusing message considering that there are already two of them.

5.2   Program development

At this point you should be able to look at complete Java methods and tell what they do. But it may not be clear yet how to go about writing them. I am going to suggest one technique that I call **incremental development**.

As an example, imagine you want to find the distance between two points, given by the coordinates (x_1, y_1) and (x_2, y_2). By the usual definition,

$$distance = \sqrt{(x_2 - x_1)^2 + (y_2 - y_1)^2} \qquad (5.1)$$

The first step is to consider what a `distance` method should look like in Java. In other words, what are the inputs (parameters) and what is the output (return value).

In this case, the two points are the parameters, and it is natural to represent them using four `doubles`, although we will see later that there is a `Point` object in Java that we could use. The return value is the distance, which will have type `double`.

Already we can write an outline of the method:

```
public static double distance
            (double x1, double y1, double x2, double y2) {
  return 0.0;
}
```

The statement `return 0.0;` is a place-keeper that is necessary in order to compile the program. Obviously, at this stage the program doesn't do anything useful, but it is worthwhile to try compiling it so we can identify any syntax errors before we make it more complicated.

In order to test the new method, we have to invoke it with sample values. Somewhere in `main` I would add:

```
double dist = distance (1.0, 2.0, 4.0, 6.0);
```

I chose these values so that the horizontal distance is 3 and the vertical distance is 4; that way, the result will be 5 (the hypotenuse of a 3-4-5 triangle). When you are testing a method, it is useful to know the right answer.

Once we have checked the syntax of the method definition, we can start adding lines of code one at a time. After each incremental change, we recompile and run the program. That way, at any point we know exactly where the error must be—in the last line we added.

The next step in the computation is to find the differences $x_2 - x_1$ and $y_2 - y_1$. I will store those values in temporary variables named `dx` and `dy`.

```
 public static double distance
            (double x1, double y1, double x2, double y2) {
  double dx = x2 - x1;
  double dy = y2 - y1;
```

```
    System.out.println ("dx is " + dx);
    System.out.println ("dy is " + dy);
    return 0.0;
}
```

I added print statements that will let me check the intermediate values before proceeding. As I mentioned, I already know that they should be 3.0 and 4.0.

When the method is finished I will remove the print statements. Code like that is called **scaffolding**, because it is helpful for building the program, but it is not part of the final product. Sometimes it is a good idea to keep the scaffolding around, but comment it out, just in case you need it later.

The next step in the development is to square dx and dy. We could use the Math.pow method, but it is simpler and faster to just multiply each term by itself.

```
public static double distance
             (double x1, double y1, double x2, double y2) {
  double dx = x2 - x1;
  double dy = y2 - y1;
  double dsquared = dx*dx + dy*dy;
  System.out.println ("dsquared is " + dsquared);
  return 0.0;
}
```

Again, I would compile and run the program at this stage and check the intermediate value (which should be 25.0).

Finally, we can use the Math.sqrt method to compute and return the result.

```
public static double distance
             (double x1, double y1, double x2, double y2) {
  double dx = x2 - x1;
  double dy = y2 - y1;
  double dsquared = dx*dx + dy*dy;
  double result = Math.sqrt (dsquared);
  return result;
}
```

Then in main, we should print and check the value of the result.

As you gain more experience programming, you might find yourself writing and debugging more than one line at a time. Nevertheless, this incremental development process can save you a lot of debugging time.

The key aspects of the process are:

- Start with a working program and make small, incremental changes. At any point, if there is an error, you will know exactly where it is.

- Use temporary variables to hold intermediate values so you can print and check them.

- Once the program is working, you might want to remove some of the scaffolding or consolidate multiple statements into compound expressions, but only if it does not make the program difficult to read.

5.3   Composition

As you should expect by now, once you define a new method, you can use it as part of an expression, and you can build new methods using existing methods. For example, what if someone gave you two points, the center of the circle and a point on the perimeter, and asked for the area of the circle?

Let's say the center point is stored in the variables xc and yc, and the perimeter point is in xp and yp. The first step is to find the radius of the circle, which is the distance between the two points. Fortunately, we have a method, distance that does that.

```
double radius = distance (xc, yc, xp, yp);
```

The second step is to find the area of a circle with that radius, and return it.

```
double area = area (radius);
return area;
```

Wrapping that all up in a method, we get:

```
public static double fred
            (double xc, double yc, double xp, double yp) {
  double radius = distance (xc, yc, xp, yp);
  double area = area (radius);
  return area;
}
```

The name of this method is fred, which may seem odd. I will explain why in the next section.

The temporary variables radius and area are useful for development and debugging, but once the program is working we can make it more concise by composing the method invocations:

```
public static double fred
            (double xc, double yc, double xp, double yp) {
  return area (distance (xc, yc, xp, yp));
}
```

5.4   Overloading

In the previous section you might have noticed that fred and area perform similar functions—finding the area of a circle—but take different parameters. For area, we have to provide the radius; for fred we provide two points.

If two methods do the same thing, it is natural to give them the same name. In other words, it would make more sense if fred were called area.

Having more than one method with the same name, which is called **overloading**, is legal in Java *as long as each version takes different parameters.* So we can go ahead and rename `fred`:

```
public static double area
            (double x1, double y1, double x2, double y2) {
  return area (distance (xc, yc, xp, yp));
}
```

When you invoke an overloaded method, Java knows which version you want by looking at the arguments that you provide. If you write:

```
double x = area (3.0);
```

Java goes looking for a method named `area` that takes a single `double` as an argument, and so it uses the first version, which interprets the argument as a radius. If you write:

```
double x = area (1.0, 2.0, 4.0, 6.0);
```

Java uses the second version of `area`. More amazing still, the second version of `area` actually invokes the first.

Many of the built-in Java commands are overloaded, meaning that there are different versions that accept different numbers or types of parameters. For example, there are versions of `print` and `println` that accept a single parameter of any type. In the Math class, there is a version of `abs` that works on `doubles`, and there is also a version for `ints`.

Although overloading is a useful feature, it should be used with caution. You might get yourself nicely confused if you are trying to debug one version of a method while accidently invoking a different one.

Actually, that reminds me of one of the cardinal rules of debugging: **make sure that the version of the program you are looking at is the version of the program that is running!** Some time you may find yourself making one change after another in your program, and seeing the same thing every time you run it. This is a warning sign that for one reason or another you are not running the version of the program you think you are. To check, stick in a `print` statement (it doesn't matter what you print) and make sure the behavior of the program changes accordingly.

5.5   Boolean expressions

Most of the operations we have seen produce results that are the same type as their operands. For example, the + operator takes two `ints` and produces an `int`, or two `doubles` and produces a `double`, etc.

The exceptions we have seen are the **relational operators**, which compare `ints` and `floats` and return either `true` or `false`. `true` and `false` are special values in Java, and together they make up a type called **boolean**. You might recall that when I defined a type, I said it was a set of values. In the case of ints, doubles and Strings, those sets are pretty big. For booleans, not so big.

Boolean expressions and variables work just like other types of expressions and variables:

```
boolean fred;
fred = true;
boolean testResult = false;
```

The first example is a simple variable declaration; the second example is an assignment, and the third example is a combination of a declaration and an assignment, sometimes called an **initialization**. The values true and false are keywords in Java, so they may appear in a different color, depending on your development environment.

As I mentioned, the result of a conditional operator is a boolean, so you can store the result of a comparison in a variable:

```
boolean evenFlag = (n%2 == 0);     // true if n is even
boolean positiveFlag = (x > 0);    // true if x is positive
```

and then use it as part of a conditional statement later:

```
if (evenFlag) {
  System.out.println ("n was even when I checked it");
}
```

A variable used in this way is frequently called a **flag**, since it flags the presence or absence of some condition.

5.6   Logical operators

There are three **logical operators** in Java: AND, OR and NOT, which are denoted by the symbols &&, || and !. The semantics (meaning) of these operators is similar to their meaning in English. For example x > 0 && x < 10 is true only if x is greater than zero AND less than 10.

evenFlag || n%3 == 0 is true if *either* of the conditions is true, that is, if evenFlag is true OR the number is divisible by 3.

Finally, the NOT operator has the effect of negating or inverting a boolean expression, so !evenFlag is true if evenFlag is false—if the number is odd.

Logical operators often provide a way to simplify nested conditional statements. For example, how would you write the following code using a single conditional?

```
if (x > 0) {
  if (x < 10) {
    System.out.println ("x is a positive single digit.");
  }
}
```

5.7 Boolean methods

Methods can return boolean values just like any other type, which is often convenient for hiding complicated tests inside methods. For example:

```
public static boolean isSingleDigit (int x) {
  if (x >= 0 && x < 10) {
    return true;
  } else {
    return false;
  }
}
```

The name of this method is `isSingleDigit`. It is common to give boolean methods names that sound like yes/no questions. The return type is `boolean`, which means that every return statement has to provide a boolean expression.

The code itself is straightforward, although it is a bit longer than it needs to be. Remember that the expression `x >= 0 && x < 10` has type boolean, so there is nothing wrong with returning it directly, and avoiding the `if` statement altogether:

```
public static boolean isSingleDigit (int x) {
  return (x >= 0 && x < 10);
}
```

In `main` you can invoke this method in the usual ways:

```
boolean bigFlag = !isSingleDigit (17);
System.out.println (isSingleDigit (2));
```

The first line assigns the value `true` to `bigFlag` only if 17 is *not* a single-digit number. The second line prints `true` because 2 is a single-digit number. Yes, `println` is overloaded to handle booleans, too.

The most common use of boolean methods is inside conditional statements

```
if (isSingleDigit (x)) {
  System.out.println ("x is little");
} else {
  System.out.println ("x is big");
}
```

5.8 More recursion

Now that we have methods that return values, you might be interested to know that we have a **complete** programming language, by which I mean that anything that can be computed can be expressed in this language. Any program ever written could be rewritten using only the language features we have used so far (actually, we would need a few commands to control devices like the keyboard, mouse, disks, etc., but that's all).

Proving this claim is a non-trivial exercise first accomplished by Alan Turing, one of the first computer scientists (well, some would argue that he was a mathematician, but a lot of the early computer scientists started as mathematicians). Accordingly, it is known as the Turing thesis. If you take a course on the Theory of Computation, you will have a chance to see the proof.

To give you an idea of what you can do with the tools we have learned so far, let's look at some methods for evaluating recursively-defined mathematical functions. A recursive definition is similar to a circular definition, in the sense that the definition contains a reference to the thing being defined. A truly circular definition is typically not very useful:

frabjuous: an adjective used to describe something that is frabjuous.

If you saw that definition in the dictionary, you might be annoyed. On the other hand, if you looked up the definition of the mathematical function **factorial**, you might get something like:

$$0! = 1$$
$$n! = n \cdot (n - 1)!$$

(Factorial is usually denoted with the symbol !, which is not to be confused with the Java logical operator ! which means NOT.) This definition says that the factorial of 0 is 1, and the factorial of any other value, n, is n multiplied by the factorial of $n - 1$. So 3! is 3 times 2!, which is 2 times 1!, which is 1 times 0!. Putting it all together, we get 3! equal to 3 times 2 times 1 times 1, which is 6.

If you can write a recursive definition of something, you can usually write a Java program to evaluate it. The first step is to decide what the parameters are for this function, and what the return type is. With a little thought, you should conclude that factorial takes an integer as a parameter and returns an integer:

```
public static int factorial (int n) {
}
```

If the argument happens to be zero, all we have to do is return 1:

```
public static int factorial (int n) {
  if (n == 0) {
    return 1;
  }
}
```

Otherwise, and this is the interesting part, we have to make a recursive call to find the factorial of $n - 1$, and then multiply it by n.

```
public static int factorial (int n) {
  if (n == 0) {
    return 1;
  } else {
```

```
        int recurse = factorial (n-1);
        int result = n * recurse;
        return result;
    }
}
```

If we look at the flow of execution for this program, it is similar to nLines from the previous chapter. If we invoke factorial with the value 3:

Since 3 is not zero, we take the second branch and calculate the factorial of $n - 1$...

> Since 2 is not zero, we take the second branch and calculate the factorial of $n - 1$...
>
> > Since 1 is not zero, we take the second branch and calculate the factorial of $n - 1$...
> >
> > > Since 0 *is* zero, we take the first branch and return the value 1 immediately without making any more recursive calls.
> >
> > The return value (1) gets multiplied by n, which is 1, and the result is returned.
>
> The return value (1) gets multiplied by n, which is 2, and the result is returned.

The return value (2) gets multiplied by n, which is 3, and the result, 6, is returned to main, or whoever invoked factorial (3).

Here is what the stack diagram looks like for this sequence of function calls:

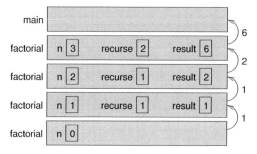

The return values are shown being passed back up the stack.

Notice that in the last instance of factorial, the local variables recurse and result do not exist because when n=0 the branch that creates them does not execute.

5.9   Leap of faith

Following the flow of execution is one way to read programs, but as you saw in the previous section, it can quickly become labarynthine. An alternative is what I call the "leap of faith." When you come to a method invocation, instead of following the flow of execution, you *assume* that the method works correctly and returns the appropriate value.

In fact, you are already practicing this leap of faith when you use built-in methods. When you invoke `Math.cos` or `drawOval`, you don't examine the implementations of those methods. You just assume that they work, because the people who wrote the built-in classes were good programmers.

Well, the same is true when you invoke one of your own methods. For example, in Section 5.7 we wrote a method called `isSingleDigit` that determines whether a number is between 0 and 9. Once we have convinced ourselves that this method is correct—by testing and examination of the code—we can use the method without ever looking at the code again.

The same is true of recursive programs. When you get to the recursive invocation, instead of following the flow of execution, you should *assume* that the recursive invocation works (yields the correct result), and then ask yourself, "Assuming that I can find the factorial of $n - 1$, can I compute the factorial of n?" In this case, it is clear that you can, by multiplying by n.

Of course, it is a bit strange to assume that the method works correctly when you have not even finished writing it, but that's why it's called a leap of faith!

5.10   One more example

In the previous example I used temporary variables to spell out the steps, and to make the code easier to debug, but I could have saved a few lines:

```
public static int factorial (int n) {
  if (n == 0) {
    return 1;
  } else {
    return n * factorial (n-1);
  }
}
```

From now on I will tend to use the more concise version, but I recommend that you use the more explicit version while you are developing code. When you have it working, you can tighten it up, if you are feeling inspired.

After `factorial`, the classic example of a recursively-defined mathematical function is `fibonacci`, which has the following definition:

$$fibonacci(0) = 1$$

$$fibonacci(1) = 1$$
$$fibonacci(n) = fibonacci(n-1) + fibonacci(n-2);$$

Translated into Java, this is

```
public static int fibonacci (int n) {
  if (n == 0 || n == 1) {
    return 1;
  } else {
    return fibonacci (n-1) + fibonacci (n-2);
  }
}
```

If you try to follow the flow of execution here, even for fairly small values of n, your head explodes. But according to the leap of faith, if we assume that the two recursive calls (yes, you can make two recursive calls) work correctly, then it is clear that we get the right result by adding them together.

5.11   Glossary

return type: The part of a method declaration that indicates what type of value the method returns.

return value: The value provided as the result of a method invocation.

dead code: Part of a program that can never be executed, often because it appears after a `return` statement.

scaffolding: Code that is used during program development but is not part of the final version.

void: A special return type that indicates a void method; that is, one that does not return a value.

overloading: Having more than one method with the same name but different parameters. When you invoke an overloaded method, Java knows which version to use by looking at the arguments you provide.

boolean: A type of variable that can contain only the two values `true` and `false`.

flag: A variable (usually `boolean`) that records a condition or status information.

conditional operator: An operator that compares two values and produces a boolean that indicates the relationship between the operands.

logical operator: An operator that combines boolean values and produces boolean values.

initialization: A statement that declares a new variable and assigns a value to it at the same time.

5.12   Exercises

Exercise 5.1   Write a class method named isDivisible that takes two integers, n and m and that returns true if n is divisible by m and false otherwise.

Exercise 5.2   What is the output of the following program? The purpose of this exercise is to make sure you understand logical operators and the flow of execution through fruitful methods.

```
public static void main (String[] args) {
    boolean flag1 = isHoopy (202);
    boolean flag2 = isFrabjuous (202);
    System.out.println (flag1);
    System.out.println (flag2);
    if (flag1 && flag2) {
        System.out.println ("ping!");
    }
    if (flag1 || flag2) {
        System.out.println ("pong!");
    }
}


public static boolean isHoopy (int x) {
    boolean hoopyFlag;
    if (x%2 == 0) {
        hoopyFlag = true;
    } else {
        hoopyFlag = false;
    }
    return hoopyFlag;
}


public static boolean isFrabjuous (int x) {
    boolean frabjuousFlag;
    if (x > 0) {
        frabjuousFlag = true;
    } else {
        frabjuousFlag = false;
    }
    return frabjuousFlag;
}
```

Exercise 5.3   The distance between two points (x_1, y_1) and (x_2, y_2) is

$$Distance = \sqrt{(x_2 - x_1)^2 + (y_2 - y_1)^2}$$

Please write a method named distance that takes four doubles as parameters—x1, y1, x2 and y2—and that prints the distance between the points.

You should assume that there is a method named sumSquares that calculates and returns the sum of the squares of its arguments. For example:

```
    double x = sumSquares (3.0, 4.0);
```
would assign the value 25.0 to x.

The point of this exercise is to write a new method that uses an existing one. You should write only one method: distance. You should not write sumSquares or main and you should not invoke distance.

Exercise 5.4   The point of this exercise is to practice the syntax of fruitful methods.

a. Dig out your solution to Exercise 3.5 and make sure you can still compile and run it.

b. Transform multadd into a fruitful method, so that instead of printing a result, it returns it.

c. Everywhere in the program that multadd gets invoked, change the invocation so that it stores the result in a variable and/or prints the result.

d. Transform yikes in the same way.

Exercise 5.5   The point of this exercise is to use a stack diagram to understand the execution of a recursive program.

```
public class Prod {

    public static void main (String[] args) {
        System.out.println (prod (1, 4));
    }

    public static int prod (int m, int n) {
        if (m == n) {
            return n;
        } else {
            int recurse = prod (m, n-1);
            int result = n * recurse;
            return result;
        }
    }
}
```

a. Draw a stack diagram showing the state of the program just before the last instance of prod completes. What is the output of this program?

b. Explain in a few words what prod does.

c. Rewrite prod without using the temporary variables recurse and result.

Exercise 5.6   The purpose of this exercise is to translate a recursive definition into a Java method. The Ackerman function is defined for non-negative integers as follows:

$$A(m,n) = \begin{cases} n+1 & \text{if} \quad m = 0 \\ A(m-1,1) & \text{if} \quad m > 0, n = 0 \\ A(m-1, A(m,n-1)) & \text{if} \quad m > 0, n > 0 \end{cases}$$

Write a method called `ack` that takes two `int`s as parameters and that computes and returns the value of the Ackerman function.

Test your implementation of Ackerman by invoking it from `main` and printing the return value.

WARNING: the return value gets very big very quickly. You should try it only for small values of m and n (not bigger than 2).

Exercise 5.7

    a. Create a program called `Recurse.java` and type in the following methods:

```
// first: returns the first character of the given String
public static char first (String s) {
    return s.charAt (0);
}

// last: returns a new String that contains all but the
// first letter of the given String
public static String rest (String s) {
    return s.substring (1, s.length());
}

// length: returns the length of the given String
public static int length (String s) {
    return s.length();
}
```

    b. Write some code in `main` that tests each of these methods. Make sure they work, and make sure you understand what they do.

    c. Write a method called `printString` that takes a String as a parameter and that prints the letters of the String, one on each line. It should be a `void` method.

    d. Write a method called `printBackward` that does the same thing as `printString` but that prints the String backwards (one character per line).

    e. Write a method called `reverseString` that takes a String as a parameter and that returns a new String as a return value. The new String should contain the same letters as the parameter, but in reverse order. For example, the output of the following code

```
String backwards = reverseString ("Allen Downey");
System.out.println (backwards);
```

    should be

```
yenwoD nellA
```

Exercise 5.8

    a. Create a new program called `Sum.java`, and type in the following two methods.

```
public static int methOne (int m, int n) {
  if (m == n) {
    return n;
  } else {
    return m + methOne (m+1, n);
  }
}

public static int methTwo (int m, int n) {
  if (m == n) {
    return n;
  } else {
    return n * methTwo (m, n-1);
  }
}
```

b. Write a few lines in main to test these methods. Invoke them a couple of times, with a few different values, and see what you get. By some combination of testing and examination of the code, figure out what these methods do, and give them more meaningful names. Add comments that describe their function abstractly.

c. Add a println statement to the beginning of both methods so that they print their arguments each time they are invoked. This is a useful technique for debugging recursive programs, since it demonstrates the flow of execution.

Exercise 5.9   Write a recursive method called power that takes a double x and an integer n and that returns x^n. Hint: a recursive definition of this operation is power (x, n) = x * power (x, n-1). Also, remember that anything raised to the zeroeth power is 1.

Exercise 5.10   (This exercise is based on page 44 of Ableson and Sussman's *Structure and Interpretation of Computer Programs*.)

The following algorithm is known as Euclid's Algorithm because it appears in Euclid's *Elements* (Book 7, ca. 300 B.C.). It may be the oldest nontrivial algorithm.

The algorithm is based on the observation that, if r is the remainder when a is divided by b, then the common divisors of a and b are the same as the common divisors of b and r. Thus we can use the equation

$$gcd(a, b) = gcd(b, r)$$

to successively reduce the problem of computing a GCD to the problem of computing the GCD of smaller and smaller pairs of integers. For example,

$$gcd(36, 20) = gcd(20, 16) = gcd(16, 4) = gcd(4, 0) = 4$$

implies that the GCD of 36 and 20 is 4. It can be shown that for any two starting numbers, this repeated reduction eventually produces a pair where the second number is 0. Then the GCD is the other number in the pair.

Write a method called gcd that takes two integer parameters and that uses Euclid's algorithm to compute and return the greatest common divisor of the two numbers.

Chapter 6

Iteration

6.1 Multiple assignment

I haven't said much about it, but it is legal in Java to make more than one assignment to the same variable. The effect of the second assignment is to replace the old value of the variable with a new value.

```
int fred = 5;
System.out.print (fred);
fred = 7;
System.out.println (fred);
```

The output of this program is 57, because the first time we print fred his value is 5, and the second time his value is 7.

This kind of **multiple assignment** is the reason I described variables as a *container* for values. When you assign a value to a variable, you change the contents of the container, as shown in the figure:

When there are multiple assignments to a variable, it is especially important to distinguish between an assignment statement and a statement of equality. Because Java uses the = symbol for assignment, it is tempting to interpret a statement like a = b as a statement of equality. It is not!

First of all, equality is commutative, and assignment is not. For example, in mathematics if $a = 7$ then $7 = a$. But in Java a = 7; is a legal assignment statement, and 7 = a; is not.

Furthermore, in mathematics, a statement of equality is true for all time. If $a = b$ now, then a will always equal b. In Java, an assignment statement can make two variables equal, but they don't have to stay that way!

```
int a = 5;
int b = a;      // a and b are now equal
a = 3;          // a and b are no longer equal
```

The third line changes the value of a but it does not change the value of b, and so they are no longer equal. In many programming languages an alternative symbol is used for assignment, such as <- or :=, in order to avoid this confusion.

Although multiple assignment is frequently useful, you should use it with caution. If the values of variables are changing constantly in different parts of the program, it can make the code difficult to read and debug.

6.2   Iteration

One of the things computers are often used for is the automation of repetitive tasks. Repeating identical or similar tasks without making errors is something that computers do well and people do poorly.

We have already seen programs that use recursion to perform repetition, such as nLines and countdown. This type of repetition is called **iteration**, and Java provides several language features that make it easier to write iterative programs.

The two features we are going to look at are the while statement and the for statement.

6.3   The while statement

Using a while statement, we can rewrite countdown:

```
public static void countdown (int n) {
  while (n > 0) {
    System.out.println (n);
    n = n-1;
  }
  System.out.println ("Blastoff!");
}
```

You can almost read a while statement as if it were English. What this means is, "While n is greater than zero, continue printing the value of n and then reducing the value of n by 1. When you get to zero, print the word 'Blastoff!'"

More formally, the flow of execution for a while statement is as follows:

1. Evaluate the condition in parentheses, yielding true or false.

2. If the condition is false, exit the while statement and continue execution at the next statement.

3. If the condition is true, execute each of the statements between the squiggly-brackets, and then go back to step 1.

This type of flow is called a **loop** because the third step loops back around to the top. Notice that if the condition is false the first time through the loop, the statements inside the loop are never executed. The statements inside the loop are sometimes called the **body** of the loop.

The body of the loop should change the value of one or more variables so that, eventually, the condition becomes false and the loop terminates. Otherwise the loop will repeat forever, which is called an **infinite** loop. An endless source of amusement for computer scientists is the observation that the directions on shampoo, "Lather, rinse, repeat," are an infinite loop.

In the case of countdown, we can prove that the loop will terminate because we know that the value of n is finite, and we can see that the value of n gets smaller each time through the loop (each **iteration**), so eventually we have to get to zero. In other cases it is not so easy to tell:

```
public static void sequence (int n) {
  while (n != 1) {
    System.out.println (n);
    if (n%2 == 0) {            // n is even
      n = n / 2;
    } else {                   // n is odd
      n = n*3 + 1;
    }
  }
}
```

The condition for this loop is n != 1, so the loop will continue until n is 1, which will make the condition false.

At each iteration, the program prints the value of n and then checks whether it is even or odd. If it is even, the value of n is divided by two. If it is odd, the value is replaced by $3n + 1$. For example, if the starting value (the argument passed to sequence) is 3, the resulting sequence is 3, 10, 5, 16, 8, 4, 2, 1.

Since n sometimes increases and sometimes decreases, there is no obvious proof that n will ever reach 1, or that the program will terminate. For some particular values of n, we can prove termination. For example, if the starting value is a power of two, then the value of n will be even every time through the loop, until we get to 1. The previous example ends with such a sequence, starting with 16.

Particular values aside, the interesting question is whether we can prove that this program terminates for *all* values of n. So far, no one has been able to prove it *or* disprove it!

6.4   Tables

One of the things loops are good for is generating and printing tabular data. For example, before computers were readily available, people had to calculate logarithms, sines and cosines, and other common mathematical functions by hand.

To make that easier, there were books containing long tables where you could find the values of various functions. Creating these tables was slow and boring, and the result tended to be full of errors.

When computers appeared on the scene, one of the initial reactions was, "This is great! We can use the computers to generate the tables, so there will be no errors." That turned out to be true (mostly), but shortsighted. Soon thereafter computers (and calculators) were so pervasive that the tables became obsolete.

Well, almost. It turns out that for some operations, computers use tables of values to get an approximate answer, and then perform computations to improve the approximation. In some cases, there have been errors in the underlying tables, most famously in the table the original Intel Pentium used to perform floating-point division.

Although a "log table" is not as useful as it once was, it still makes a good example of iteration. The following program prints a sequence of values in the left column and their logarithms in the right column:

```
double x = 1.0;
while (x < 10.0) {
  System.out.println (x + "   " + Math.log(x));
  x = x + 1.0;
}
```

The output of this program is

```
1.0   0.0
2.0   0.6931471805599453
3.0   1.0986122886681098
4.0   1.3862943611198906
5.0   1.6094379124341003
6.0   1.791759469228055
7.0   1.9459101490553132
8.0   2.0794415416798357
9.0   2.1972245773362196
```

Looking at these values, can you tell what base the `log` function uses by default?

Since powers of two are so important in computer science, we often want to find logarithms with respect to base 2. To find that, we have to use the following formula:

$$\log_2 x = log_e x / log_e 2 \qquad (6.1)$$

Changing the `print` statement to

```
        System.out.println (x + "   " + Math.log(x) / Math.log(2.0));
```

yields

```
1.0    0.0
2.0    1.0
3.0    1.5849625007211563
4.0    2.0
5.0    2.321928094887362
6.0    2.584962500721156
7.0    2.807354922057604
8.0    3.0
9.0    3.1699250014423126
```

We can see that 1, 2, 4 and 8 are powers of two, because their logarithms base 2 are round numbers. If we wanted to find the logarithms of other powers of two, we could modify the program like this:

```
double x = 1.0;
while (x < 100.0) {
  System.out.println (x + "   " + Math.log(x) / Math.log(2.0));
  x = x * 2.0;
}
```

Now instead of adding something to x each time through the loop, which yields an arithmetic sequence, we multiply x by something, yielding a **geometric** sequence. The result is:

```
1.0    0.0
2.0    1.0
4.0    2.0
8.0    3.0
16.0   4.0
32.0   5.0
64.0   6.0
```

Log tables may not be useful any more, but for computer scientists, knowing the powers of two is! Some time when you have an idle moment, you should memorize the powers of two up to 65536 (that's 2^{16}).

6.5   Two-dimensional tables

A two-dimensional table is a table where you choose a row and a column and read the value at the intersection. A multiplication table is a good example. Let's say you wanted to print a multiplication table for the values from 1 to 6.

A good way to start is to write a simple loop that prints the multiples of 2, all on one line.

```
int i = 1;
while (i <= 6) {
  System.out.print (2*i + "   ");
```

```
    i = i + 1;
  }
  System.out.println ("");
```

The first line initializes a variable named i, which is going to act as a counter, or **loop variable**. As the loop executes, the value of i increases from 1 to 6, and then when i is 7, the loop terminates. Each time through the loop, we print the value 2*i followed by three spaces. Since we are using the print command rather than println, all the output appears on a single line.

As I mentioned in Section 2.4, in some environments the output from print gets stored without being displayed until println is invoked. If the program terminates, and you forget to invoke println, you may never see the stored output.

The output of this program is:

2   4   6   8   10   12

So far, so good. The next step is to **encapsulate** and **generalize**.

6.6   Encapsulation and generalization

Encapsulation usually means taking a piece of code and wrapping it up in a method, allowing you to take advantage of all the things methods are good for. We have seen two examples of encapsulation, when we wrote printParity in Section 4.3 and isSingleDigit in Section 5.7.

Generalization means taking something specific, like printing multiples of 2, and making it more general, like printing the multiples of any integer.

Here's a method that encapsulates the loop from the previous section and generalizes it to print multiples of n.

```
  public static void printMultiples (int n) {
    int i = 1;
    while (i <= 6) {
      System.out.print (n*i + "    ");
      i = i + 1;
    }
    System.out.println ("");
  }
```

To encapsulate, all I had to do was add the first line, which declares the name, parameter, and return type. To generalize, all I had to do was replace the value 2 with the parameter n.

If I invoke this method with the argument 2, I get the same output as before. With argument 3, the output is:

3   6   9   12   15   18

and with argument 4, the output is

4   8   12   16   20   24

By now you can probably guess how we are going to print a multiplication table: we'll invoke printMultiples repeatedly with different arguments. In fact, we are going to use another loop to iterate through the rows.

```
int i = 1;
while (i <= 6) {
  printMultiples (i);
  i = i + 1;
}
```

First of all, notice how similar this loop is to the one inside printMultiples. All I did was replace the print statement with a method invocation.

The output of this program is

```
1    2    3    4     5    6
2    4    6    8     10   12
3    6    9    12    15   18
4    8    12   16    20   24
5    10   15   20    25   30
6    12   18   24    30   36
```

which is a (slightly sloppy) multiplication table. If the sloppiness bothers you, Java provides methods that give you more control over the format of the output, but I'm not going to get into that here.

6.7 Methods

In the last section I mentioned "all the things methods are good for." About this time, you might be wondering what exactly those things are. Here are some of the reasons methods are useful:

- By giving a name to a sequence of statements, you make your program easier to read and debug.

- Dividing a long program into methods allows you to separate parts of the program, debug them in isolation, and then compose them into a whole.

- Methods facilitate both recursion and iteration.

- Well-designed methods are often useful for many programs. Once you write and debug one, you can reuse it.

6.8 More encapsulation

To demonstrate encapsulation again, I'll take the code from the previous section and wrap it up in a method:

```
public static void printMultTable () {
  int i = 1;
  while (i <= 6) {
    printMultiples (i);
    i = i + 1;
  }
}
```

The process I am demonstrating is a common development plan. You develop code gradually by adding lines to main or someplace else, and then when you get it working, you extract it and wrap it up in a method.

The reason this is useful is that you sometimes don't know when you start writing exactly how to divide the program into methods. This approach lets you design as you go along.

6.9   Local variables

About this time, you might be wondering how we can use the same variable i in both printMultiples and printMultTable. Didn't I say that you can only declare a variable once? And doesn't it cause problems when one of the methods changes the value of the variable?

The answer to both questions is "no," because the i in printMultiples and the i in printMultTable are *not the same variable*. They have the same name, but they do not refer to the same storage location, and changing the value of one of them has no effect on the other.

Variables that are declared inside a method definition are called **local variables** because they are local to their own methods. You cannot access a local variable from outside its "home" method, and you are free to have multiple variables with the same name, as long as they are not in the same method.

It is often a good idea to use different variable names in different methods, to avoid confusion, but there are good reasons to reuse names. For example, it is common to use the names i, j and k as loop variables. If you avoid using them in one method just because you used them somewhere else, you will probably make the program harder to read.

6.10   More generalization

As another example of generalization, imagine you wanted a program that would print a multiplication table of any size, not just the 6x6 table. You could add a parameter to printMultTable:

```
public static void printMultTable (int high) {
  int i = 1;
  while (i <= high) {
```

```
    printMultiples (i);
     i = i + 1;
  }
}
```

I replaced the value 6 with the parameter high. If I invoke printMultTable
with the argument 7, I get

```
1   2   3   4    5    6
2   4   6   8    10   12
3   6   9   12   15   18
4   8   12  16   20   24
5   10  15  20   25   30
6   12  18  24   30   36
7   14  21  28   35   42
```

which is fine, except that I probably want the table to be square (same number of rows and columns), which means I have to add another parameter to
printMultiples, to specify how many columns the table should have.

Just to be annoying, I will also call this parameter high, demonstrating that
different methods can have parameters with the same name (just like local
variables):

```
  public static void printMultiples (int n, int high) {
    int i = 1;
    while (i <= high) {
      System.out.print (n*i + "   ");
      i = i + 1;
    }
    newLine ();
  }

  public static void printMultTable (int high) {
    int i = 1;
    while (i <= high) {
      printMultiples (i, high);
      i = i + 1;
    }
  }
```

Notice that when I added a new parameter, I had to change the first line of the
method (the interface or prototype), and I also had to change the place where
the method is invoked in printMultTable. As expected, this program generates
a square 7x7 table:

```
1   2   3   4    5    6    7
2   4   6   8    10   12   14
3   6   9   12   15   18   21
4   8   12  16   20   24   28
5   10  15  20   25   30   35
6   12  18  24   30   36   42
7   14  21  28   35   42   49
```

When you generalize a method appropriately, you often find that the resulting program has capabilities you did not intend. For example, you might notice that the multiplication table is symmetric, because $ab = ba$, so all the entries in the table appear twice. You could save ink by printing only half the table. To do that, you only have to change one line of `printMultTable`. Change

```
        printMultiples (i, high);
```

to

```
        printMultiples (i, i);
```

and you get

```
1
2    4
3    6    9
4    8    12   16
5    10   15   20   25
6    12   18   24   30   36
7    14   21   28   35   42   49
```

I'll leave it up to you to figure out how it works.

6.11   Glossary

loop: A statement that executes repeatedly while or until some condition is satisfied.

infinite loop: A loop whose condition is always true.

body: The statements inside the loop.

iteration: One pass through (execution of) the body of the loop, including the evaluation of the condition.

encapsulate: To divide a large complex program into components (like methods) and isolate the components from each other (for example, by using local variables).

local variable: A variable that is declared inside a method and that exists only within that method. Local variables cannot be accessed from outside their home method, and do not interfere with any other methods.

generalize: To replace something unnecessarily specific (like a constant value) with something appropriately general (like a variable or parameter). Generalization makes code more versatile, more likely to be reused, and sometimes even easier to write.

development plan: A process for developing a program. In this chapter, I demonstrated a style of development based on developing code to do simple, specific things, and then encapsulating and generalizing. In Section 5.2 I demonstrated a technique I called incremental development. In later chapters I will suggest other styles of development.

6.12   Exercises

Exercise 6.1

```
public static void main (String[] args) {
    loop (10);
}

public static void loop (int n) {
    int i = n;
    while (i > 1) {
        System.out.println (i);
        if (i%2 == 0) {
            i = i/2;
        } else {
            i = i+1;
        }
    }
}
```

a. Draw a table that shows the value of the variables i and n during the execution of loop. The table should contain one column for each variable and one line for each iteration.

b. What is the output of this program?

Exercise 6.2

a. Encapsulate the following code fragment, transforming it into a method that takes a String as an argument and that returns (and doesn't print) the final value of count.

b. In a sentence, describe abstractly what the resulting method does.

c. Assuming that you have already generalized this method so that it works on any String, what else could you do to generalize it more?

```
String s = "((3 + 7) * 2)";
int len = s.length ();

int i = 0;
int count = 0;

while (i < len) {
    char c = s.charAt(i);

    if (c == '(') {
        count = count + 1;
    } else if (c == ')') {
        count = count - 1;
    }
    i = i + 1;
}

System.out.println (count);
```

Exercise 6.3   Let's say you are given a number, a, and you want to find its square root. One way to do that is to start with a very rough guess about the answer, x_0, and then improve the guess using the following formula:

$$x_1 = (x_0 + a/x_0)/2 \qquad (6.2)$$

For example, if we want to find the square root of 9, and we start with $x_0 = 6$, then $x_1 = (6 + 9/6)/2 = 15/4 = 3.75$, which is closer.

We can repeat the procedure, using x_1 to calculate x_2, and so on. In this case, $x_2 = 3.075$ and $x_3 = 3.00091$. So that is converging very quickly on the right answer (which is 3).

Write a method called `squareRoot` that takes a `double` as a parameter and that returns an approximation of the square root of the parameter, using this algorithm. You may not use the built-in method `Math.sqrt`.

As your initial guess, you should use $a/2$. Your method should iterate until it gets two consecutive estimates that differ by less than 0.0001; in other words, until the absolute value of $x_n - x_{n-1}$ is less than 0.0001. You can use the built-in method `Math.abs` to calculate the absolute value.

Exercise 6.4   In Exercise 5.9 we wrote a recursive version of `power`, which takes a double `x` and an integer `n` and returns x^n. Now write an iterative method to perform the same calculation.

Exercise 6.5   Section 5.10 presents a recursive method that computes the factorial function. Write an iterative version of `factorial`.

Exercise 6.6   One way to calculate e^x is to use the infinite series expansion

$$e^x = 1 + x + x^2/2! + x^3/3! + x^4/4! + \ldots \qquad (6.3)$$

If the loop variable is named `i`, then the ith term is equal to $x^i/i!$.

a. Write a method called `myexp` that adds up the first `n` terms of the series shown above. You can use the `factorial` method from Section 5.10 or your iterative version.

b. You can make this method much more efficient if you realize that in each iteration the numerator of the term is the same as its predecessor multiplied by `x` and the denominator is the same as its predecessor multiplied by `i`. Use this observation to eliminate the use of `Math.pow` and `factorial`, and check that you still get the same result.

c. Write a method called `check` that takes a single parameter, `x`, and that prints the values of `x`, `Math.exp(x)` and `myexp(x)` for various values of `x`. The output should look something like:

```
1.0     2.708333333333333       2.718281828459045
```

HINT: you can use the String `"\t"` to print a tab character between columns of a table.

d. Vary the number of terms in the series (the second argument that `check` sends to `myexp`) and see the effect on the accuracy of the result. Adjust this value until the estimated value agrees with the "correct" answer when x is 1.

e. Write a loop in `main` that invokes `check` with the values 0.1, 1.0, 10.0, and 100.0. How does the accuracy of the result vary as x varies? Compare the number of digits of agreement rather than the difference between the actual and estimated values.

f. Add a loop in `main` that checks `myexp` with the values -0.1, -1.0, -10.0, and -100.0. Comment on the accuracy.

Exercise 6.7   One way to evaluate e^{-x^2} is to use the infinite series expansion

$$e^{-x^2} = 1 - 2x + 3x^2/2! - 4x^3/3! + 5x^4/4! - \dots \qquad (6.4)$$

In other words, we need to add up a series of terms where the ith term is equal to $(-1)^i(i+1)x^i/i!$. Write a method named `gauss` that takes x and n as arguments and that returns the sum of the first n terms of the series. You should not use `factorial` or `pow`.

Chapter 7

Strings and things

7.1 Invoking methods on objects

In Java and other object-oriented languages, objects are collections of related data that come with a set of methods. These methods operate on the objects, performing computations and sometimes modifying the object's data.

Of the types we have seen so far, only Strings are objects. Based on the definition of object, you might ask "What is the data contained in a String object?" and "What are the methods we can invoke on String objects?"

The data contained in a String object are the letters of the string. There are quite a few methods that operate on Strings, but I will only use a few in this book. The rest are documented at

http://java.sun.com/j2se/1.4.1/docs/api/java/lang/String.html

The first method we will look at is charAt, which allows you to extract letters from a String. In order to store the result, we need a variable type that can store individual letters (as opposed to strings). Individual letters are called characters, and the variable type that stores them is called char.

chars work just like the other types we have seen:

```java
char fred = 'c';
if (fred == 'c') {
  System.out.println (fred);
}
```

Character values appear in single quotes ('c'). Unlike string values (which appear in double quotes), character values can contain only a single letter or symbol.

Here's how the charAt method is used:

```java
String fruit = "banana";
char letter = fruit.charAt(1);
System.out.println (letter);
```

The syntax `fruit.charAt` indicates that I am invoking the `charAt` method on the object named `fruit`. I am passing the argument 1 to this method, which indicates that I would like to know the first letter of the string. The result is a character, which is stored in a `char` named `letter`. When I print the value of `letter`, I get a surprise:

a

a is not the first letter of `"banana"`. Unless you are a computer scientist. For perverse reasons, computer scientists always start counting from zero. The 0th letter ("zeroeth") of `"banana"` is b. The 1th letter ("oneth") is a and the 2th ("twoeth") letter is n.

If you want the zeroeth letter of a string, you have to pass zero as an argument:

```
char letter = fruit.charAt(0);
```

7.2   Length

The second `String` method we'll look at is `length`, which returns the number of characters in the string. For example:

```
int length = fruit.length();
```

`length` takes no arguments, as indicated by `()`, and returns an integer, in this case 6. Notice that it is legal to have a variable with the same name as a method (although it can be confusing for human readers).

To find the last letter of a string, you might be tempted to try something like

```
int length = fruit.length();
char last = fruit.charAt (length);        // WRONG!!
```

That won't work. The reason is that there is no 6th letter in `"banana"`. Since we started counting at 0, the 6 letters are numbered from 0 to 5. To get the last character, you have to subtract 1 from `length`.

```
int length = fruit.length();
char last = fruit.charAt (length-1);
```

7.3   Traversal

A common thing to do with a string is start at the beginning, select each character in turn, do something to it, and continue until the end. This pattern of processing is called a **traversal**. A natural way to encode a traversal is with a `while` statement:

```
int index = 0;
while (index < fruit.length()) {
  char letter = fruit.charAt (index);
  System.out.println (letter);
  index = index + 1;
}
```

This loop traverses the string and prints each letter on a line by itself. Notice that the condition is `index < fruit.length()`, which means that when `index` is equal to the length of the string, the condition is false and the body of the loop is not executed. The last character we access is the one with the index `fruit.length()-1`.

The name of the loop variable is `index`. An **index** is a variable or value used to specify one member of an ordered set (in this case the set of characters in the string). The index indicates (hence the name) which one you want. The set has to be ordered so that each letter has an index and each index refers to a single character.

As an exercise, write a method that takes a `String` as an argument and that prints the letters backwards, all on one line.

7.4   Run-time errors

Way back in Section 1.3.2 I talked about run-time errors, which are errors that don't appear until a program has started running. In Java run-time errors are called **exceptions**.

So far, you probably haven't seen many run-time errors, because we haven't been doing many things that can cause one. Well, now we are. If you use the `charAt` command and you provide an index that is negative or greater than `length-1`, you will get an exception: specifically, a `StringIndexOutOfBoundsException`. Try it and see how it looks.

If your program causes an exception, it prints an error message indicating the type of exception and where in the program it occurred. Then the program terminates.

7.5   Reading documentation

If you go to

`http://java.sun.com/j2se/1.4/docs/api/java/lang/String.html`

and click on `charAt`, you get the following documentation (or something like it):

```
public char charAt(int index)

Returns the character at the specified index.
An index ranges from 0 to length() - 1.

Parameters: index - the index of the character.

Returns: the character at the specified index of this string.
        The first character is at index 0.
```

Throws: StringIndexOutOfBoundsException if the index is out of range.

The first line is the method's **prototype**, which indicates the name of the method, the type of the parameters, and the return type.

The next line describes what the method does. The following lines explain the parameters and return values. In this case the explanations are a bit redundant, but the documentation is supposed to fit a standard format. The last line explains what exceptions, if any, can be caused by this method.

7.6   The indexOf method

In some ways, indexOf is the opposite of charAt. charAt takes an index and returns the character at that index. indexOf takes a character and finds the index where that character appears.

charAt fails if the index is out of range, and causes an exception. indexOf fails if the character does not appear in the string, and returns the value -1.

```
String fruit = "banana";
int index = fruit.indexOf('a');
```

This finds the index of the letter 'a' in the string. In this case, the letter appears three times, so it is not obvious what indexOf should do. According to the documentation, it returns the index of the *first* appearance.

In order to find subsequent appearances, there is an alternative version of indexOf (for an explanation of this kind of overloading, see Section 5.4). It takes a second argument that indicates where in the string to start looking. If we invoke

```
int index = fruit.indexOf('a', 2);
```

it will start at the tweeth letter (the first n) and find the second a, which is at index 3. If the letter happens to appear at the starting index, the starting index is the answer. Thus,

```
int index = fruit.indexOf('a', 5);
```

returns 5. Based on the documentation, it is a little tricky to figure out what happens if the starting index is out of range:

> indexOf returns the index of the first occurrence of the character in the character sequence represented by this object that is greater than or equal to fromIndex, or -1 if the character does not occur.

One way to figure out what this means is to try out a couple of cases. Here are the results of my experiments:

- If the starting index is greater than or equal to length(), the result is -1, indicating that the letter does not appear at any index greater than the starting index.

- If the starting index is negative, the result is 1, indicating the first appearance of the letter at an index greater than the starting index.

If you go back and look at the documentation, you'll see that this behavior is consistent with the definition, even if it was not immediately obvious. Now that we have a better idea how indexOf works, we can use it as part of a program.

7.7   Looping and counting

The following program counts the number of times the letter 'a' appears in a string:

```
String fruit = "banana";
int length = fruit.length();
int count = 0;

int index = 0;
while (index < length) {
  if (fruit.charAt(index) == 'a') {
    count = count + 1;
  }
  index = index + 1;
}
System.out.println (count);
```

This program demonstrates a common idiom, called a **counter**. The variable count is initialized to zero and then incremented each time we find an 'a' (to **increment** is to increase by one; it is the opposite of **decrement**, and unrelated to **excrement**, which is a noun). When we exit the loop, count contains the result: the total number of a's.

As an exercise, encapsulate this code in a method named countLetters, and generalize it so that it accepts the string and the letter as arguments.

As a second exercise, rewrite the method so that it uses indexOf to locate the a's, rather than checking the characters one by one.

7.8   Increment and decrement operators

Incrementing and decrementing are such common operations that Java provides special operators for them. The ++ operator adds one to the current value of an int or char. -- subtracts one. Neither operator works on doubles, booleans or Strings.

Technically, it is legal to increment a variable and use it in an expression at the same time. For example, you might see something like:

```
System.out.println (i++);
```

Looking at this, it is not clear whether the increment will take effect before or after the value is printed. Because expressions like this tend to be confusing, I would discourage you from using them. In fact, to discourage you even more, I'm not going to tell you what the result is. If you really want to know, you can try it.

Using the increment operators, we can rewrite the letter-counter:

```
int index = 0;
while (index < length) {
  if (fruit.charAt(index) == 'a') {
    count++;
  }
  index++;
}
```

It is a common error to write something like

```
index = index++;                   // WRONG!!
```

Unfortunately, this is syntactically legal, so the compiler will not warn you. The effect of this statement is to leave the value of `index` unchanged. This is often a difficult bug to track down.

Remember, you can write `index = index +1;`, or you can write `index++;`, but you shouldn't mix them.

7.9   Strings are immutable

As you look over the documentation of the `String` methods, you might notice `toUpperCase` and `toLowerCase`. These methods are often a source of confusion, because it sounds like they have the effect of changing (or mutating) an existing string. Actually, neither these methods nor any others can change a string, because strings are **immutable**.

When you invoke `toUpperCase` on a `String`, you get a *new* `String` as a return value. For example:

```
String name = "Alan Turing";
String upperName = name.toUpperCase ();
```

After the second line is executed, `upperName` contains the value `"ALAN TURING"`, but `name` still contains `"Alan Turing"`.

7.10   Strings are incomparable

It is often necessary to compare strings to see if they are the same, or to see which comes first in alphabetical order. It would be nice if we could use the comparison operators, like `==` and `>`, but we can't.

In order to compare `Strings`, we have to use the `equals` and `compareTo` methods. For example:

```
String name1 = "Alan Turing";
String name2 = "Ada Lovelace";

if (name1.equals (name2)) {
  System.out.println ("The names are the same.");
}

int flag = name1.compareTo (name2);
if (flag == 0) {
  System.out.println ("The names are the same.");
} else if (flag < 0) {
  System.out.println ("name1 comes before name2.");
} else if (flag > 0) {
  System.out.println ("name2 comes before name1.");
}
```

The syntax here is a little weird. To compare two things, you have to invoke a method on one of them and pass the other as an argument.

The return value from `equals` is straightforward enough; `true` if the strings contain the same characters, and `false` otherwise.

The return value from `compareTo` is a little odd. It is the difference between the first characters in the strings that differ. If the strings are equal, it is 0. If the first string (the one on which the method is invoked) comes first in the alphabet, the difference is negative. Otherwise, the difference is positive. In this case the return value is positive 8, because the second letter of "Ada" comes before the second letter of "Alan" by 8 letters.

Using `compareTo` is often tricky, and I never remember which way is which without looking it up, but the good news is that the interface is pretty standard for comparing many types of objects, so once you get it you are all set.

Just for completeness, I should admit that it is *legal*, but very seldom *correct*, to use the == operator with `Strings`. But what that means will not make sense until later, so for now, don't do it.

7.11 Glossary

object: A collection of related data that comes with a set of methods that operate on it. The only objects we have used so far are `Strings`.

index: A variable or value used to select one of the members of an ordered set, like a character from a string.

traverse: To iterate through all the elements of a set performing a similar operation on each.

counter: A variable used to count something, usually initialized to zero and then incremented.

increment: Increase the value of a variable by one. The increment operator in Java is ++.

decrement: Decrease the value of a variable by one. The decrement operator in Java is --.

exception: A run time error. Exceptions cause the execution of a program to terminate.

7.12   Exercises

Exercise 7.1

The point of this exercise is to try out some of the String operations and fill in some of the details that aren't covered in the chapter.

   a. Create a new program named Test.java and write a main method that contains expressions that combine various types using the + operator. For example, what happens when you "add" a String and a char? Does it perform addition or concatenation? What is the type of the result? (How can you determine the type of the result?)

   b. Make a bigger copy of the following table and fill it in. At the intersection of each pair of types, you should indicate whether it is legal to use the + operator with these types, what operation is performed (addition or concatenation), and what the type of the result is.

	boolean	char	int	String
boolean				
char				
int				
String				

   c. Think about some of the choices the designers of Java made when they filled in this table. How many of the entries seem reasonable, as if there were no other reasonable choice? How many seem like arbitrary choices from several equally reasonable possibilities? How many seem stupid?

   d. Here's a puzzler: normally, the statement x++ is exactly equivalent to x = x + 1. Unless x is a char! In that case, x++ is legal, but x = x + 1 causes an error. Try it out and see what the error message is, then see if you can figure out what is going on.

Exercise 7.2

What is the output of this program? Describe in a sentence, abstractly, what bing does (not how it works).

```
public class Mystery {

    public static String bing (String s) {
        int i = s.length() - 1;
        String total = "";
```

```
        while (i >= 0 ) {
            char ch = s.charAt (i);
            System.out.println (i + "      " + ch);

            total = total + ch;
            i--;
        }
        return total;
    }

    public static void main (String[] args) {
        System.out.println (bing ("Allen"));
    }
}
```

Exercise 7.3   A friend of yours shows you the following method and explains that if number is any two-digit number, the program will output the number backwards. He claims that if number is 17, the method will output 71.

Is he right? If not, explain what the program actually does and modify it so that it does the right thing.

```
    int number = 17;
    int lastDigit = number%10;
    int firstDigit = number/10;
    System.out.println (lastDigit + firstDigit);
```

Exercise 7.4   What is the output of the following program?

```
public class Rarefy {

    public static void rarefy (int x) {
        if (x == 0) {
            return;
        } else {
            rarefy (x/2);
        }

        System.out.print (x%2);
    }

    public static void main (String[] args) {
        rarefy (5);
        System.out.println ("");
    }
}
```

Explain in 4-5 words what the method rarefy really does.

Exercise 7.5

   a. Create a new program named Palindrome.java.

b. Write a method named `first` that takes a String and returns the first letter, and one named `last` that returns the last letter.

c. Write a method named `middle` that takes a String and returns a substring that contains everything *except* the first and last characters.

Hint: read the documentation of the `substring` method in the `String` class. Run a few tests to make sure you understand how `substring` works before you try to write `middle`.

What happens if you invoke `middle` on a string that has only two letters? One letter? No letters?

d. The usual definition of a palindrome is a word that reads the same both forward and backward, like "otto" and "palindromeemordnilap." An alternative way to define a property like this is to specify a way of testing for the property. For example, we might say, "a single letter is a palindrome, and a two-letter word is a palindrome if the letters are the same, and any other word is a palindrome if the first letter is the same as the last and the middle is a palindrome."

Write a recursive method named `isPalindrome` that takes a `String` and that returns a boolean indicating whether the word is a palindrome or not.

e. Once you have a working palindrome checker, look for ways to simplify it by reducing the number of conditions you check. Hint: it might be useful to adopt the definition that the empty string is a palindrome.

f. On a piece of paper, figure out a strategy for checking palindromes iteratively. There are several possible approaches, so make sure you have a solid plan before you start writing code.

g. Implement your strategy in a method called `isPalindromeIter`.

Exercise 7.6   A word is said to be "abecedarian" if the letters in the word appear in alphabetical order. For example, the following are all 6-letter English abecedarian words.

abdest, acknow, acorsy, adempt, adipsy, agnosy, befist, behint, beknow, bijoux, biopsy, cestuy, chintz, deflux, dehors, dehort, deinos, diluvy, dimpsy

a. Describe an algorithm for checking whether a given word (String) is abecedarian, assuming that the word contains only lower-case letters. Your algorithm can be iterative or recursive.

b. Implement your algorithm in a method called `isAbecedarian`.

Exercise 7.7   A dupledrome is a word that contains only double letters, like "llaammaa" or "ssaabb". I conjecture that there are no dupledromes in common English use. To test that conjecture, I would like a program that reads words from the dictionary one at a time and checks them for dupledromity.

Write a method called `isDupledrome` that takes a String and returns a boolean indicating whether the word is a dupledrome.

Exercise 7.8

When names are recorded in a computer, they are sometimes written with the first name first, like "Allen Downey," and sometimes with the last name first and a comma, like "Downey, Allen." That can make it difficult to compare names and put them in alphabetical order.

A related problem is that some people have names with capital letters in funny places, like my friend Beth DeSombre, or no capitals at all, like the poet e.e. cummings. When computers compare characters, they usually put all the capital letters before the lower-case letters. As a result, computers often put names with capitals in the wrong order.

If you are curious, find a local phone book like a campus directory and see if you can figure out the alphabetizing scheme. Look for multiple-word names like Van Houten and names with nonstandard capitalization, like desJardins. See if you can figure out the sorting rules. If you have access to a European phone book, try that, too, and see if the rules are different.

The result of all this nonstandardization is that it is usually not right to sort names using simple String comparison. A common solution is to keep two versions of each name: the printable version and an internal format used for sorting.

In this exercise, you will write a method that compares two names by converting them to a standard format. We will work from the bottom up, writing some helper methods and then compareName.

    a. Create a new program called Name.java. In the documentation of String, read about find and toLower and compareTo. Write some simple code to test each of them and make sure you understand how they work.

    b. Write a method called hasComma that takes a name as an argument and that returns a boolean indicating whether it contains a comma. If it does, you can assume that it is in last name first format.

    c. Write a method called convertName that takes a name as an argument. It should check whether it contains a comma. If it does, it should just return the string.

      If not, then it should assume that the name is in first name first format, and it should return a new string that contains the name converted to last name first format.

    d. Write a method called compareName that takes two names as arguments and that returns -1 if the first comes before the second alphabetically, 0 if the names are equal alphabetically, and 1 otherwise. Your method should be case-insensitive, meaning that it doesn't matter whether the letters are upper- or lower-case.

Exercise 7.9

    a. The Captain Crunch decoder ring works by taking each letter in a string and adding 13 to it. For example, 'a' becomes 'n' and 'b' becomes 'o'. The letters "wrap around" at the end, so 'z' becomes 'm'.

      Write a method that takes a String and that returns a new String containing the encoded version. You should assume that the String contains upper and lower case letters, and spaces, but no other punctuation. Lower case letters should be tranformed into other lower case letters; upper into upper. You should not encode the spaces.

b. Generalize the Captain Crunch method so that instead of adding 13 to the letters, it adds any given amount. Now you should be able to encode things by adding 13 and decode them by adding -13. Try it.

Chapter 8

Interesting objects

8.1 What's interesting?

Although `String`s are objects, they are not very interesting objects, because

- They are immutable.

- They have no instance variables.

- You don't have to use the `new` command to create one.

In this chapter, we are going to use two new object types that are part of the Java language, `Point` and `Rectangle`. Right from the start, I want to make it clear that these points and rectangles are not graphical objects that appear on the screen. They are variables that contain data, just like `int`s and `double`s. Like other variables, they are used internally to perform computations.

The definitions of the `Point` and `Rectangle` classes are in the `java.awt` package, so we have to import them.

8.2 Packages

The built-in Java classes are divided into a number of **packages**, including `java.lang`, which contains almost all of the classes we have seen so far, and `java.awt`, which contains classes that pertain to the Java **Abstract Window Toolkit** (AWT), which contains classes for windows, buttons, graphics, etc.

In order to use a package, you have to **import** it, which is why the program in Section D.1 starts with `import java.awt.*`. The * indicates that we want to import all the classes in the AWT package. If you want, you can name the classes you want to import explicitly, but there is no great advantage. The classes in `java.lang` are imported automatically, which is why most of our programs haven't required an `import` statement.

All `import` statements appear at the beginning of the program, outside the class definition.

8.3 Point objects

At the most basic level, a point is two numbers (coordinates) that we treat collectively as a single object. In mathematical notation, points are often written in parentheses, with a comma separating the coordinates. For example, $(0,0)$ indicates the origin, and (x, y) indicates the point x units to the right and y units up from the origin.

In Java, a point is represented by a `Point` object. To create a new point, you have to use the `new` command:

```
Point blank;
blank = new Point (3, 4);
```

The first line is a conventional variable declaration: `blank` has type `Point`. The second line is kind of funny-looking; it invokes the `new` command, specifies the type of the new object, and provides arguments. It will probably not surprise you that the arguments are the coordinates of the new point, $(3, 4)$.

The result of the `new` command is a **reference** to the new point. I'll explain references more later; for now the important thing is that the variable `blank` contains a reference to the newly-created object. There is a standard way to diagram this assignment, shown in the figure.

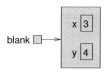

As usual, the name of the variable `blank` appears outside the box and its value appears inside the box. In this case, that value is a reference, which is shown graphically with a dot and an arrow. The arrow points to the object we're referring to.

The big box shows the newly-created object with the two values in it. The names x and y are the names of the **instance variables**.

Taken together, all the variables, values, and objects in a program are called the **state**. Diagrams like this that show the state of the program are called **state diagrams**. As the program runs, the state changes, so you should think of a state diagram as a snapshot of a particular point in the execution.

8.4 Instance variables

The pieces of data that make up an object are sometimes called components, records, or fields. In Java they are called instance variables because each object, which is an **instance** of its type, has its own copy of the instance variables.

It's like the glove compartment of a car. Each car is an instance of the type "car," and each car has its own glove compartment. If you asked me to get something from the glove compartment of your car, you would have to tell me which car is yours.

Similarly, if you want to read a value from an instance variable, you have to specify the object you want to get it from. In Java this is done using "dot notation."

```
int x = blank.x;
```

The expression `blank.x` means "go to the object `blank` refers to, and get the value of `x`." In this case we assign that value to a local variable named x. Notice that there is no conflict between the local variable named x and the instance variable named x. The purpose of dot notation is to identify *which* variable you are referring to unambiguously.

You can use dot notation as part of any Java expression, so the following are legal.

```
System.out.println (blank.x + ", " + blank.y);
int distance = blank.x * blank.x + blank.y * blank.y;
```

The first line prints 3, 4; the second line calculates the value 25.

8.5 Objects as parameters

You can pass objects as parameters in the usual way. For example

```
public static void printPoint (Point p) {
  System.out.println ("(" + p.x + ", " + p.y + ")");
}
```

is a method that takes a point as an argument and prints it in the standard format. If you invoke `printPoint (blank)`, it will print (3, 4). Actually, Java has a built-in method for printing `Points`. If you invoke `System.out.println (blank)`, you get

`java.awt.Point[x=3,y=4]`

This is a standard format Java uses for printing objects. It prints the name of the type, followed by the contents of the object, including the names and values of the instance variables.

As a second example, we can rewrite the `distance` method from Section 5.2 so that it takes two `Points` as parameters instead of four `doubles`.

```
public static double distance (Point p1, Point p2) {
  double dx = (double)(p2.x - p1.x);
  double dy = (double)(p2.y - p1.y);
  return Math.sqrt (dx*dx + dy*dy);
}
```

The typecasts are not really necessary; I just added them as a reminder that the instance variables in a `Point` are integers.

8.6   Rectangles

Rectangles are similar to points, except that they have four instance variables,
named x, y, width and height. Other than that, everything is pretty much the
same.

```
Rectangle box = new Rectangle (0, 0, 100, 200);
```

creates a new Rectangle object and makes box refer to it. The figure shows
the effect of this assignment.

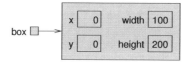

If you print box, you get

`java.awt.Rectangle[x=0,y=0,width=100,height=200]`

Again, this is the result of a built-in Java method that knows how to print
Rectangle objects.

8.7   Objects as return types

You can write methods that return objects. For example, findCenter takes a
Rectangle as an argument and returns a Point that contains the coordinates
of the center of the Rectangle:

```
public static Point findCenter (Rectangle box) {
  int x = box.x + box.width/2;
  int y = box.y + box.height/2;
  return new Point (x, y);
}
```

Notice that you can use new to create a new object, and then immediately use
the result as a return value.

8.8   Objects are mutable

You can change the contents of an object by making an assignment to one of
its instance variables. For example, to "move" a rectangle without changing its
size, you could modify the x and y values:

```
box.x = box.x + 50;
box.y = box.y + 100;
```

The result is shown in the figure:

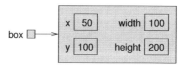

We could take this code and encapsulate it in a method, and generalize it to move the rectangle by any amount:

```
public static void moveRect (Rectangle box, int dx, int dy) {
    box.x = box.x + dx;
    box.y = box.y + dy;
}
```

The variables dx and dy indicate how far to move the rectangle in each direction. Invoking this method has the effect of modifying the Rectangle that is passed as an argument.

```
Rectangle box = new Rectangle (0, 0, 100, 200);
moveRect (box, 50, 100);
System.out.println (box);
```

prints java.awt.Rectangle[x=50,y=100,width=100,height=200].

Modifying objects by passing them as arguments to methods can be useful, but it can also make debugging more difficult because it is not always clear which method invocations do or do not modify their arguments. Later, I will discuss some pros and cons of this programming style.

In the meantime, we can enjoy the luxury of Java's built-in methods, which include translate, which does exactly the same thing as moveRect, although the syntax for invoking it is a little different. Instead of passing the Rectangle as an argument, we invoke translate on the Rectangle and pass only dx and dy as arguments.

```
box.translate (50, 100);
```

The effect is exactly the same.

8.9   Aliasing

Remember that when you make an assignment to an object variable, you are assigning a *reference* to an object. It is possible to have multiple variables that refer to the same object. For example, this code:

```
Rectangle box1 = new Rectangle (0, 0, 100, 200);
Rectangle box2 = box1;
```

generates a state diagram that looks like this:

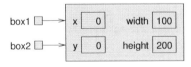

Both box1 and box2 refer or "point" to the same object. In other words, this object has two names, box1 and box2. When a person uses two names, it's called **aliasing**. Same thing with objects.

When two variables are aliased, any changes that affect one variable also affect the other. For example:

```
System.out.println (box2.width);
box1.grow (50, 50);
System.out.println (box2.width);
```

The first line prints 100, which is the width of the `Rectangle` referred to by `box2`. The second line invokes the `grow` method on `box1`, which expands the `Rectangle` by 50 pixels in every direction (see the documentation for more details). The effect is shown in the figure:

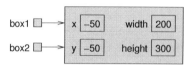

As should be clear from this figure, whatever changes are made to `box1` also apply to `box2`. Thus, the value printed by the third line is 200, the width of the expanded rectangle. (As an aside, it is perfectly legal for the coordinates of a `Rectangle` to be negative.)

As you can tell even from this simple example, code that involves aliasing can get confusing fast, and it can be very difficult to debug. In general, aliasing should be avoided or used with care.

8.10   `null`

When you create an object variable, remember that you are creating a *reference* to an object. Until you make the variable point to an object, the value of the variable is `null`. `null` is a special value in Java (and a Java keyword) that is used to mean "no object."

The declaration `Point blank;` is equivalent to this initialization

```
Point blank = null;
```

and is shown in the following state diagram:

blank ☐

The value `null` is represented by a dot with no arrow.

If you try to use a null object, either by accessing an instance variable or invoking a method, you will get a `NullPointerException`. The system will print an error message and terminate the program.

```
Point blank = null;
int x = blank.x;              // NullPointerException
blank.translate (50, 50);     // NullPointerException
```

On the other hand, it is legal to pass a null object as an argument or receive one as a return value. In fact, it is common to do so, for example to represent an empty set or indicate an error condition.

8.11   Garbage collection

In Section 8.9 we talked about what happens when more than one variable refers to the same object. What happens when *no* variable refers to an object? For example:

```
Point blank = new Point (3, 4);
blank = null;
```

The first line creates a new `Point` object and makes `blank` refer to it. The second line changes `blank` so that instead of referring to the object, it refers to nothing (the null object).

If no one refers to an object, then no one can read or write any of its values, or invoke a method on it. In effect, it ceases to exist. We could keep the object in memory, but it would only waste space, so periodically as your program runs, the Java system looks for stranded objects and reclaims them, in a process called **garbage collection**. Later, the memory space occupied by the object will be available to be used as part of a new object.

You don't have to do anything to make garbage collection work, and in general you will not be aware of it.

8.12   Objects and primitives

There are two kinds of types in Java, primitive types and object types. Primitives, like `int` and `boolean` begin with lower-case letters; object types begin with upper-case letters. This distinction is useful because it reminds us of some of the differences between them:

- When you declare a primitive variable, you get storage space for a primitive value. When you declare an object variable, you get a space for a reference to an object. In order to get space for the object itself, you have to use the `new` command.

- If you don't initialize a primitive type, it is given a default value that depends on the type. For example, 0 for `int`s and `true` for `boolean`s. The default value for object types is `null`, which indicates no object.

- Primitive variables are well isolated in the sense that there is nothing you can do in one method that will affect a variable in another method. Object variables can be tricky to work with because they are not as well isolated. If you pass a reference to an object as an argument, the method you invoke might modify the object, in which case you will see the effect. The same is true when you invoke a method on an object. Of course, that can be a good thing, but you have to be aware of it.

There is one other difference between primitives and object types. You cannot add new primitives to the Java language (unless you get yourself on the standards committee), but you can create new object types! We'll see how in the next chapter.

8.13 Glossary

package: A collection of classes. The built-in Java classes are organized in packages.

AWT: The Abstract Window Toolkit, one of the biggest and most commonly-used Java packages.

instance: An example from a category. My cat is an instance of the category "feline things." Every object is an instance of some class.

instance variable: One of the named data items that make up an object. Each object (instance) has its own copy of the instance variables for its class.

reference: A value that indicates an object. In a state diagram, a reference appears as an arrow.

aliasing: The condition when two or more variables refer to the same object.

garbage collection: The process of finding objects that have no references and reclaiming their storage space.

state: A complete description of all the variables and objects and their values, at a given point during the execution of a program.

state diagram: A snapshot of the state of a program, shown graphically.

8.14 Exercises

Exercise 8.1

a. For the following program, draw a stack diagram showing the local variables and parameters of `main` and `fred`, and show any objects those variables refer to.

b. What is the output of this program?

```
public static void main (String[] args)
{
    int x = 5;
    Point blank = new Point (1, 2);

    System.out.println (fred (x, blank));
    System.out.println (x);
```

```
    System.out.println (blank.x);
    System.out.println (blank.y);
}

public static int fred (int x, Point p)
{
    x = x + 7;
    return x + p.x + p.y;
}
```

The point of this exercise is to make sure you understand the mechanism for passing Objects as parameters.

Exercise 8.2

    a. For the following program, draw a stack diagram showing the state of the program just before distance returns. Include all variables and parameters and the objects those variables refer to.

    b. What is the output of this program?

```
public static double distance (Point p1, Point p2) {
    int dx = p1.x - p2.x;
    int dy = p1.y - p2.y;
    return Math.sqrt (dx*dx + dy*dy);
}

public static Point findCenter (Rectangle box) {
    int x = box.x + box.width/2;
    int y = box.y + box.height/2;
    return new Point (x, y);
}

public static void main (String[] args) {
    Point blank = new Point (5, 8);

    Rectangle rect = new Rectangle (0, 2, 4, 4);
    Point center = findCenter (rect);

    double dist = distance (center, blank);

    System.out.println (dist);
}
```

Exercise 8.3   The method grow is part of the built-in Rectangle class. Here is the documentation of it (from the Sun web page):

```
public void grow(int h, int v)
```

Grows the rectangle both horizontally and vertically.

This method modifies the rectangle so that it is h units larger on both the left and right side, and v units larger at both the top and bottom.

The new rectangle has (x - h, y - v) as its top-left corner, a width
of width + 2h, and a height of height + 2v.

If negative values are supplied for h and v, the size of the rectangle
decreases accordingly. The grow method does not check whether the
resulting values of width and height are non-negative.

  a. What is the output of the following program?

  b. Draw a state diagram that shows the state of the program just before the end
     of main. Include all local variables and the objects they refer to.

  c. At the end of main, are p1 and p2 aliased? Why or why not?

```
public static void printPoint (Point p) {
    System.out.println ("(" + p.x + ", " + p.y + ")");
}

public static Point findCenter (Rectangle box) {
    int x = box.x + box.width/2;
    int y = box.y + box.height/2;
    return new Point (x, y);
}

public static void main (String[] args) {

    Rectangle box1 = new Rectangle (2, 4, 7, 9);
    Point p1 = findCenter (box1);
    printPoint (p1);

    box1.grow (1, 1);
    Point p2 = findCenter (box1);
    printPoint (p2);
}
```

Exercise 8.4   You are probably getting sick of the factorial method by now, but
we're going to do one more version.

  a. Create a new program called Big.java and start by writing an iterative version
     of factorial.

  b. Print a table of the integers from 0 to 30 along with their factorials. At some
     point around 15, you will probably see that the answers are not right any more.
     Why not?

  c. BigIntegers are built-in objects that can represent arbitrarily big integers. There
     is no upper bound except the limitations of memory size and processing speed.
     Print the documentation for the BigInteger class in the java.math package,
     and read it.

  d. There are several ways to create a new BigInteger, but the one I recommend
     uses valueOf. The following code converts an integer to a BigInteger:

```
int x = 17;
BigInteger big = BigInteger.valueOf (x);
```

Type in this code and try out a few simple cases like creating a BigInteger and printing it. Notice that `println` knows how to print BigIntegers! Don't forget to add `import java.math.BigInteger` to the beginning of your program.

e. Unfortunately, because BigIntegers are not primitive types, we cannot use the usual math operators on them. Instead we have to use object methods like `add`. In order to add two BigIntegers, you have to invoke `add` on one of the objects and pass the other as an argument. For example:

```
BigInteger small = BigInteger.valueOf (17);
BigInteger big = BigInteger.valueOf (1700000000);
BigInteger total = small.add (big);
```

Try out some of the other methods, like `multiply` and `pow`.

f. Convert `factorial` so that it performs its calculation using BigIntegers, and then returns the BigInteger as a result. You can leave the parameter alone—it will still be an integer.

g. Try printing the table again with your modified factorial function. Is it correct up to 30? How high can you make it go? I calculated the factorial of all the numbers from 0 to 999, but my machine is pretty slow, so it took a while. The last number, 999!, has 2565 digits.

Exercise 8.5   Many encryption algorithms depends on the ability to raise large integers to an integer power. Here is a method that implements a (reasonably) fast algorithm for integer exponentiation:

```
public static int pow (int x, int n) {
    if (n==0) return 1;

    // find x to the n/2 recursively
    int t = pow (x, n/2);

    // if n is even, the result is t squared
    // if n is odd, the result is t squared times x

    if (n%2 == 0) {
      return t*t;
    } else {
      return t*t*x;
    }
}
```

The problem with this method is that it will only work if the result is smaller than 2 billion. Rewrite it so that the result is a `BigInteger`. The parameters should still be integers, though.

You can use the BigInteger methods `add` and `multiply`, but don't use the built-in `pow` method, which would spoil the fun.

Chapter 9

Create your own objects

9.1 Class definitions and object types

Every time you write a class definition, you create a new object type, with the same name as the class. Way back in Section 1.5, when we defined the class named Hello, we also created an object type named Hello. We didn't create any variables with type Hello, and we didn't use the new command to create any Hello objects, but we could have!

That example doesn't make much sense, since there is no reason to create a Hello object, and it is not clear what it would be good for if we did. In this chapter, we will look at some examples of class definitions that create *useful* new object types.

Here are the most important ideas in this chapter:

- Defining a new class also creates a new object type with the same name.

- A class definition is like a template for objects: it determines what instance variables the objects have and what methods can operate on them.

- Every object belongs to some object type; hence, it is an instance of some class.

- When you invoke the new command to create an object, Java invokes a special method called a **constructor** to initialize the instance variables. You provide one or more constructors as part of the class definition.

- Typically all the methods that operate on a type go in the class definition for that type.

Here are some syntax issues about class definitions:

- Class names (and hence object types) always begin with a capital letter, which helps distinguish them from primitive types and variable names.

- You usually put one class definition in each file, and the name of the file must be the same as the name of the class, with the suffix .java. For example, the Time class is defined in the file named Time.java.

- In any program, one class is designated as the **startup class**. The startup class must contain a method named main, which is where the execution of the program begins. Other classes *may* have a method named main, but it will not be executed.

With those issues out of the way, let's look at an example of a user-defined type, Time.

9.2   Time

A common motivation for creating a new Object type is to take several related pieces of data and encapsulate them into an object that can be manipulated (passed as an argument, operated on) as a single unit. We have already seen two built-in types like this, Point and Rectangle.

Another example, which we will implement ourselves, is Time, which is used to record the time of day. The various pieces of information that form a time are the hour, minute and second. Because every Time object will contain these data, we need to create instance variables to hold them.

The first step is to decide what type each variable should be. It seems clear that hour and minute should be integers. Just to keep things interesting, let's make second a double, so we can record fractions of a second.

Instance variables are declared at the beginning of the class definition, outside of any method definition, like this:

```
class Time {
  int hour, minute;
  double second;
}
```

All by itself, this code fragment is a legal class definition. The state diagram for a Time object would look like this:

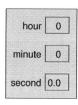

After declaring the instance variables, the next step is usually to define a constructor for the new class.

9.3   Constructors

The usual role of a constructor is to initialize the instance variables. The syntax for constructors is similar to that of other methods, with three exceptions:

- The name of the constructor is the same as the name of the class.

- Constructors have no return type and no return value.

- The keyword `static` is omitted.

Here is an example for the `Time` class:

```java
public Time () {
  this.hour = 0;
  this.minute = 0;
  this.second = 0.0;
}
```

Notice that where you would expect to see a return type, between `public` and `Time`, there is nothing. That's how we (and the compiler) can tell that this is a constructor.

This constructor does not take any arguments, as indicated by the empty parentheses (). Each line of the constructor initializes an instance variable to an arbitrary default value (in this case, midnight). The name `this` is a special keyword that is the name of the object we are creating. You can use `this` the same way you use the name of any other object. For example, you can read and write the instance variables of `this`, and you can pass `this` as an argument to other methods.

But you do not declare `this` and you do not use `new` to create it. In fact, you are not even allowed to make an assignment to it! `this` is created by the system; all you have to do is store values in its instance variables.

A common error when writing constructors is to put a `return` statement at the end. Resist the temptation.

9.4   More constructors

Constructors can be overloaded, just like other methods, which means that you can provide multiple constructors with different parameters. Java knows which constructor to invoke by matching the arguments of the `new` command with the parameters of the constructors.

It is very common to have one constructor that takes no arguments (shown above), and one constructor that takes a parameter list that is identical to the list of instance variables. For example:

```
public Time (int hour, int minute, double second) {
  this.hour = hour;
  this.minute = minute;
  this.second = second;
}
```

The names and types of the parameters are exactly the same as the names and types of the instance variables. All the constructor does is copy the information from the parameters to the instance variables.

If you go back and look at the documentation for Points and Rectangles, you will see that both classes provide constructors like this. Overloading constructors provides the flexibility to create an object first and then fill in the blanks, or to collect all the information before creating the object.

So far this might not seem very interesting, and in fact it is not. Writing constructors is a boring, mechanical process. Once you have written two, you will find that you can churn them out in your sleep, just by looking at the list of instance variables.

9.5   Creating a new object

Although constructors look like methods, you never invoke them directly. Instead, when you use the new command, the system allocates space for the new object and then invokes your constructor to initialize the instance variables.

The following program demonstrates two ways to create and initialize Time objects:

```
class Time {
  int hour, minute;
  double second;

  public Time () {
    this.hour = 0;
    this.minute = 0;
    this.second = 0.0;
  }

  public Time (int hour, int minute, double second) {
    this.hour = hour;
    this.minute = minute;
    this.second = second;
  }

  public static void main (String[] args) {

    // one way to create and initialize a Time object
    Time t1 = new Time ();
```

```
   t1.hour = 11;
   t1.minute = 8;
   t1.second = 3.14159;
   System.out.println (t1);

   // another way to do the same thing
   Time t2 = new Time (11, 8, 3.14159);
   System.out.println (t2);
  }
}
```

As an exercise, figure out the flow of execution through this program.

In `main`, the first time we invoke the `new` command, we provide no arguments, so Java invokes the first constructor. The next few lines assign values to each of the instance variables.

The second time we invoke the `new` command, we provide arguments that match the parameters of the second constructor. This way of initializing the instance variables is more concise (and slightly more efficient), but it can be harder to read, since it is not as clear which values are assigned to which instance variables.

9.6   Printing an object

The output of this program is:

```
Time@80cc7c0
Time@80cc807
```

When Java prints the value of a user-defined object type, it prints the name of the type and a special hexadecimal (base 16) code that is unique for each object. This code is not meaningful in itself; in fact, it can vary from machine to machine and even from run to run. But it can be useful for debugging, in case you want to keep track of individual objects.

In order to print objects in a way that is more meaningful to users (as opposed to programmers), you usually want to write a method called something like printTime:

```
  public static void printTime (Time t) {
    System.out.println (t.hour + ":" + t.minute + ":" + t.second);
  }
```

Compare this method to the version of `printTime` in Section 3.10.

The output of this method, if we pass either `t1` or `t2` as an argument, is `11:8:3.14159`. Although this is recognizable as a time, it is not quite in the standard format. For example, if the number of minutes or seconds is less than 10, we expect a leading 0 as a place-keeper. Also, we might want to drop the decimal part of the seconds. In other words, we want something like `11:08:03`.

In most languages, there are simple ways to control the output format for numbers. In Java there are no simple ways.

Java provides very powerful tools for printing formatted things like times and dates, and also for interpreting formatted input. Unfortunately, these tools are not very easy to use, so I am going to leave them out of this book. If you want, though, you can take a look at the documentation for the Date class in the java.util package.

9.7   Operations on objects

Even though we can't print times in an optimal format, we can still write methods that manipulate Time objects. In the next few sections, I will demonstrate several of the possible interfaces for methods that operate on objects. For some operations, you will have a choice of several possible interfaces, so you should consider the pros and cons of each of these:

pure function: Takes objects and/or primitives as arguments but does not modify the objects. The return value is either a primitive or a new object created inside the method.

modifier: Takes objects as arguments and modifies some or all of them. Often returns void.

fill-in method: One of the arguments is an "empty" object that gets filled in by the method. Technically, this is a type of modifier.

9.8   Pure functions

A method is considered a pure function if the result depends only on the arguments, and it has no side effects like modifying an argument or printing something. The only result of invoking a pure function is the return value.

One example is after, which compares two Times and returns a boolean that indicates whether the first operand comes after the second:

```
public static boolean after (Time time1, Time time2) {
    if (time1.hour > time2.hour) return true;
    if (time1.hour < time2.hour) return false;

    if (time1.minute > time2.minute) return true;
    if (time1.minute < time2.minute) return false;

    if (time1.second > time2.second) return true;
    return false;
}
```

What is the result of this method if the two times are equal? Does that seem like the appropriate result for this method? If you were writing the documentation for this method, would you mention that case specifically?

A second example is addTime, which calculates the sum of two times. For example, if it is 9:14:30, and your breadmaker takes 3 hours and 35 minutes, you could use addTime to figure out when the bread will be done.

Here is a rough draft of this method that is not quite right:

```
public static Time addTime (Time t1, Time t2) {
  Time sum = new Time ();
  sum.hour = t1.hour + t2.hour;
  sum.minute = t1.minute + t2.minute;
  sum.second = t1.second + t2.second;
  return sum;
}
```

Although this method returns a Time object, it is not a constructor. You should go back and compare the syntax of a method like this with the syntax of a constructor, because it is easy to get confused.

Here is an example of how to use this method. If currentTime contains the current time and breadTime contains the amount of time it takes for your breadmaker to make bread, then you could use addTime to figure out when the bread will be done.

```
Time currentTime = new Time (9, 14, 30.0);
Time breadTime = new Time (3, 35, 0.0);
Time doneTime = addTime (currentTime, breadTime);
printTime (doneTime);
```

The output of this program is 12:49:30.0, which is correct. On the other hand, there are cases where the result is not correct. Can you think of one?

The problem is that this method does not deal with cases where the number of seconds or minutes adds up to more than 60. In that case, we have to "carry" the extra seconds into the minutes column, or extra minutes into the hours column.

Here's a second, corrected version of this method.

```
public static Time addTime (Time t1, Time t2) {
  Time sum = new Time ();
  sum.hour = t1.hour + t2.hour;
  sum.minute = t1.minute + t2.minute;
  sum.second = t1.second + t2.second;

  if (sum.second >= 60.0) {
    sum.second -= 60.0;
    sum.minute += 1;
  }
  if (sum.minute >= 60) {
    sum.minute -= 60;
    sum.hour += 1;
  }
  return sum;
```

```
}
```

Although it's correct, it's starting to get big. Later, I will suggest an alternative approach to this problem that will be much shorter.

This code demonstrates two operators we have not seen before, += and -=. These operators provide a concise way to increment and decrement variables. They are similar to ++ and --, except (1) they work on `doubles` as well as `ints`, and (2) the amount of the increment does not have to be 1. The statement `sum.second -= 60.0;` is equivalent to `sum.second = sum.second - 60;`

9.9 Modifiers

As an example of a modifier, consider `increment`, which adds a given number of seconds to a `Time` object. Again, a rough draft of this method looks like:

```
public static void increment (Time time, double secs) {
  time.second += secs;

  if (time.second >= 60.0) {
    time.second -= 60.0;
    time.minute += 1;
  }
  if (time.minute >= 60) {
    time.minute -= 60;
    time.hour += 1;
  }
}
```

The first line performs the basic operation; the remainder deals with the same cases we saw before.

Is this method correct? What happens if the argument `secs` is much greater than 60? In that case, it is not enough to subtract 60 once; we have to keep doing it until `second` is below 60. We can do that by simply replacing the `if` statements with `while` statements:

```
public static void increment (Time time, double secs) {
  time.second += secs;

  while (time.second >= 60.0) {
    time.second -= 60.0;
    time.minute += 1;
  }
  while (time.minute >= 60) {
    time.minute -= 60;
    time.hour += 1;
  }
}
```

This solution is correct, but not very efficient. Can you think of a solution that does not require iteration?

9.10   Fill-in methods

Occasionally you will see methods like addTime written with a different interface
(different arguments and return values). Instead of creating a new object every
time addTime is invoked, we could require the caller to provide an "empty"
object where addTime should store the result. Compare the following with the
previous version:

```
public static void addTimeFill (Time t1, Time t2, Time sum) {
  sum.hour = t1.hour + t2.hour;
  sum.minute = t1.minute + t2.minute;
  sum.second = t1.second + t2.second;

  if (sum.second >= 60.0) {
    sum.second -= 60.0;
    sum.minute += 1;
  }
  if (sum.minute >= 60) {
    sum.minute -= 60;
    sum.hour += 1;
  }
}
```

One advantage of this approach is that the caller has the option of reusing the
same object repeatedly to perform a series of additions. This can be slightly
more efficient, although it can be confusing enough to cause subtle errors. For
the vast majority of programming, it is worth spending a little run time to avoid
a lot of debugging time.

9.11   Which is best?

Anything that can be done with modifiers and fill-in methods can also be done
with pure functions. In fact, there are programming languages, called **functional** programming languages, that only allow pure functions. Some programmers believe that programs that use pure functions are faster to develop and
less error-prone than programs that use modifiers. Nevertheless, there are times
when modifiers are convenient, and some cases where functional programs are
less efficient.

In general, I recommend that you write pure functions whenever it is reasonable
to do so, and resort to modifiers only if there is a compelling advantage. This
approach might be called a functional programming style.

9.12   Incremental development vs. planning

In this chapter I have demonstrated an approach to program development I
refer to as **rapid prototyping with iterative improvement**. In each case,

I wrote a rough draft (or prototype) that performed the basic calculation, and then tested it on a few cases, correcting flaws as I found them.

Although this approach can be effective, it can lead to code that is unnecessarily complicated—since it deals with many special cases—and unreliable—since it is hard to convince yourself that you have found *all* the errors.

An alternative is high-level planning, in which a little insight into the problem can make the programming much easier. In this case the insight is that a Time is really a three-digit number in base 60! The second is the "ones column," the minute is the "60's column", and the hour is the "3600's column."

When we wrote addTime and increment, we were effectively doing addition in base 60, which is why we had to "carry" from one column to the next.

Thus an alternative approach to the whole problem is to convert Times into doubles and take advantage of the fact that the computer already knows how to do arithmetic with doubles. Here is a method that converts a Time into a double:

```
public static double convertToSeconds (Time t) {
  int minutes = t.hour * 60 + t.minute;
  double seconds = minutes * 60 + t.second;
  return seconds;
}
```

Now all we need is a way to convert from a double to a Time object. We could write a method to do it, but it might make more sense to write it as a third constructor:

```
public Time (double secs) {
  this.hour = (int) (secs / 3600.0);
  secs -= this.hour * 3600.0;
  this.minute = (int) (secs / 60.0);
  secs -= this.minute * 60;
  this.second = secs;
}
```

This constructor is a little different from the others, since it involves some calculation along with assignments to the instance variables.

You might have to think a bit to convince yourself that the technique I am using to convert from one base to another is correct. Assuming you are convinced, we can use these methods to rewrite addTime:

```
public static Time addTime (Time t1, Time t2) {
  double seconds = convertToSeconds (t1) + convertToSeconds (t2);
  return new Time (seconds);
}
```

This is much shorter than the original version, and it is much easier to demonstrate that it is correct (assuming, as usual, that the methods it invokes are correct). As an exercise, rewrite increment the same way.

9.13   Generalization

In some ways converting from base 60 to base 10 and back is harder than just dealing with times. Base conversion is more abstract; our intuition for dealing with times is better.

But if we have the insight to treat times as base 60 numbers, and make the investment of writing the conversion methods (`convertToSeconds` and the third constructor), we get a program that is shorter, easier to read and debug, and more reliable.

It is also easier to add more features later. For example, imagine subtracting two `Times` to find the duration between them. The naive approach would be to implement subtraction complete with "borrowing." Using the conversion methods would be much easier.

Ironically, sometimes making a problem harder (more general) makes it easier (fewer special cases, fewer opportunities for error).

9.14   Algorithms

When you write a general solution for a class of problems, as opposed to a specific solution to a single problem, you have written an **algorithm**. I mentioned this word in Chapter 1, but did not define it carefully. It is not easy to define, so I will try a couple of approaches.

First, consider some things that are not algorithms. For example, when you learned to multiply single-digit numbers, you probably memorized the multiplication table. In effect, you memorized 100 specific solutions, so that knowledge is not really algorithmic.

But if you were "lazy," you probably cheated by learning a few tricks. For example, to find the product of n and 9, you can write $n - 1$ as the first digit and $10 - n$ as the second digit. This trick is a general solution for multiplying any single-digit number by 9. That's an algorithm!

Similarly, the techniques you learned for addition with carrying, subtraction with borrowing, and long division are all algorithms. One of the characteristics of algorithms is that they do not require any intelligence to carry out. They are mechanical processes in which each step follows from the last according to a simple set of rules.

In my opinion, it is embarrassing that humans spend so much time in school learning to execute algorithms that, quite literally, require no intelligence.

On the other hand, the process of designing algorithms is interesting, intellectually challenging, and a central part of what we call programming.

Some of the things that people do naturally, without difficulty or conscious thought, are the most difficult to express algorithmically. Understanding natural language is a good example. We all do it, but so far no one has been able to explain *how* we do it, at least not in the form of an algorithm.

Later you will have the opportunity to design simple algorithms for a variety of problems.

9.15   Glossary

class: Previously, I defined a class as a collection of related methods. In this chapter we learned that a class definition is also a template for a new type of object.

instance: A member of a class. Every object is an instance of some class.

constructor: A special method that initializes the instance variables of a newly-constructed object.

project: A collection of one or more class definitions (one per file) that make up a program.

startup class: The class that contains the `main` method where execution of the program begins.

function: A method whose result depends only on its parameters, and that has no side-effects other than returning a value.

functional programming style: A style of program design in which the majority of methods are functions.

modifier: A method that changes one or more of the objects it receives as parameters, and usually returns `void`.

fill-in method: A type of method that takes an "empty" object as a parameter and fills in its instance variables instead of generating a return value. This type of method is usually not the best choice.

algorithm: A set of instructions for solving a class of problems by a mechanical process.

9.16   Exercises

Exercise 9.1   In the board game Scrabble[1], each tile contains a letter, which is used to spell words, and a score, which is used to determine the value of a word.

   a. Write a definition for a class named `Tile` that represents Scrabble tiles. The instance variables should be a character named `letter` and an integer named `value`.

---

[1]Scrabble is a registered trademark owned in the U.S.A and Canada by Hasbro Inc., and in the rest of the world by J.W. Spear & Sons Limited of Maidenhead, Berkshire, England, a subsidiary of Mattel Inc.

b. Write a constructor that takes parameters named `letter` and `value` and initializes the instance variables.

c. Write a method named `printTile` that takes a `Tile` object as a parameter and prints the instance variables in some reader-friendly format.

d. Write a method named `testTile` that creates a Tile object with the letter Z and the value 10, and then uses `printTile` to print the state of the object.

The point of this exercise is to practice the mechanical part of creating a new class definition and code that tests it.

Exercise 9.2   Write a class definition for `Date`, an object type that contains three integers, `year`, `month` and `day`. This class should provide two constructors. The first should take no parameters. The second should take parameters named `year`, `month` and `day`, and use them to initialize the instance variables.

Add code to `main` that creates a new `Date` object named `birthday`. The new object should contain your birthdate. You can use either constructor.

Exercise 9.3

A rational number is a number that can be represented as the ratio of two integers. For example, 2/3 is a rational number, and you can think of 7 as a rational number with an implicit 1 in the denominator. For this assignment, you are going to write a class definition for rational numbers.

a. Examine the following program and make sure you understand what it does:

```
public class Complex
{
    double real, imag;

    // simple constructor
    public Complex () {
        this.real = 0.0;  this.imag = 0.0;
    }

    // constructor that takes arguments
    public Complex (double real, double imag) {
        this.real = real;  this.imag = imag;
    }

    public static void printComplex (Complex c) {
        System.out.println (c.real + " + " + c.imag + "i");
    }

    // conjugate is a modifier
    public static void conjugate (Complex c) {
        c.imag = -c.imag;
    }

    // abs is a function that returns a primitive
    public static double abs (Complex c) {
        return Math.sqrt (c.real * c.real + c.imag * c.imag);
```

```
        }

        // add is a function that returns a new Complex object
        public static Complex add (Complex a, Complex b) {
            return new Complex (a.real + b.real, a.imag + b.imag);
        }

        public static void main(String args[]) {

            // use the first constructor
            Complex x = new Complex ();
            x.real = 1.0;
            x.imag = 2.0;

            // use the second constructor
            Complex y = new Complex (3.0, 4.0);

            System.out.println (Complex.abs (y));

            Complex.conjugate (x);
            Complex.printComplex (x);
            Complex.printComplex (y);

            Complex s = Complex.add (x, y);
            Complex.printComplex (s);
        }
    }
```

b. Create a new program called `Rational.java` that defines a class named `Rational`. A `Rational` object should have two integer instance variables to store the numerator and denominator of a rational number.

c. Write a constructor that takes no arguments and that sets the two instance variables to zero.

d. Write a method called `printRational` that takes a Rational object as an argument and prints it in some reasonable format.

e. Write a `main` method that creates a new object with type Rational, sets its instance variables to some values, and prints the object.

f. At this stage, you have a minimal testable (debuggable) program. Test it and, if necessary, debug it.

g. Write a second constructor for your class that takes two arguments and that uses them to initalize the instance variables.

h. Write a method called `negate` that reverses the sign of a rational number. This method should be a modifier, so it should return `void`. Add lines to `main` to test the new method.

i. Write a method called `invert` that inverts the number by swapping the numerator and denominator. Remember the swap pattern we have seen before. Add lines to `main` to test the new method.

j. Write a method called `toDouble` that converts the rational number to a double (floating-point number) and returns the result. This method is a pure function; it does not modify the object. As always, test the new method.

k. Write a modifier named `reduce` that reduces a rational number to its lowest terms by finding the GCD of the numerator and denominator and then dividing top and bottom by the GCD. This method should be a pure function; it should not modify the instance variables of the object on which it is invoked.

You may want to write a method called `gcd` that finds the greatest common divisor of the numerator and the denominator (See Exercise 5.10).

l. Write a method called `add` that takes two Rational numbers as arguments and returns a new Rational object. The return object, not surprisingly, should contain the sum of the arguments.

There are several ways to add fractions. You can use any one you want, but you should make sure that the result of the operation is reduced so that the numerator and denominator have no common divisor (other than 1).

The purpose of this exercise is to write a class definition that includes a variety of methods, including constructors, modifiers and pure functions.

Chapter 10

Arrays

An **array** is a set of values where each value is identified by an index. You can make an array of ints, doubles, or any other type, but all the values in an array have to have the same type.

Syntactically, array types look like other Java types except they are followed by []. For example, int[] is the type "array of integers" and double[] is the type "array of doubles."

You can declare variables with these types in the usual ways:

```
int[] count;
double[] values;
```

Until you initialize these variables, they are set to null. To create the array itself, use the new command.

```
count = new int[4];
values = new double[size];
```

The first assignment makes count refer to an array of 4 integers; the second makes values refer to an array of doubles. The number of elements in values depends on size. You can use any integer expression as an array size.

The following figure shows how arrays are represented in state diagrams:

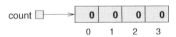

The large numbers inside the boxes are the **elements** of the array. The small numbers outside the boxes are the indices used to identify each box. When you allocate a new array, the elements are initialized to zero.

10.1 Accessing elements

To store values in the array, use the [] operator. For example count[0] refers to the "zeroeth" element of the array, and count[1] refers to the "oneth" element.

You can use the [] operator anywhere in an expression:

```
count[0] = 7;
count[1] = count[0] * 2;
count[2]++;
count[3] -= 60;
```

All of these are legal assignment statements. Here is the effect of this code fragment:

By now you should have noticed that the four elements of this array are numbered from 0 to 3, which means that there is no element with the index 4. This should sound familiar, since we saw the same thing with `String` indices. Nevertheless, it is a common error to go beyond the bounds of an array, which will cause an `ArrayOutOfBoundsException`. As with all exceptions, you get an error message and the program quits.

You can use any expression as an index, as long as it has type `int`. One of the most common ways to index an array is with a loop variable. For example:

```
int i = 0;
while (i < 4) {
  System.out.println (count[i]);
  i++;
}
```

This is a standard `while` loop that counts from 0 up to 4, and when the loop variable i is 4, the condition fails and the loop terminates. Thus, the body of the loop is only executed when i is 0, 1, 2 and 3.

Each time through the loop we use i as an index into the array, printing the ith element. This type of array traversal is very common. Arrays and loops go together like fava beans and a nice Chianti.

10.2   Copying arrays

When you copy an array variable, remember that you are copying a reference to the array. For example:

```
double[] a = new double [3];
double[] b = a;
```

This code creates one array of three `doubles`, and sets two different variables to refer to it. This situation is a form of aliasing.

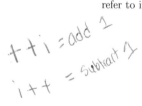

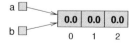

Any changes in either array will be reflected in the other. This is not usually the behavior you want; instead, you should make a copy of the array, by allocating a new array and copying each element from one to the other.

```
double[] b = new double [3];

int i = 0;
while (i < 4) {
  b[i] = a[i];
  i++;
}
```

10.3   for loops

The loops we have written so far have a number of elements in common. All of them start by initializing a variable; they have a test, or condition, that depends on that variable; and inside the loop they do something to that variable, like increment it.

This type of loop is so common that there is an alternative loop statement, called for, that expresses it more concisely. The general syntax looks like this:

```
for (INITIALIZER; CONDITION; INCREMENTOR) {
  BODY
}
```

This statement is exactly equivalent to

```
INITIALIZER;
while (CONDITION) {
  BODY
  INCREMENTOR
}
```

except that it is more concise and, since it puts all the loop-related statements in one place, it is easier to read. For example:

```
for (int i = 0; i < 4; i++) {
  System.out.println (count[i]);
}
```

is equivalent to

```
int i = 0;
while (i < 4) {
  System.out.println (count[i]);
  i++;
}
```

As an exercise, write a for loop to copy the elements of an array.

10.4   Arrays and objects

In many ways, arrays behave like objects:

- When you declare an array variable, you get a reference to an array.

- You have to use the `new` command to create the array itself.

- When you pass an array as an argument, you pass a reference, which means that the invoked method can change the contents of the array.

Some of the objects we have looked at, like `Rectangles`, are similar to arrays, in the sense that they are named collection of values. This raises the question, "How is an array of 4 integers different from a Rectangle object?"

If you go back to the definition of "array" at the beginning of the chapter, you will see one difference, which is that the elements of an array are identified by indices, whereas the elements (instance variables) of an object have names (like `x`, `width`, etc.).

Another difference between arrays and objects is that all the elements of an array have to be the same type. Although that is also true of `Rectangles`, we have seen other objects that have instance variables with different types (like `Time`).

10.5   Array length

Actually, arrays do have one named instance variable: `length`. Not surprisingly, it contains the length of the array (number of elements). It is a good idea to use this value as the upper bound of a loop, rather than a constant value. That way, if the size of the array changes, you won't have to go through the program changing all the loops; they will work correctly for any size array.

```
for (int i = 0; i < a.length; i++) {
  b[i] = a[i];
}
```

The last time the body of the loop gets executed, `i` is `a.length - 1`, which is the index of the last element. When `i` is equal to `a.length`, the condition fails and the body is not executed, which is a good thing, since it would cause an exception. This code assumes that the array `b` contains at least as many elements as `a`.

As an exercise, write a method called `cloneArray` that takes an array of integers as a parameter, creates a new array that is the same size, copies the elements from the first array into the new one, and then returns a reference to the new array.

10.6   Random numbers

Most computer programs do the same thing every time they are executed, so they are said to be **deterministic**. Usually, determinism is a good thing, since we expect the same calculation to yield the same result. For some applications, though, we would like the computer to be unpredictable. Games are an obvious example, but there are many more.

Making a program truly **nondeterministic** turns out to be not so easy, but there are ways to make it at least seem nondeterministic. One of them is to generate random numbers and use them to determine the outcome of the program. Java provides a built-in method that generates **pseudorandom** numbers, which are not truly random in the mathematical sense, but for our purposes, they will do.

Check out the documentation of the `random` method in the `Math` class. The return value is a `double` between 0.0 and 1.0. To be precise, it is greater than or equal to 0.0 and strictly less than 1.0. Each time you invoke `random` you get the next number in a pseudorandom sequence. To see a sample, run this loop:

```
for (int i = 0; i < 10; i++) {
  double x = Math.random ();
  System.out.println (x);
}
```

To generate a random `double` between 0.0 and an upper bound like `high`, you can multiply `x` by `high`. How would you generate a random number between `low` and `high`? How would you generate a random integer?

Exercise 10.1   Write a method called `randomDouble` that takes two doubles, `low` and `high`, and that returns a random double x so that $low \leq x < high$.

Exercise 10.2   Write a method called `randomInt` that takes two arguments, `low` and `high`, and that returns a random integer between `low` and `high` (including both).

10.7   Array of random numbers

If your implementation of `randomInt` is correct, then every value in the range from `low` to `high` should have the same probability. If you generate a long series of numbers, every value should appear, at least approximately, the same number of times.

One way to test your method is to generate a large number of random values, store them in an array, and count the number of times each value occurs.

The following method takes a single argument, the size of the array. It allocates a new array of integers, fills it with random values, and returns a reference to the new array.

```
public static int[] randomArray (int n) {
  int[] a = new int[n];
```

```
    for (int i = 0; i<a.length; i++) {
      a[i] = randomInt (0, 100);
    }
    return a;
  }
```

The return type is `int[]`, which means that this method returns an array of integers. To test this method, it is convenient to have a method that prints the contents of an array.

```
  public static void printArray (int[] a) {
    for (int i = 0; i<a.length; i++) {
      System.out.println (a[i]);
    }
  }
```

The following code generates an array and prints it:

```
    int numValues = 8;
    int[] array = randomArray (numValues);
    printArray (array);
```

On my machine the output is

27
6
54
62
54
2
44
81

which is pretty random-looking. Your results may differ.

If these were exam scores, and they would be pretty bad exam scores, the teacher might present the results to the class in the form of a **histogram**, which is a set of counters that keeps track of the number of times each value appear.

For exam scores, we might have ten counters to keep track of how many students scored in the 90s, the 80s, etc. The next few sections develop code to generate a histogram.

10.8   Counting

A good approach to problems like this is to think of simple methods that are easy to write, and that might turn out to be useful. Then you can combine them into a solution. Of course, it is not easy to know ahead of time which methods are likely to be useful, but as you gain experience you will have a better idea.

Also, it is not always obvious what sort of things are easy to write, but a good approach is to look for subproblems that fit a pattern you have seen before.

Back in Section 7.7 we looked at a loop that traversed a string and counted the number of times a given letter appeared. You can think of this program as an example of a pattern called "traverse and count." The elements of this pattern are:

- A set or container that can be traversed, like an array or a string.

- A test that you can apply to each element in the container.

- A counter that keeps track of how many elements pass the test.

In this case, the container is an array of integers. The test is whether or not a given score falls in a given range of values.

Here is a method called `inRange` that counts the number of elements in an array that fall in a given range. The parameters are the array and two integers that specify the lower and upper bounds of the range.

```
public static int inRange (int[] a, int low, int high) {
    int count = 0;
    for (int i=0; i<a.length; i++) {
        if (a[i] >= low && a[i] < high) count++;
    }
    return count;
}
```

In my description of the method, I wasn't very careful about whether something equal to `low` or `high` falls in the range, but you can see from the code that `low` is in and `high` is out. That should keep us from counting any elements twice.

Now we can could the number of scores in the ranges we are interested in:

```
int[] scores = randomArray (30);
int a = inRange (scores, 90, 100);
int b = inRange (scores, 80, 90);
int c = inRange (scores, 70, 80);
int d = inRange (scores, 60, 70);
int f = inRange (scores, 0, 60);
```

10.9   The histogram

The code we have so far is a bit repetitive, but it is acceptable as long as the number of ranges want is small. But now imagine that we want to keep track of the number of times each score appears, all 100 possible values. Would you want to write:

```
int count0 = inRange (scores, 0, 1);
int count1 = inRange (scores, 1, 2);
int count2 = inRange (scores, 2, 3);
...
int count3 = inRange (scores, 99, 100);
```

I don't think so. What we really want is a way to store 100 integers, preferably so we can use an index to access each one. Immediately, you should be thinking "array!"

The counting pattern is the same whether we use a single counter or an array of counters. In this case, we initialize the array outside the loop; then, inside the loop, we invoke inRange and store the result:

```
int[] counts = new int [100];

for (int i = 0; i<100; i++) {
    counts[i] = inRange (scores, i, i+1);
}
```

The only tricky thing here is that we are using the loop variable in two roles: as in index into the array, and as the parameter to inRange.

10.10   A single-pass solution

Although this code works, it is not as efficient as it could be. Every time it invokes inRange, it traverses the entire array. As the number of ranges increases, that gets to be a lot of traversals.

It would be better to make a single pass through the array, and for each value, compute which range it falls in. Then we could increment the appropriate counter. In this example, that computation is trivial, because we can use the value itself as an index into the array of counters.

Here is code that traverses an array of scores, once, and generates a histogram.

```
int[] counts = new int [100];

for (int i = 0; i < scores.length; i++) {
    int index = scores[i];
    counts[index]++;
}
```

Exercise 10.3   Encapsulate this code in a method called scoreHist that takes an array of scores and returns a histogram of the values in the array.

Modify the method so that the histogram has only 10 counters, and count the number of scores in each range of 10 values; that is, the 90s, the 80s, etc.

10.11   Glossary

array: A named collection of values, where all the values have the same type, and each value is identified by an index.

collection: Any data structure that contains a set of items or elements.

element: One of the values in an array. The [] operator selects elements of an array.

index: An integer variable or value used to indicate an element of an array.

deterministic: A program that does the same thing every time it is invoked.

pseudorandom: A sequence of numbers that appear to be random, but which are actually the product of a deterministic computation.

histogram: An array of integers where each integer counts the number of values that fall into a certain range.

10.12   Exercises

Exercise 10.4   Write a class method named `areFactors` that takes an integer n and an array of integers, and that returns true if the numbers in the array are all factors of n (which is to say that n is divisible by all of them). HINT: See Exercise 5.1.

Exercise 10.5   Write a method that takes an array of integers and an integer named `target` as arguments, and that returns the first index where `target` appears in the array, if it does, and -1 otherwise.

Exercise 10.6   Write a method called `arrayHist` that takes an array of integers and that returns a new histogram array. The histogram should contain 11 elements with the following contents:

```
element 0 -- number of elements in the array that are <= 0
        1 -- number of elements in the array that are == 1
        2 -- number of elements in the array that are == 2
        ...
        9 -- number of elements in the array that are == 9
       10 -- number of elements in the array that are >= 10
```

Exercise 10.7   Some programmers disagree with the general rule that variables and methods should be given meaningful names. Instead, they think variables and methods should be named after fruit.

For each of the following methods, write one sentence that describes abstractly what the method does. For each variable, identify the role it plays.

```
public static int banana (int[] a) {
    int grape = 0;
    int i = 0;
    while (i < a.length) {
        grape = grape + a[i];
        i++;
    }
    return grape;
}
```

Integer [ ] ^
Integer P

```java
public static int apple (int[] a, int p) {
    int i = 0;
    int pear = 0;
    while (i < a.length) {
        if (a[i] == p) pear++;
        i++;
    }
    return pear;
}


public static int grapefruit (int[] a, int p) {
    for (int i = 0; i<a.length; i++) {
        if (a[i] == p) return i;
    }
    return -1;
}
```

The purpose of this exercise is to practice reading code and recognizing the solution patterns we have seen.

Exercise 10.8

a. What is the output of the following program?

b. Draw a stack diagram that shows the state of the program just before mus returns.

c. Describe in a few words what mus does.

```java
public static int[] make (int n) {
    int[] a = new int[n];

    for (int i=0; i<n; i++) {
        a[i] = i+1;
    }
    return a;
}


public static void dub (int[] jub) {
    for (int i=0; i<jub.length; i++) {
        jub[i] *= 2;
    }
}


public static int mus (int[] zoo) {
    int fus = 0;
    for (int i=0; i<zoo.length; i++) {
        fus = fus + zoo[i];
    }
    return fus;
}


public static void main (String[] args) {
    int[] bob = make (5);
```

```
    dub (bob);

    System.out.println (mus (bob));
}
```

Exercise 10.9   Many of the patterns we have seen for traversing arrays can also
be written recursively. It is not common to do so, but it is a useful exercise.

  a. Write a method called `maxInRange` that takes an array of integers and a range
     of indices (`lowIndex` and `highIndex`), and that finds the maximum value in the
     array, considering only the elements between `lowIndex` and `highIndex`, including
     both ends.

     This method should be recursive. If the length of the range is 1, that is, if
     `lowIndex == highIndex`, we know immediately that the sole element in the
     range must be the maximum. So that's the base case.

     If there is more than one element in the range, we can break the array into two
     pieces, find the maximum in each of the pieces, and then find the maximum of
     each of the piece-maxima.

  b. Methods like `maxInRange` can be awkward to use. To find the largest element
     in an array, we have to provide a range that includes the entire array.

         `double max = maxInRange (array, 0, a.length-1);`

     Write a method called `max` that takes an array as a parameter and that uses
     `maxInRange` to find and return the largest value. Methods like `max` are sometimes
     called **wrapper methods** because they provide a layer of abstraction around
     an awkward method and provide an interface to the outside world that is easier
     to use. The method that actually performs the computation is called the **helper
     method**. We will see this pattern again in Section 14.9.

  c. Write a recursive version of `find` using the wrapper-helper pattern. `find` should
     take an array of integers and a target integer. It should return the index of the
     first location where the target integer appears in the array, or -1 if it does not
     appear.

Exercise 10.10   One not-very-efficient way to sort the elements of an array is to
find the largest element and swap it with the first element, then find the second-largest
element and swap it with the second, and so on.

  a. Write a method called `indexOfMaxInRange` that takes an array of integers, finds
     the largest element in the given range, and returns *its index*. You can modify
     your recursive version of `maxInRange` or you can write an iterative version from
     scratch.

  b. Write a method called `swapElement` that takes an array of integers and two
     indices, and that swaps the elements at the given indices.

  c. Write a method called `sortArray` that takes an array of integers and that uses
     `indexOfMaxInRange` and `swapElement` to sort the array from largest to smallest.

Exercise 10.11   Write a method called `letterHist` that takes a String as a parameter and that returns a histogram of the letters in the String. The zeroeth element of

the histogram should contain the number of a's in the String (upper and lower case); the 25th element should contain the number of z's. Your solution should only traverse the String once.

Exercise 10.12   A word is said to be a "doubloon" if every letter that appears in the word appears exactly twice. For example, the following are all the doubloons I found in my dictionary.

> Abba, Anna, appall, appearer, appeases, arraigning, beriberi, bilabial, boob, Caucasus, coco, Dada, deed, Emmett, Hannah, horseshoer, intestines, Isis, mama, Mimi, murmur, noon, Otto, papa, peep, reappear, redder, sees, Shanghaiings, Toto

Write a method called `isDoubloon` that returns `true` if the given word is a doubloon and `false` otherwise.

Exercise 10.13   In Scrabble each player has a set of tiles with letters on them, and the object of the game is to use those letters to spell words. The scoring system is complicated, but as a rough guide longer words are often worth more than shorter words.

Imagine you are given your set of tiles as a String, like `"qijibo"` and you are given another String to test, like `"jib"`. Write a method called `testWord` that takes these two Strings and returns true if the set of tiles can be used to spell the word. You might have more than one tile with the same letter, but you can only use each tile once.

Exercise 10.14   In real Scrabble, there are some blank tiles that can be used as wild cards; that is, a blank tile can be used to represent any letter.

Think of an algorithm for `testWord` that deals with wild cards. Don't get bogged down in details of implementation like how to represent wild cards. Just describe the algorithm, using English, pseudocode, or Java.

Chapter 11

Arrays of Objects

11.1 Composition

By now we have seen several examples of composition (the ability to combine language features in a variety of arrangements). One of the first examples we saw was using a method invocation as part of an expression. Another example is the nested structure of statements: you can put an `if` statement within a `while` loop, or within another `if` statement, etc.

Having seen this pattern, and having learned about arrays and objects, you should not be surprised to learn that you can have arrays of objects. In fact, you can also have objects that contain arrays (as instance variables); you can have arrays that contain arrays; you can have objects that contain objects, and so on.

In the next two chapters we will look at some examples of these combinations, using `Card` objects as an example.

11.2 Card objects

If you are not familiar with common playing cards, now would be a good time to get a deck, or else this chapter might not make much sense. There are 52 cards in a deck, each of which belongs to one of four suits and one of 13 ranks. The suits are Spades, Hearts, Diamonds and Clubs (in descending order in Bridge). The ranks are Ace, 2, 3, 4, 5, 6, 7, 8, 9, 10, Jack, Queen and King. Depending on what game you are playing, the rank of the Ace may be higher than King or lower than 2.

If we want to define a new object to represent a playing card, it is pretty obvious what the instance variables should be: `rank` and `suit`. It is not as obvious what type the instance variables should be. One possibility is `String`s, containing things like `"Spade"` for suits and `"Queen"` for ranks. One problem with this implementation is that it would not be easy to compare cards to see which had higher rank or suit.

An alternative is to use integers to **encode** the ranks and suits. By "encode," I do not mean what some people think, which is to encrypt, or translate into a secret code. What a computer scientist means by "encode" is something like "define a mapping between a sequence of numbers and the things I want to represent." For example,

Spades	$\mapsto$	3
Hearts	$\mapsto$	2
Diamonds	$\mapsto$	1
Clubs	$\mapsto$	0

The obvious feature of this mapping is that the suits map to integers in order, so we can compare suits by comparing integers. The mapping for ranks is fairly obvious; each of the numerical ranks maps to the corresponding integer, and for face cards:

Jack	$\mapsto$	11
Queen	$\mapsto$	12
King	$\mapsto$	13

The reason I am using mathematical notation for these mappings is that they are not part of the Java program. They are part of the program design, but they never appear explicitly in the code. The class definition for the `Card` type looks like this:

```
class Card
{
    int suit, rank;

    public Card () {
        this.suit = 0;   this.rank = 0;
    }

    public Card (int suit, int rank) {
        this.suit = suit;   this.rank = rank;
    }
}
```

As usual, I am providing two constructors, one of which takes a parameter for each instance variable and the other of which takes no parameters.

To create an object that represents the 3 of Clubs, we would use the **new** command:

```
    Card threeOfClubs = new Card (0, 3);
```

The first argument, 0 represents the suit Clubs.

11.3   The printCard method

When you create a new class, the first step is usually to declare the instance variables and write constructors. The second step is often to write the standard methods that every object should have, including one that prints the object, and one or two that compare objects. I will start with printCard.

In order to print Card objects in a way that humans can read easily, we want to map the integer codes onto words. A natural way to do that is with an array of Strings. You can create an array of Strings the same way you create an array of primitive types:

```
String[] suits = new String [4];
```

Then we can set the values of the elements of the array.

```
suits[0] = "Clubs";
suits[1] = "Diamonds";
suits[2] = "Hearts";
suits[3] = "Spades";
```

Creating an array and initializing the elements is such a common operation that Java provides a special syntax for it:

```
String[] suits = { "Clubs", "Diamonds", "Hearts", "Spades" };
```

The effect of this statement is identical to that of the separate declaration, allocation, and assignment. A state diagram of this array might look like:

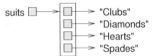

The elements of the array are *references* to the Strings, rather than Strings themselves. This is true of all arrays of objects, as I will discuss in more detail later. For now, all we need is another array of Strings to decode the ranks:

```
String[] ranks = { "narf", "Ace", "2", "3", "4", "5", "6",
             "7", "8", "9", "10", "Jack", "Queen", "King" };
```

The reason for the "narf" is to act as a place-keeper for the zeroeth element of the array, which will never be used. The only valid ranks are 1–13. This wasted element is not necessary, of course. We could have started at 0, as usual, but it is best to encode 2 as 2, and 3 as 3, etc.

Using these arrays, we can select the appropriate Strings by using the suit and rank as indices. In the method printCard,

```
public static void printCard (Card c) {
    String[] suits = { "Clubs", "Diamonds", "Hearts", "Spades" };
    String[] ranks = { "narf", "Ace", "2", "3", "4", "5", "6",
                 "7", "8", "9", "10", "Jack", "Queen", "King" };

    System.out.println (ranks[c.rank] + " of " + suits[c.suit]);
}
```

the expression suits[c.suit] means "use the instance variable suit from the object c as an index into the array named suits, and select the appropriate string." The output of this code

```
Card card = new Card (1, 11);
printCard (card);
```

is Jack of Diamonds.

11.4   The sameCard method

The word "same" is one of those things that occur in natural language that seem perfectly clear until you give it some thought, and then you realize there is more to it than you expected.

For example, if I say "Chris and I have the same car," I mean that his car and mine are the same make and model, but they are two different cars. If I say "Chris and I have the same mother," I mean that his mother and mine are one and the same. So the idea of "sameness" is different depending on the context.

When you talk about objects, there is a similar ambiguity. For example, if two Cards are the same, does that mean they contain the same data (rank and suit), or they are actually the same Card object?

To see if two references refer to the same object, we can use the == operator. For example:

```
Card card1 = new Card (1, 11);
Card card2 = card1;

if (card1 == card2) {
    System.out.println ("card1 and card2 are the same object.");
}
```

This type of equality is called **shallow equality** because it only compares the references, not the contents of the objects.

To compare the contents of the objects—**deep equality**—it is common to write a method with a name like sameCard.

```
public static boolean sameCard (Card c1, Card c2) {
    return (c1.suit == c2.suit && c1.rank == c2.rank);
}
```

Now if we create two different objects that contain the same data, we can use sameCard to see if they represent the same card:

```
Card card1 = new Card (1, 11);
Card card2 = new Card (1, 11);

if (sameCard (card1, card2)) {
    System.out.println ("card1 and card2 are the same card.");
}
```

In this case, card1 and card2 are two different objects that contain the same data

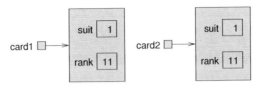

so the condition is true. What does the state diagram look like when card1 == card2 is true?

In Section 7.10 I said that you should never use the == operator on Strings because it does not do what you expect. Instead of comparing the contents of the String (deep equality), it checks whether the two Strings are the same object (shallow equality).

11.5   The compareCard method

For primitive types, there are conditional operators that compare values and determine when one is greater or less than another. These operators (< and > and the others) don't work for object types. For Strings there is a built-in compareTo method. For Cards we have to write our own, which we will call compareCard. Later, we will use this method to sort a deck of cards.

Some sets are completely ordered, which means that you can compare any two elements and tell which is bigger. For example, the integers and the floating-point numbers are totally ordered. Some sets are unordered, which means that there is no meaningful way to say that one element is bigger than another. For example, the fruits are unordered, which is why we cannot compare apples and oranges. In Java, the boolean type is unordered; we cannot say that true is greater than false.

The set of playing cards is partially ordered, which means that sometimes we can compare cards and sometimes not. For example, I know that the 3 of Clubs is higher than the 2 of Clubs, and the 3 of Diamonds is higher than the 3 of Clubs. But which is better, the 3 of Clubs or the 2 of Diamonds? One has a higher rank, but the other has a higher suit.

In order to make cards comparable, we have to decide which is more important, rank or suit. To be honest, the choice is completely arbitrary. For the sake of choosing, I will say that suit is more important, because when you buy a new deck of cards, it comes sorted with all the Clubs together, followed by all the Diamonds, and so on.

With that decided, we can write compareCard. It will take two Cards as parameters and return 1 if the first card wins, -1 if the second card wins, and 0 if they tie (indicating deep equality). It is sometimes confusing to keep those return values straight, but they are pretty standard for comparison methods.

First we compare the suits:

```
if (c1.suit > c2.suit) return 1;
if (c1.suit < c2.suit) return -1;
```

If neither statement is true, then the suits must be equal, and we have to compare ranks:

```
if (c1.rank > c2.rank) return 1;
if (c1.rank < c2.rank) return -1;
```

If neither of these is true, the ranks must be equal, so we return 0. In this ordering, aces will appear lower than deuces (2s).

As an exercise, fix it so that aces are ranked higher than Kings, and encapsulate this code in a method.

11.6   Arrays of cards

The reason I chose Cards as the objects for this chapter is that there is an obvious use for an array of cards—a deck. Here is some code that creates a new deck of 52 cards:

```
Card[] deck = new Card [52];
```

Here is the state diagram for this object:

The important thing to see here is that the array contains only *references* to objects; it does not contain any Card objects. The values of the array elements are initialized to null. You can access the elements of the array in the usual way:

```
if (deck[3] == null) {
    System.out.println ("No cards yet!");
}
```

But if you try to access the instance variables of the non-existent Cards, you will get a NullPointerException.

```
deck[2].rank;              // NullPointerException
```

Nevertheless, that is the correct syntax for accessing the rank of the "twoeth" card in the deck (really the third—we started at zero, remember?). This is another example of composition, the combination of the syntax for accessing an element of an array and an instance variable of an object.

The easiest way to populate the deck with Card objects is to write a nested loop:

```
int index = 0;
for (int suit = 0; suit <= 3; suit++) {
    for (int rank = 1; rank <= 13; rank++) {
```

```
        deck[index] = new Card (suit, rank);
        index++;
    }
}
```

The outer loop enumerates the suits, from 0 to 3. For each suit, the inner loop enumerates the ranks, from 1 to 13. Since the outer loop iterates 4 times, and the inner loop iterates 13 times, the total number of times the body is executed is 52 (13 times 4).

I used the variable index to keep track of where in the deck the next card should go. The following state diagram shows what the deck looks like after the first two cards have been allocated:

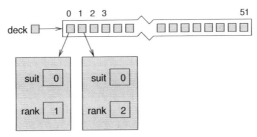

Exercise 11.1 Encapsulate this deck-building code in a method called buildDeck that takes no parameters and that returns a fully-populated array of Cards.

11.7 The printDeck method

Whenever you are working with arrays, it is convenient to have a method that will print the contents of the array. We have seen the pattern for traversing an array several times, so the following method should be familiar:

```
public static void printDeck (Card[] deck) {
    for (int i=0; i<deck.length; i++) {
        printCard (deck[i]);
    }
}
```

Since deck has type Card[], an element of deck has type Card. Therefore, deck[i] is a legal argument for printCard.

11.8 Searching

The next method I want to write is findCard, which searches through an array of Cards to see whether it contains a certain card. It may not be obvious why this method would be useful, but it gives me a chance to demonstrate two ways to go searching for things, a linear search and a bisection search.

Linear search is the more obvious of the two; it involves traversing the deck and comparing each card to the one we are looking for. If we find it we return the index where the card appears. If it is not in the deck, we return -1.

```
public static int findCard (Card[] deck, Card card) {
    for (int i = 0; i< deck.length; i++) {
        if (sameCard (deck[i], card)) return i;
    }
    return -1;
}
```

The arguments of `findCard` are named `card` and `deck`. It might seem odd to have a variable with the same name as a type (the `card` variable has type `Card`). This is legal and common, although it can sometimes make code hard to read. In this case, though, I think it works.

The method returns as soon as it discovers the card, which means that we do not have to traverse the entire deck if we find the card we are looking for. If the loop terminates without finding the card, we know the card is not in the deck and return -1.

If the cards in the deck are not in order, there is no way to search that is faster than this. We have to look at every card, since otherwise there is no way to be certain the card we want is not there.

But when you look for a word in a dictionary, you don't search linearly through every word. The reason is that the words are in alphabetical order. As a result, you probably use an algorithm that is similar to a bisection search:

1. Start in the middle somewhere.

2. Choose a word on the page and compare it to the word you are looking for.

3. If you found the word you are looking for, stop.

4. If the word you are looking for comes after the word on the page, flip to somewhere later in the dictionary and go to step 2.

5. If the word you are looking for comes before the word on the page, flip to somewhere earlier in the dictionary and go to step 2.

If you ever get to the point where there are two adjacent words on the page and your word comes between them, you can conclude that your word is not in the dictionary. The only alternative is that your word has been misfiled somewhere, but that contradicts our assumption that the words are in alphabetical order.

In the case of a deck of cards, if we know that the cards are in order, we can write a version of `findCard` that is much faster. The best way to write a bisection search is with a recursive method. That's because bisection is naturally recursive.

The trick is to write a method called findBisect that takes two indices as parameters, low and high, indicating the segment of the array that should be searched (including both low and high).

1. To search the array, choose an index between low and high (call it mid) and compare it to the card you are looking for.

2. If you found it, stop.

3. If the card at mid is higher than your card, search in the range from low to mid-1.

4. If the card at mid is lower than your card, search in the range from mid+1 to high.

Steps 3 and 4 look suspiciously like recursive invocations. Here's what this all looks like translated into Java code:

```java
public static int findBisect (Card[] deck, Card card, int low, int high) {
    int mid = (high + low) / 2;
    int comp = compareCard (deck[mid], card);

    if (comp == 0) {
        return mid;
    } else if (comp > 0) {
        return findBisect (deck, card, low, mid-1);
    } else {
        return findBisect (deck, card, mid+1, high);
    }
}
```

Rather than call compareCard three times, I called it once and stored the result.

Although this code contains the kernel of a bisection search, it is still missing a piece. As it is currently written, if the card is not in the deck, it will recurse forever. We need a way to detect this condition and deal with it properly (by returning -1).

The easiest way to tell that your card is not in the deck is if there are *no* cards in the deck, which is the case if high is less than low. Well, there are still cards in the deck, of course, but what I mean is that there are no cards in the segment of the deck indicated by low and high.

With that line added, the method works correctly:

```java
public static int findBisect (Card[] deck, Card card, int low, int high) {
    System.out.println (low + ", " + high);

    if (high < low) return -1;

    int mid = (high + low) / 2;
    int comp = deck[mid].compareCard (card);
```

```
    if (comp == 0) {
        return mid;
    } else if (comp > 0) {
        return findBisect (deck, card, low, mid-1);
    } else {
        return findBisect (deck, card, mid+1, high);
    }
}
```

I added a print statement at the beginning so I could watch the sequence of recursive calls and convince myself that it would eventually reach the base case. I tried out the following code:

```
    Card card1 = new Card (1, 11);
    System.out.println (findBisect (deck, card1, 0, 51));
```

And got the following output:

```
0, 51
0, 24
13, 24
19, 24
22, 24
23
```

Then I made up a card that is not in the deck (the 15 of Diamonds), and tried to find it. I got the following:

```
0, 51
0, 24
13, 24
13, 17
13, 14
13, 12
-1
```

These tests don't prove that this program is correct. In fact, no amount of testing can prove that a program is correct. On the other hand, by looking at a few cases and examining the code, you might be able to convince yourself.

The number of recursive calls is fairly small, typically 6 or 7. That means we only had to invoke compareCard 6 or 7 times, compared to up to 52 times if we did a linear search. In general, bisection is much faster than a linear search, and even more so for large arrays.

Two common errors in recusive programs are forgetting to include a base case and writing the recursive call so that the base case is never reached. Either error will cause an infinite recursion, in which case Java will (eventually) throw a StackOverflowException.

11.9   Decks and subdecks

Looking at the interface to `findBisect`

```
public static int findBisect (Card[] deck, Card card, int low, int high)
```

it might make sense to think of three of the parameters, `deck`, `low` and `high`, as a single parameter that specifies a **subdeck**. This way of thinking is quite common, and I sometimes think of it as an **abstract parameter**. What I mean by "abstract," is something that is not literally part of the program text, but which describes the function of the program at a higher level.

For example, when you invoke a method and pass an array and the bounds `low` and `high`, there is nothing that prevents the invoked method from accessing parts of the array that are out of bounds. So you are not literally sending a subset of the deck; you are really sending the whole deck. But as long as the recipient plays by the rules, it makes sense to think of it, abstractly, as a subdeck.

There is one other example of this kind of abstraction that you might have noticed in Section 9.7, when I referred to an "empty" data structure. The reason I put "empty" in quotation marks was to suggest that it is not literally accurate. All variables have values all the time. When you create them, they are given default values. So there is no such thing as an empty object.

But if the program guarantees that the current value of a variable is never read before it is written, then the current value is irrelevant. Abstractly, it makes sense to think of such a variable as "empty."

This kind of thinking, in which a program comes to take on meaning beyond what is literally encoded, is a very important part of thinking like a computer scientist. Sometimes, the word "abstract" gets used so often and in so many contexts that it comes to lose its meaning. Nevertheless, abstraction is a central idea in computer science (as well as many other fields).

A more general definition of "abstraction" is "The process of modeling a complex system with a simplified description in order to suppress unnecessary details while capturing relevant behavior."

11.10   Glossary

encode: To represent one set of values using another set of values, by constructing a mapping between them.

shallow equality: Equality of references. Two references that point to the same object.

deep equality: Equality of values. Two references that point to objects that have the same value.

abstract parameter: A set of parameters that act together as a single parameter.

abstraction: The process of interpreting a program (or anything else) at a higher level than what is literally represented by the code.

11.11   Exercises

Exercise 11.2   Imagine a card game in which the objective is to get a collection of cards with a total score of 21. The total score for a hand is the total of the scores for all the cards. The score for each card is as follows: aces count as 1, all face cards count as ten; for all other cards the score is the same as the rank. Example: the hand (Ace, 10, Jack, 3) has a total score of $1 + 10 + 10 + 3 = 24$.

Write a method called `handScore` that takes an array of cards as an argument and that adds up (and returns) the total score. You should assume that the ranks of the cards are encoded according to the mapping in Section 11.2, with Aces encoded as 1.

Exercise 11.3   The `printCard` method in Section 11.3 takes a Card object and returns a string representation of the card.

Write a class method for the `Card` class called `parseCard` that takes a String and returns the corresponding card. You can assume that the String contains the name of a card in a valid format, as if it had been produced by `printCard`.

In other words, the string will contain a single space between the rank and the word "of," and between the word "of" and the suit. If the string does not contain a legal card name, the method should return a null object.

The purpose of this problem is to review the concept of parsing and implement a method that parses a specific set of strings.

Exercise 11.4   Write a method called `suitHist` that takes an array of Cards as a parameter and that returns a histogram of the suits in the hand. Your solution should only traverse the array once.

Exercise 11.5   Write a method called `isFlush` that takes an array of Cards as a parameter and that returns `true` if the hand contains a flush, and `false` otherwise. A flush is a poker hand that contains five or more cards of the same suit.

Chapter 12

Objects of Arrays

12.1 The Deck class

In the previous chapter, we worked with an array of objects, but I also mentioned that it is possible to have an object that contains an array as an instance variable. In this chapter we are going to create a new object, called a Deck, that contains an array of Cards as an instance variable.

The class definition looks like this

```
class Deck {
    Card[] cards;

    public Deck (int n) {
        cards = new Card[n];
    }
}
```

The name of the instance variable is cards to help distinguish the Deck object from the array of Cards that it contains. Here is a state diagram showing what a Deck object looks like with no cards allocated:

As usual, the constructor initializes the instance variable, but in this case it uses the new command to create the array of cards. It doesn't create any cards to go in it, though. For that we could write another constructor that creates a standard 52-card deck and populates it with Card objects:

```
public Deck () {
    cards = new Card[52];
    int index = 0;
    for (int suit = 0; suit <= 3; suit++) {
```

```
        for (int rank = 1; rank <= 13; rank++) {
            cards[index] = new Card (suit, rank);
            index++;
        }
    }
}
```

Notice how similar this method is to `buildDeck`, except that we had to change
the syntax to make it a constructor. To invoke it, we use the `new` command:

```
    Deck deck = new Deck ();
```

Now that we have a `Deck` class, it makes sense to put all the methods that
pertain to Decks in the `Deck` class definition. Looking at the methods we have
written so far, one obvious candidate is `printDeck` (Section 11.7). Here's how
it looks, rewritten to work with a `Deck` object:

```
public static void printDeck (Deck deck) {
    for (int i=0; i<deck.cards.length; i++) {
        Card.printCard (deck.cards[i]);
    }
}
```

The most obvious thing we have to change is the type of the parameter, from
`Card[]` to `Deck`. The second change is that we can no longer use `deck.length`
to get the length of the array, because `deck` is a `Deck` object now, not an array.
It contains an array, but it is not, itself, an array. Therefore, we have to write
`deck.cards.length` to extract the array from the `Deck` object and get the
length of the array.

For the same reason, we have to use `deck.cards[i]` to access an element of
the array, rather than just `deck[i]`. The last change is that the invocation of
`printCard` has to say explicitly that `printCard` is defined in the `Card` class.

For some of the other methods, it is not obvious whether they should be included
in the `Card` class or the `Deck` class. For example, `findCard` takes a `Card` and a
`Deck` as arguments; you could reasonably put it in either class. As an exercise,
move `findCard` into the `Deck` class and rewrite it so that the first parameter is
a `Deck` object rather than an array of `Cards`.

12.2   Shuffling

For most card games you need to be able to shuffle the deck; that is, put the
cards in a random order. In Section 10.6 we saw how to generate random
numbers, but it is not obvious how to use them to shuffle a deck.

One possibility is to model the way humans shuffle, which is usually by dividing
the deck in two and then reassembling the deck by choosing alternately from
each deck. Since humans usually don't shuffle perfectly, after about 7 iterations
the order of the deck is pretty well randomized. But a computer program would
have the annoying property of doing a perfect shuffle every time, which is not

really very random. In fact, after 8 perfect shuffles, you would find the deck back in the same order you started in. For a discussion of that claim, see `http://www.wiskit.com/marilyn/craig.html` or do a web search with the keywords "perfect shuffle."

A better shuffling algorithm is to traverse the deck one card at a time, and at each iteration choose two cards and swap them.

Here is an outline of how this algorithm works. To sketch the program, I am using a combination of Java statements and English words that is sometimes called **pseudocode**:

```
for (int i=0; i<deck.length; i++) {
    // choose a random number between i and deck.cards.length
    // swap the ith card and the randomly-chosen card
}
```

The nice thing about using pseudocode is that it often makes it clear what methods you are going to need. In this case, we need something like `randomInt`, which chooses a random integer between the parameters `low` and `high`, and `swapCards` which takes two indices and switches the cards at the indicated positions.

You can probably figure out how to write `randomInt` by looking at Section 10.6, although you will have to be careful about possibly generating indices that are out of range.

You can also figure out `swapCards` yourself. The only tricky thing is to decide whether to swap just the references to the cards or the contents of the cards. Does it matter which one you choose? Which is faster?

I will leave the remaining implementation of these methods as an exercise.

12.3   Sorting

Now that we have messed up the deck, we need a way to put it back in order. Ironically, there is an algorithm for sorting that is very similar to the algorithm for shuffling. This algorithm is sometimes called **selection sort** because it works by traversing the array repeatedly and selecting the lowest remaining card each time.

During the first iteration we find the lowest card and swap it with the card in the 0th position. During the ith, we find the lowest card to the right of i and swap it with the ith card.

Here is pseudocode for selection sort:

```
for (int i=0; i<deck.length; i++) {
    // find the lowest card at or to the right of i
    // swap the ith card and the lowest card
}
```

Again, the pseudocode helps with the design of the **helper methods**. In this case we can use swapCards again, so we only need one new one, called findLowestCard, that takes an array of cards and an index where it should start looking.

Once again, I am going to leave the implementation up to the reader.

12.4   Subdecks

How should we represent a hand or some other subset of a full deck? One possibility is to create a new class called Hand, which might extend Deck. Another possibility, the one I will demonstrate, is to represent a hand with a Deck object that happens to have fewer than 52 cards.

We might want a method, subdeck, that takes a Deck and a range of indices, and that returns a new Deck that contains the specified subset of the cards:

```
public static Deck subdeck (Deck deck, int low, int high) {
    Deck sub = new Deck (high-low+1);

    for (int i = 0; i<sub.cards.length; i++) {
        sub.cards[i] = deck.cards[low+i];
    }
    return sub;
}
```

The length of the subdeck is high-low+1 because both the low card and high card are included. This sort of computation can be confusing, and lead to "off-by-one" errors. Drawing a picture is usually the best way to avoid them.

Because we provide an argument with the new command, the contructor that gets invoked will be the first one, which only allocates the array and doesn't allocate any cards. Inside the for loop, the subdeck gets populated with copies of the references from the deck.

The following is a state diagram of a subdeck being created with the parameters low=3 and high=7. The result is a hand with 5 cards that are shared with the original deck; i.e. they are aliased.

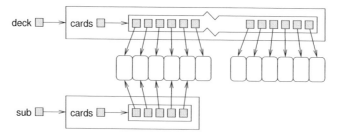

I have suggested that aliasing is not generally a good idea, since changes in one subdeck will be reflected in others, which is not the behavior you would expect from real cards and decks. But if the objects in question are immutable, then aliasing is less dangerous. In this case, there is probably no reason ever to change the rank or suit of a card. Instead we will create each card once and then treat it as an immutable object. So for `Cards` aliasing is a reasonable choice.

12.5   Shuffling and dealing

In Section 12.2 I wrote pseudocode for a shuffling algorithm. Assuming that we have a method called `shuffleDeck` that takes a deck as an argument and shuffles it, we can create and shuffle a deck:

```
Deck deck = new Deck ();
shuffleDeck (deck);
```

Then, to deal out several hands, we can use subdeck:

```
Deck hand1 = subdeck (deck, 0, 4);
Deck hand2 = subdeck (deck, 5, 9);
Deck pack = subdeck (deck, 10, 51);
```

This code puts the first 5 cards in one hand, the next 5 cards in the other, and the rest into the pack.

When you thought about dealing, did you think we should give out one card at a time to each player in the round-robin style that is common in real card games? I thought about it, but then realized that it is unnecessary for a computer program. The round-robin convention is intended to mitigate imperfect shuffling and make it more difficult for the dealer to cheat. Neither of these is an issue for a computer.

This example is a useful reminder of one of the dangers of engineering metaphors: sometimes we impose restrictions on computers that are unnecessary, or expect capabilities that are lacking, because we unthinkingly extend a metaphor past its breaking point. Beware of misleading analogies.

12.6   Mergesort

In Section 12.3, we saw a simple sorting algorithm that turns out not to be very efficient. In order to sort n items, it has to traverse the array n times, and each traversal takes an amount of time that is proportional to n. The total time, therefore, is proportional to n^2.

In this section I will sketch a more efficient algorithm called **mergesort**. To sort n items, mergesort takes time proportional to $n \log n$. That may not seem impressive, but as n gets big, the difference between n^2 and $n \log n$ can be enormous. Try out a few values of n and see.

The basic idea behind mergesort is this: if you have two subdecks, each of which has been sorted, it is easy (and fast) to merge them into a single, sorted deck. Try this out with a deck of cards:

1. Form two subdecks with about 10 cards each and sort them so that when they are face up the lowest cards are on top. Place both decks face up in front of you.

2. Compare the top card from each deck and choose the lower one. Flip it over and add it to the merged deck.

3. Repeat step two until one of the decks is empty. Then take the remaining cards and add them to the merged deck.

The result should be a single sorted deck. Here's what this looks like in pseudocode:

```
public static Deck merge (Deck d1, Deck d2) {
    // create a new deck big enough for all the cards
    Deck result = new Deck (d1.cards.length + d2.cards.length);

    // use the index i to keep track of where we are in
    // the first deck, and the index j for the second deck
    int i = 0;
    int j = 0;

    // the index k traverses the result deck
    for (int k = 0; k<result.cards.length; k++) {

        // if d1 is empty, d2 wins; if d2 is empty, d1 wins;
        // otherwise, compare the two cards

        // add the winner to the new deck
    }
    return result;
}
```

The best way to test merge is to build and shuffle a deck, use subdeck to form two (small) hands, and then use the sort routine from the previous chapter to sort the two halves. Then you can pass the two halves to merge to see if it works.

If you can get that working, try a simple implementation of mergeSort:

```
public static Deck mergeSort (Deck deck) {
    // find the midpoint of the deck
    // divide the deck into two subdecks
    // sort the subdecks using sortDeck
    // merge the two halves and return the result
}
```

Then, if you get that working, the real fun begins! The magical thing about mergesort is that it is recursive. At the point where you sort the subdecks, why should you invoke the old, slow version of `sort`? Why not invoke the spiffy new `mergeSort` you are in the process of writing?

Not only is that a good idea, it is *necessary* in order to achieve the performance advantage I promised. In order to make it work, though, you have to add a base case so that it doesn't recurse forever. A simple base case is a subdeck with 0 or 1 cards. If `mergesort` receives such a small subdeck, it can return it unmodified, since it is already sorted.

The recursive version of `mergesort` should look something like this:

```
public static Deck mergeSort (Deck deck) {
    // if the deck is 0 or 1 cards, return it

    // find the midpoint of the deck
    // divide the deck into two subdecks
    // sort the subdecks using mergesort
    // merge the two halves and return the result
}
```

As usual, there are two ways to think about recursive programs: you can think through the entire flow of execution, or you can make the "leap of faith." I have deliberately constructed this example to encourage you to make the leap of faith.

When you were using `sortDeck` to sort the subdecks, you didn't feel compelled to follow the flow of execution, right? You just assumed that the `sortDeck` method would work because you already debugged it. Well, all you did to make `mergeSort` recursive was replace one sorting algorithm with another. There is no reason to read the program differently.

Well, actually, you have to give some thought to getting the base case right and making sure that you reach it eventually, but other than that, writing the recursive version should be no problem. Good luck!

12.7   Glossary

pseudocode: A way of designing programs by writing rough drafts in a combination of English and Java.

helper method: Often a small method that does not do anything enormously useful by itself, but which helps another, more useful, method.

12.8   Exercises

Exercise 12.1   Write a version of `findBisect` that takes a subdeck as an argument, rather than a deck and an index range (see Section 11.8). Which version is more error-prone? Which version do you think is more efficient?

Exercise 12.2   In the previous version of the Card class, a deck is implemented as an array of Cards. For example, when we pass a "deck" as a parameter, the actual type of the parameter is Card[].

In this chapter, we developed an alternative representation for a deck, an object type named Deck that contains an array of cards as an instance variable. In this exercise, you will implement the new representation of a deck.

a. Add a second file, named Deck.java to the program. This file will contain the definition of the Deck class.

b. Type in the constructors for the Deck class as shown in Section 12.1.

c. Of the methods currently in the Card class, decide which ones would be more appropriate as members of the new Deck class. Move them there and make any changes necessary to get the program to compile and run again.

d. Look over the program and identify every place where an array of Cards is being used to represent a deck. Modify the program throughout so that it uses a Deck object instead. You can use the version of printDeck in Section 12.1 as an example.

It is probably a good idea to make this transformation one method at a time, and test the program after each change. On the other hand, if you are confident you know what you are doing, you can make most of the changes with search-and-replace commands.

Exercise 12.3   The goal of this exercise is to implement the shuffling and sorting algorithms from this chapter.

a. Write a method called swapCards that takes a deck (array of cards) and two indices, and that switches the cards at those two locations.
   HINT: it should switch the references to the two cards, rather than the contents of the two objects. This is not only faster, but it makes it easier to deal with the case where cards are aliased.

b. Write a method called shuffleDeck that uses the algorithm in Section 12.2. You might want to use the randomInt method from Exercise 10.2.

c. Write a method called findLowestCard that uses the compareCard method to find the lowest card in a given range of the deck (from lowIndex to highIndex, including both).

d. Write a method called sortDeck that arranges a deck of cards from lowest to highest.

Exercise 12.4   In order to make life more difficult for card-counters, many casinos now use automatic shuffling machines that can do incremental shuffling, which means that after each hand, the used cards are returned to the deck and, instead of reshuffling the entire deck, the new cards are inserted in random locations.

Write a method called incrementalShuffle that takes a Deck and a Card and that inserts the card into the deck at a random location. This is an example of an **incremental algorithm**.

Exercise 12.5 The goal of this exercise is to write a program that generates random poker hands and classifies them, so that we can estimate the probability of the various poker hands. Don't worry if you don't play poker; I'll tell you everything you need to know.

a. As a warmup, write a program that uses shuffleDeck and subdeck to generate and print four random poker hands with five cards each. Did you get anything good? Here are the possible poker hands, in increasing order of value:

   pair: two cards with the same rank

   two pair: two pairs of cards with the same rank

   three of a kind: three cards with the same rank

   straight: five cards with ranks in sequence

   flush: five cards with the same suit

   full house: three cards with one rank, two cards with another

   four of a kind: four cards with the same rank

   straight flush: five cards in sequence and with the same suit

b. Write a method called isFlush that takes a Deck as a parameter and returns a boolean indicating whether the hand contains a flush.

c. Write a method called isThreeKind that takes a hand and returns a boolean indicating whether the hand contains Three of a Kind.

d. Write a loop that generates a few thousand hands and checks whether they contain a flush or three of a kind. Estimate the probability of getting one of those hands.

e. Write methods that test for the other poker hands. Some are easier than others. You might find it useful to write some general-purpose helper methods that can be used for more than one test.

f. In some poker games, players get seven cards each, and they form a hand with the best five of the seven. Modify your program to generate seven-card hands and recompute the probabilities.

Exercise 12.6 As a special challenge, think of algorithms to check for various poker hands if there are wild cards. For example, if "deuces are wild," that means that if you have a card with rank 2, you can use it to represent any card in the deck.

Exercise 12.7 The goal of this exercise is to implement mergesort.

a. Using the pseudocode in Section 12.6, write the method called merge. Be sure to test it before trying to use it as part of a mergeSort.

b. Write the simple version of mergeSort, the one that divides the deck in half, uses sortDeck to sort the two halves, and uses merge to create a new, fully-sorted deck.

c. Write the fully recursive version of mergeSort. Remember that sortDeck is a modifier and mergeSort is a function, which means that they get invoked differently:

```
sortDeck (deck);              // modifies existing deck
deck = mergeSort (deck);      // replaces old deck with new
```

Chapter 13

Object-oriented programming

13.1 Programming languages and styles

There are many programming languages in the world, and almost as many programming styles (sometimes called paradigms). Three styles that have appeared in this book are procedural, functional, and object-oriented. Although Java is usually thought of as an object-oriented language, it is possible to write Java programs in any style. The style I have demonstrated in this book is pretty much procedural. Existing Java programs and the built-in Java packages are written in a mixture of all three styles, but they tend to be more object-oriented than the programs in this book.

It's not easy to define what object-oriented programming is, but here are some of its characteristics:

- Object definitions (classes) usually correspond to relevant real-world objects. For example, in Chapter 12.1, the creation of the Deck class was a step toward object-oriented programming.

- The majority of methods are object methods (the kind you invoke on an object) rather than class methods (the kind you just invoke). So far all the methods we have written have been class methods. In this chapter we will write some object methods.

- The language feature most associated with object-oriented programming is **inheritance**. I will cover inheritance later in this chapter.

Recently object-oriented programming has become quite popular, and there are people who claim that it is superior to other styles in various ways. I hope that by exposing you to a variety of styles I have given you the tools you need to understand and evaluate these claims.

13.2   Object and class methods

There are two types of methods in Java, called **class methods** and **object methods**. So far, every method we have written has been a class method. Class methods are identified by the keyword `static` in the first line. Any method that does not have the keyword `static` is an object method.

Although we have not written any object methods, we have invoked some. Whenever you invoke a method "on" an object, it's an object method. For example, `charAt` and the other methods we invoked on `String` objects are all object methods.

Anything that can be written as a class method can also be written as an object method, and vice versa. Sometimes it is just more natural to use one or the other. For reasons that will be clear soon, object methods are often shorter than the corresponding class methods.

13.3   The current object

When you invoke a method on an object, that object becomes **the current object**. Inside the method, you can refer to the instance variables of the current object by name, without having to specify the name of the object.

Also, you can refer to the current object using the keyword `this`. We have already seen `this` used in constructors. In fact, you can think of constructors as being a special kind of object method.

13.4   Complex numbers

As a running example for the rest of this chapter we will consider a class definition for complex numbers. Complex numbers are useful for many branches of mathematics and engineering, and many computations are performed using complex arithmetic. A complex number is the sum of a real part and an imaginary part, and is usually written in the form $x + yi$, where x is the real part, y is the imaginary part, and i represents the square root of -1. Thus, $i \cdot i = -1$.

The following is a class definition for a new object type called `Complex`:

```
class Complex
{
    // instance variables
    double real, imag;

    // constructor
    public Complex () {
        this.real = 0.0;  this.imag = 0.0;
    }
```

```
// constructor
public Complex (double real, double imag) {
    this.real = real;
    this.imag = imag;
}
```
}

There should be nothing surprising here. The instance variables are doubles that contain the real and imaginary parts. The two constructors are the usual kind: one takes no parameters and assigns default values to the instance variables, the other takes parameters that are identical to the instance variables. As we have seen before, the keyword `this` is used to refer to the object being initialized.

In `main`, or anywhere else we want to create `Complex` objects, we have the option of creating the object and then setting the instance variables, or doing both at the same time:

```
Complex x = new Complex ();
x.real = 1.0;
x.imag = 2.0;
Complex y = new Complex (3.0, 4.0);
```

13.5   A function on `Complex` numbers

Let's look at some of the operations we might want to perform on complex numbers. The absolute value of a complex number is defined to be $\sqrt{x^2 + y^2}$. The `abs` method is a pure function that computes the absolute value. Written as a class method, it looks like this:

```
// class method
public static double abs (Complex c) {
    return Math.sqrt (c.real * c.real + c.imag * c.imag);
}
```

This version of `abs` calculates the absolute value of `c`, the `Complex` object it receives as a parameter. The next version of `abs` is an object method; it calculates the absolute value of the current object (the object the method was invoked on). Thus, it does not receive any parameters:

```
// object method
public double abs () {
    return Math.sqrt (real*real + imag*imag);
}
```

I removed the keyword `static` to indicate that this is an object method. Also, I eliminated the unnecessary parameter. Inside the method, I can refer to the instance variables `real` and `imag` by name without having to specify an object. Java knows implicitly that I am referring to the instance variables of the current object. If I wanted to make it explicit, I could have used the keyword `this`:

```
// object method
public double abs () {
```

```
    return Math.sqrt (this.real * this.real + this.imag * this.imag);
}
```

But that would be longer and not really any clearer. To invoke this method, we invoke it on an object, for example

```
    Complex y = new Complex (3.0, 4.0);
    double result = y.abs();
```

13.6 Another function on `Complex` numbers

Another operation we might want to perform on complex numbers is addition. You can add complex numbers by adding the real parts and adding the imaginary parts. Written as a class method, that looks like:

```
public static Complex add (Complex a, Complex b) {
    return new Complex (a.real + b.real, a.imag + b.imag);
}
```

To invoke this method, we would pass both operands as arguments:

```
    Complex sum = add (x, y);
```

Written as an object method, it would take only one argument, which it would add to the current object:

```
public Complex add (Complex b) {
    return new Complex (real + b.real, imag + b.imag);
}
```

Again, we can refer to the instance variables of the current object implicitly, but to refer to the instance variables of b we have to name b explicitly using dot notation. To invoke this method, you invoke it on one of the operands and pass the other as an argument.

```
    Complex sum = x.add (y);
```

From these examples you can see that the current object (`this`) can take the place of one of the parameters. For this reason, the current object is sometimes called an **implicit parameter**.

13.7 A modifier

As yet another example, we'll look at `conjugate`, which is a modifier method that transforms a `Complex` number into its complex conjugate. The complex conjugate of $x + yi$ is $x - yi$.

As a class method, this looks like:

```
public static void conjugate (Complex c) {
    c.imag = -c.imag;
}
```

As an object method, it looks like

```
public void conjugate () {
    imag = -imag;
}
```

By now you should be getting the sense that converting a method from one kind to another is a mechanical process. With a little practice, you will be able to do it without giving it much thought, which is good because you should not be constrained to writing one kind of method or the other. You should be equally familiar with both so that you can choose whichever one seems most appropriate for the operation you are writing.

For example, I think that add should be written as a class method because it is a symmetric operation of two operands, and it makes sense for both operands to appear as parameters. To me, it seems odd to invoke the method on one of the operands and pass the other as an argument.

On the other hand, simple operations that apply to a single object can be written most concisely as object methods (even if they take some additional arguments).

13.8   The toString method

Every object type has a method called toString that generates a string representation of the object. When you print an object using print or println, Java invokes the object's toString method. The default version of toString returns a string that contains the type of the object and a unique identifier (see Section 9.6). When you define a new object type, you can **override** the default behavior by providing a new method with the behavior you want.

Here is what toString might look like for the Complex class:

```
public String toString () {
    return real + " + " + imag + "i";
}
```

The return type for toString is String, naturally, and it takes no parameters. You can invoke toString in the usual way:

```
Complex x = new Complex (1.0, 2.0);
String s = x.toString ();
```

or you can invoke it indirectly through println:

```
System.out.println (x);
```

In this case, the output is 1.0 + 2.0i.

This version of toString does not look good if the imaginary part is negative. As an exercise, write a better version.

13.9   The equals method

When you use the == operator to compare two objects, what you are really asking is, "Are these two things the same object?" That is, do both objects refer to the same location in memory.

For many types, that is not the appropriate definition of equality. For example, two complex numbers are equal if their real parts are equal and their imaginary parts are equal. They don't have to be the same object.

When you define a new object type, you can provide your own definition of equality by providing an object method called equals. For the Complex class, this looks like:

```
public boolean equals (Complex b) {
    return (real == b.real && imag == b.imag);
}
```

By convention, equals is always an object method that returns a boolean.

The documentation of equals in the Object class provides some guidelines you should keep in mind when you make up your own definition of equality:

> The equals method implements an equivalence relation:
>
> - It is reflexive: for any reference value x, x.equals(x) should return true.
>
> - It is symmetric: for any reference values x and y, x.equals(y) should return true if and only if y.equals(x) returns true.
>
> - It is transitive: for any reference values x, y, and z, if x.equals(y) returns true and y.equals(z) returns true, then x.equals(z) should return true.
>
> - It is consistent: for any reference values x and y, multiple invocations of x.equals(y) consistently return true or consistently return false.
>
> - For any reference value x, x.equals(null) should return false.

The definition of equals I provided satisfies all these conditions except one. Which one? As an exercise, fix it.

13.10   Invoking one object method from another

As you might expect, it is legal and common to invoke one object method from another. For example, to normalize a complex number, you divide both parts by the absolute value. It may not be obvious why this is useful, but it is.

Let's write the method normalize as an object method, and let's make it a modifier.

```
public void normalize () {
    double d = this.abs();
    real = real/d;
    imag = imag/d;
}
```

The first line finds the absolute value of the current object by invoking `abs` on the current object. In this case I named the current object explicitly, but I could have left it out. If you invoke one object method within another, Java assumes that you are invoking it on the current object.

Exercise 13.1   Rewrite `normalize` as a pure function. Then rewrite it as a class method.

13.11   Oddities and errors

If you have both object methods and class methods in the same class definition, it is easy to get confused. A common way to organize a class definition is to put all the constructors at the beginning, followed by all the object methods and then all the class methods.

You can have an object method and a class method with the same name, as long as they do not have the same number and types of parameters. As with other kinds of overloading, Java decides which version to invoke by looking at the arguments you provide.

Now that we know what the keyword `static` means, you have probably figured out that `main` is a class method, which means that there is no "current object" when it is invoked.

Since there is no current object in a class method, it is an error to use the keyword `this`. If you try, you might get an error message like: "Undefined variable: this." Also, you cannot refer to instance variables without using dot notation and providing an object name. If you try, you might get "Can't make a static reference to nonstatic variable..." This is not one of the better error messages, since it uses some non-standard language. For example, by "nonstatic variable" it means "instance variable." But once you know what it means, you know what it means.

13.12   Inheritance

The language feature that is most often associated with object-oriented programming is **inheritance**. Inheritance is the ability to define a new class that is a modified version of a previously-defined class (including built-in classes).

The primary advantage of this feature is that you can add new methods or instance variables to an existing class without modifying the existing class. This is particularly useful for built-in classes, since you can't modify them even if you want to.

The reason inheritance is called "inheritance" is that the new class inherits all the instance variables and methods of the existing class. Extending this metaphor, the existing class is sometimes called the **parent** class.

13.13   Drawable rectangles

An an example of inheritance, we are going to take the existing `Rectangle` class and make it "drawable." That is, we are going to create a new class called `DrawableRectangle` that will have all the instance variables and methods of a `Rectangle`, plus an additional method called `draw` that will take a `Graphics` object as a parameter and draw the rectangle.

The class definition looks like this:

```
import java.awt.*;

class DrawableRectangle extends Rectangle {

    public void draw (Graphics g) {
        g.drawRect (x, y, width, height);
    }
}
```

Yes, that's really all there is in the whole class definition. The first line imports the `java.awt` package, which is where `Rectangle` and `Graphics` are defined.

The next line indicates that `DrawableRectangle` inherits from `Rectangle`. The keyword `extends` is used to identify the class we are inheriting from, which is called the **parent class**.

The rest is the definition of the `draw` method, which refers to the instance variables `x`, `y`, `width` and `height`. It might seem odd to refer to instance variables that don't appear in this class definition, but remember that they are inherited from the parent class.

To create and draw a `DrawableRectangle`, you could use the following:

```
public static void draw (Graphics g, int x, int y, int width, int height) {
    DrawableRectangle dr = new DrawableRectangle ();
    dr.x = 10;        dr.y = 10;
    dr.width = 200;  dr.height = 200;
    dr.draw (g);
}
```

The parameters of `draw` are a `Graphics` object and the bounding box of the drawing area (not the coordinates of the rectangle).

It might seem odd to use the `new` command for a class that has no constructors. `DrawableRectangle` inherits the default constructor of its parent class, so there is no problem there.

We can set the instance variables of `dr` and invoke methods on it in the usual way. When we invoke `draw`, Java invokes the method we defined in `DrawableRectangle`. If we invoked `grow` or some other `Rectangle` method on `dr`, Java would know to use the method defined in the parent class.

13.14 The class hierarchy

In Java, all classes extend some other class. The most basic class is called Object. It contains no instance variables, but it does provide the methods equals and toString, among others.

Many classes extend Object, including almost all of the classes we have written and many of the built-in classes, like Rectangle. Any class that does not explicitly name a parent inherits from Object by default.

Some inheritance chains are longer, though. For example, in Appendix D.6, the Slate class extends Frame, which extends Window, which extends Container, which extends Component, which extends Object. No matter how long the chain, Object is the ultimate parent of all classes.

All the classes in Java can be organized into a "family tree" that is called the class hierarchy. Object usually appears at the top, with all the "child" classes below. If you look at the documentation of Frame, for example, you will see the part of the hierarchy that makes up Frame's pedigree.

13.15 Object-oriented design

Inheritance is a powerful feature. Some programs that would be complicated without it can be written concisely and simply with it. Also, inheritance can facilitate code reuse, since you can customize the behavior of build-in classes without having to modify them.

On the other hand, inheritance can make programs difficult to read, since it is sometimes not clear, when a method is invoked, where to find the definition. For example, one of the methods you can invoke on a Slate is getBounds. Can you find the documentation for getBounds? It turns out that getBounds is defined in the parent of the parent of the parent of the parent of Slate.

Also, many of the things that can be done using inheritance can be done almost as elegantly (or more so) without it.

13.16 Glossary

object method: A method that is invoked on an object, and that operates on that object, which is referred to by the keyword this in Java or "the current object" in English. Object methods do not have the keyword static.

class method: A method with the keyword static. Class methods are not invoked on objects and they do not have a current object.

current object: The object on which an object method is invoked. Inside the method, the current object is referred to by this.

`this:` The keyword that refers to the current object.

implicit: Anything that is left unsaid or implied. Within an object method, you can refer to the instance variables implicitly (without naming the object).

explicit: Anything that is spelled out completely. Within a class method, all references to the instance variables have to be explicit.

13.17   Exercises

Exercise 13.2

Transform the following class method into an object method.

```
public static double abs (Complex c) {
    return Math.sqrt (c.real * c.real + c.imag * c.imag);
}
```

Exercise 13.3   Transform the following object method into a class method.

```
public boolean equals (Complex b) {
    return (real == b.real && imag == b.imag);
}
```

Exercise 13.4

This exercise is a continuation of Exercise 9.3. The purpose is to practice the syntax of object methods and get familiar with the relevant error messages.

a. Transform the methods in the `Rational` class from class methods to object methods, and make the necessary changes in `main`.

b. Make a few mistakes. Try invoking class methods as if they were object methods and vice-versa. Try to get a sense for what is legal and what is not, and for the error messages that you get when you mess things up.

c. Think about the pros and cons of class and object methods. Which is more concise (usually)? Which is a more natural way to express computation (or, maybe more fairly, what kind of computations can be expressed most naturally using each style)?

Chapter 14

Linked lists

14.1 References in objects

In the last chapter we saw that the instance variables of an object can be arrays, and I mentioned that they can be objects, too.

One of the more interesting possibilities is that an object can contain a reference to another object of the same type. There is a common data structure, the **list**, that takes advantage of this feature.

Lists are made up of **nodes**, where each node contains a reference to the next node in the list. In addition, each node usually contains a unit of data called the **cargo**. In our first example, the cargo will be a single integer, but later we will write a **generic** list that can contain objects of any type.

14.2 The Node class

As usual when we write a new class, we'll start with the instance variables, one or two constructors and toString so that we can test the basic mechanism of creating and displaying the new type.

```java
public class Node {
    int cargo;
    Node next;

    public Node () {
        cargo = 0;
        next = null;
    }

    public Node (int cargo, Node next) {
        this.cargo = cargo;
```

```
        this.next = next;
    }

    public String toString () {
        return cargo + "";
    }
}
```

The declarations of the instance variables follow naturally from the specification, and the rest follows mechanically from the instance variables. The expression `cargo + ""` is an awkward but concise way to convert an integer to a String.

To test the implementation so far, we would put something like this in `main`:

```
Node node = new Node (1, null);
System.out.println (node);
```

The result is simply

1

To make it interesting, we need a list with more than one node!

```
Node node1 = new Node (1, null);
Node node2 = new Node (2, null);
Node node3 = new Node (3, null);
```

This code creates three nodes, but we don't have a list yet because the nodes are not **linked**. The state diagram looks like this:

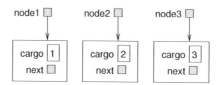

To link up the nodes, we have to make the first node refer to the second and the second node refer to the third.

```
node1.next = node2;
node2.next = node3;
node3.next = null;
```

The reference of the third node is `null`, which indicates that it is the end of the list. Now the state diagram looks like:

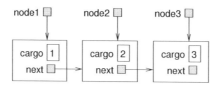

Now we know how to create nodes and link them into lists. What might be less clear at this point is why.

14.3   Lists as collections

The thing that makes lists useful is that they are a way of assembling multiple objects into a single entity, sometimes called a collection. In the example, the first node of the list serves as a reference to the entire list.

If we want to pass the list as a parameter, all we have to pass is a reference to the first node. For example, the method printList takes a single node as an argument. Starting with the head of the list, it prints each node until it gets to the end (indicated by the null reference).

```
public static void printList (Node list) {
    Node node = list;

    while (node != null) {
        System.out.print (node);
        node = node.next;
    }
    System.out.println ();
}
```

To invoke this method we just have to pass a reference to the first node:

```
printList (node1);
```

Inside printList we have a reference to the first node of the list, but there is no variable that refers to the other nodes. We have to use the next value from each node to get to the next node.

This diagram shows the value of list and the values that node takes on:

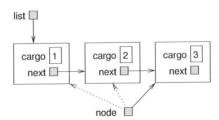

This way of moving through a list is called a **traversal**, just like the similar pattern of moving through the elements of an array. It is common to use a loop variable like node to refer to each of the nodes in the list in succession.

The output of this method is

123

By convention, lists are printed in parentheses with commas between the elements, as in (1, 2, 3). As an exercise, modify printList so that it generates output in this format.

As another exercise, rewrite printList using a for loop instead of a while loop.

14.4   Lists and recursion

Recursion and lists go together like fava beans and a nice Chianti. For example, here is a recursive algorithm for printing a list backwards:

1. Separate the list into two pieces: the first node (called the head) and the rest (called the tail).

2. Print the tail backwards.

3. Print the head.

Of course, Step 2, the recursive call, assumes that we have a way of printing a list backwards. But *if* we assume that the recursive call works—the leap of faith—then we can convince ourselves that this algorithm works.

All we need is a base case, and a way of proving that for any list we will eventually get to the base case. A natural choice for the base case is a list with a single element, but an even better choice is the empty list, represented by null.

```
public static void printBackward (Node list) {
    if (list == null) return;

    Node head = list;
    Node tail = list.next;

    printBackward (tail);
    System.out.print (head);
}
```

The first line handles the base case by doing nothing. The next two lines split the list into head and tail. The last two lines print the list.

We invoke this method exactly as we invoked printList:

```
        printBackward (node1);
```

The result is a backwards list.

Can we prove that this method will always terminate? In other words, will it always reach the base case? In fact, the answer is no. There are some lists that will make this method crash.

14.5   Infinite lists

There is nothing to prevent a node from referring back to an earlier node in the list, including itself. For example, this figure shows a list with two nodes, one of which refers to itself.

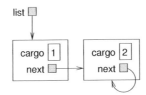

If we invoke `printList` on this list, it will loop forever. If we invoke `printBackward` it will recurse infinitely. This sort of behavior makes infinite lists difficult to work with.

Nevertheless, they are occasionally useful. For example, we might represent a number as a list of digits and use an infinite list to represent a repeating fraction.

Regardless, it is problematic that we cannot prove that `printList` and `printBackward` terminate. The best we can do is the hypothetical statement, "If the list contains no loops, then these methods will terminate." This sort of claim is called a **precondition**. It imposes a constraint on one of the parameters and describes the behavior of the method if the constraint is satisfied. We will see more examples soon.

14.6   The fundamental ambiguity theorem

There is a part of `printBackward` that might have raised an eyebrow:

```
Node head = list;
Node tail = list.next;
```

After the first assignment, `head` and `list` have the same type and the same value. So why did I create a new variable?

The reason is that the two variables play different roles. We think of `head` as a reference to a single node, and we think of `list` as a reference to the first node of a list. These "roles" are not part of the program; they are in the mind of the programmer.

The second assignment creates a new reference to the second node in the list, but in this case we think of it as a list. So, even though `head` and `tail` have the same type, they play different roles.

This ambiguity is useful, but it can make programs with lists difficult to read. I often use variable names like `node` and `list` to document how I intend to use a variable, and sometimes I create additional variables to disambiguate.

I could have written `printBackward` without `head` and `tail`, but I think it makes it harder to understand:

```
public static void printBackward (Node list) {
    if (list == null) return;

    printBackward (list.next);
```

```
        System.out.print (list);
    }
```

Looking at the two function calls, we have to remember that `printBackward` treats its argument as a list and `print` treats its argument as a single object.

Always keep in mind the **fundamental ambiguity theorem**:

> A variable that refers to a node might treat the node as a single object or as the first in a list of nodes.

14.7   Object methods for nodes

You might have wondered why `printList` and `printBackward` are class methods. I have made the claim that anything that can be done with class methods can also be done with object methods; it's just a question of which form is cleaner.

In this case there is a legitimate reason to choose class methods. It is legal to send `null` as an argument to a class method, but it is not legal to invoke an object method on a null object.

```
Node node = null;
printList (node);        // legal
node.printList ();       // NullPointerException
```

This limitation makes it awkward to write list-manipulating code in a clean, object-oriented style. A little later we will see a way to get around this, though.

14.8   Modifying lists

Obviously one way to modify a list is to change the cargo of one of the nodes, but the more interesting operations are the ones that add, remove, or reorder the nodes.

As an example, we'll write a method that removes the second node in the list and returns a reference to the removed node.

```
    public static Node removeSecond (Node list) {
        Node first = list;
        Node second = list.next;

        // make the first node refer to the third
        first.next = second.next;

        // separate the second node from the rest of the list
        second.next = null;
        return second;
    }
```

Again, I am using temporary variables to make the code more readable. Here is how to use this method.

```
printList (node1);
Node removed = removeSecond (node1);
printList (removed);
printList (node1);
```

The output is

```
(1, 2, 3)        the original list
(2)              the removed node
(1, 3)           the modified list
```

Here is a state diagram showing the effect of this operation.

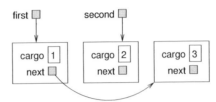

What happens if we invoke this method and pass a list with only one element (a **singleton**)? What happens if we pass the empty list as an argument? Is there a precondition for this method?

14.9   Wrappers and helpers

For some list operations it is useful to divide the labor into two methods. For example, to print a list backwards in the conventional list format, (3, 2, 1) we can use the printBackwards method to print 3, 2, but we need a separate method to print the parentheses and the first node. We'll call it printBackwardNicely.

```
public static void printBackwardNicely (Node list) {
    System.out.print ("(");

    if (list != null) {
        Node head = list;
        Node tail = list.next;
        printBackward (tail);
        System.out.print (head);
    }
    System.out.println (")");
}
```

Again, it is a good idea to check methods like this to see if they work with special cases like an empty list or a singleton.

Elsewhere in the program, when we use this method, we will invoke
printBackwardNicely directly and it will invoke printBackward on our behalf. In that sense, printBackwardNicely acts as a **wrapper**, and it uses
printBackward as a helper.

14.10   The `IntList` class

There are a number of subtle problems with the way we have been implementing
lists. In a reversal of cause and effect, I will propose an alternative implementation first and then explain what problems it solves.

First, we will create a new class called IntList. Its instance variables are an
integer that contains the length of the list and a reference to the first node in
the list. IntList objects serve as handles for manipulating lists of Node objects.

```
public class IntList {
    int length;
    Node head;

    public IntList () {
        length = 0;
        head = null;
    }
}
```

One nice thing about the IntList class is that it gives us a natural place to put
wrapper functions like printBackwardNicely, which we can make an object
method in the IntList class.

```
    public void printBackward () {
        System.out.print ("(");

        if (head != null) {
            Node tail = head.next;
            Node.printBackward (tail);
            System.out.print (head);
        }
        System.out.println (")");
    }
```

Just to make things confusing, I renamed printBackwardNicely. Now there
are two methods named printBackward: one in the Node class (the helper) and
one in the IntList class (the wrapper). In order for the wrapper to invoke the
helper, it has to identify the class explicitly (Node.printBackward).

So, one of the benefits of the IntList class is that it provides a nice place to put
wrapper functions. Another is that it makes it easier to add or remove the first
element of a list. For example, addFirst is an object method for IntLists; it
takes an int as an argument and puts it at the beginning of the list.

```
public void addFirst (int i) {
    Node node = new Node (i, head);
    head = node;
    length++;
}
```

As always, to check code like this it is a good idea to think about the special cases. For example, what happens if the list is initially empty?

14.11   Invariants

Some lists are "well-formed;" others are not. For example, if a list contains a loop, it will cause many of our methods to crash, so we might want to require that lists contain no loops. Another requirement is that the `length` value in the `IntList` object should be equal to the actual number of nodes in the list.

Requirements like this are called **invariants** because, ideally, they should be true of every object all the time. Specifying invariants for objects is a useful programming practice because it makes it easier to prove the correctness of code, check the integrity of data structures, and detect errors.

One thing that is sometimes confusing about invariants is that there are some times when they are violated. For example, in the middle of `addFirst`, after we have added the node, but before we have incremented `length`, the invariant is violated. This kind of violation is acceptable; in fact, it is often impossible to modify an object without violating an invariant for at least a little while. Normally the requirement is that every method that violates an invariant must restore the invariant.

If there is any significant stretch of code in which the invariant is violated, it is important for the comments to make that clear, so that no operations are performed that depend on the invariant.

14.12   Glossary

list: A data structure that implements a collection using a sequence of linked nodes.

node: An element of a list, usually implemented as an object that contains a reference to another object of the same type.

cargo: An item of data contained in a node.

link: An object reference embedded in an object.

generic data structure: A kind of data structure that can contain data of any type.

precondition: An assertion that must be true in order for a method to work correctly.

invariant: An assertion that should be true of an object at all times (except maybe while the object is being modified).

wrapper method: A method that acts as a middle-man between a caller and a helper method, often offering an interface that is cleaner than the helper method's.

14.13   Exercises

Exercise 14.1

Start by downloading the file IntList.java from http://thinkapjava.com/code/ IntList. It contains the definitions of IntList and Node from this chapter, along with code that demonstrates and tests some of the methods. Compile and run the program. The output should look like this:

```
(1, 2, 3)
(3, 2, 1)
```

The following exercises ask you to write additional object methods in the IntList class, but you might want to write some helper methods in the Node class as well.

After you write each method, add code to main and test it. Be sure to test special cases like empty lists and singletons.

For each method, identify any preconditions that are necessary for the method to work and add comments that document them. Your comments should also indicate whether each method is a constructor, function, or modifier.

    a. Write a method named removeFirst that removes the first node from a list and returns its cargo.

    b. Write a method named set that takes an index, i, and an item of cargo, and that replaces the cargo of the ith node with the given cargo.

    c. Write a method named add that takes an index, i, and an item of cargo, and that adds a new node containing the given cargo in the ith position.

    d. Write a method named addLast that takes an item of cargo and adds it to the end of the list.

    e. Write a method called reverse that modifies an IntList, reversing the order of the nodes.

    f. Write a method named append that takes an IntList as a parameter and appends a *copy* of the nodes from the parameter list onto the current list. You should be able to take advantage of code you have already written.

    g. Write a method named checkLength that returns true if the length field equals the number of nodes in the list, and false otherwise. The method should not cause an exception under any circumstances, and it should terminate even if the list contains a loop.

Exercise 14.2   One way to represent very large numbers is with a list of digits, usually stored in reverse order. For example, the number 123 might be represented with the list $(3, 2, 1)$.

Write a method that compares two numbers represented as IntLists and returns 1 if the first is larger, -1 if the second is larger, and 0 if they are equal.

Chapter 15

Stacks

15.1 Abstract data types

The data types we have looked at so far are all concrete, in the sense that we have completely specified how they are implemented. For example, the `Card` class represents a card using two integers. As I discussed at the time, that is not the only way to represent a card; there are many alternative implementations.

An **abstract data type**, or ADT, specifies a set of operations (or methods) and the semantics of the operations (what they do) but it does not specify the implementation of the operations. That's what makes it abstract.

Why is that useful?

- It simplifies the task of specifying an algorithm if you can denote the operations you need without having to think at the same time about how the operations are performed.

- Since there are usually many ways to implement an ADT, it might be useful to write an algorithm that can be used with any of the possible implementations.

- Well-known ADTs, like the `Stack` ADT in this chapter, are often implemented in standard libraries so they can be written once and used by many programmers.

- The operations on ADTs provide a common high-level language for specifying and talking about algorithms.

When we talk about ADTs, we often distinguish the code that uses the ADT, called the **client** code, from the code that implements the ADT, called **provider** code because it provides a standard set of services.

15.2   The Stack ADT

In this chapter we will look at one common ADT, the stack. A stack is a collection, meaning that it is a data structure that contains multiple elements. Other collections we have seen include arrays and lists.

As I said, an ADT is defined by a set of operations. Stacks can perform the following set of operations:

constructor: Create a new, empty stack.

push: Add a new item to the stack.

pop: Remove and return an item from the stack. The item that is returned is always the last one that was added.

isEmpty: Check whether the stack is empty.

A stack is sometimes called a "last in, first out," or LIFO data structure, because the last item added is the first to be removed.

15.3   The Java Stack Object

Java provides a built-in object type called Stack that implements the Stack ADT. You should make some effort to keep these two things—the ADT and the Java implementation—straight. Before using the Stack class, we have to import it from java.util.

Then the syntax for constructing a new Stack is

```
Stack stack = new Stack ();
```

Initially the stack is empty, as we can confirm with the isEmpty method, which returns a boolean:

```
System.out.println (stack.isEmpty ());
```

A stack is a generic data structure, which means that we can add any type of item to it. In the Java implementation, though, we can only add object types. For our first example, we'll use Node objects, as defined in the previous chapter. Let's start by creating and printing a short list.

```
IntList list = new IntList ();
list.addFirst (3);
list.addFirst (2);
list.addFirst (1);
list.print ();
```

The output is (1, 2, 3). To put a Node object onto the stack, use the push method:

```
stack.push (list.head);
```

The following loop traverses the list and pushes all the nodes onto the stack:

```
for (Node node = list.head; node != null; node = node.next) {
    stack.push (node);
}
```

We can remove an element from the stack with the pop method.

```
Object obj = stack.pop ();
```

The return type from pop is Object! That's because the stack implementation doesn't really know the type of the objects it contains. When we pushed the Node objects, they were automatically converted to Objects. When we get them back from the stack, we have to cast them back to Nodes.

```
Node node = (Node) obj;
System.out.println (node);
```

Unfortunately, the burden falls on the programmer to keep track of the objects in the stack and cast them back to the right type when they are removed. If you try to cast an object to the wrong type, you get a ClassCastException.

The following loop is a common idiom for popping all the elements from a stack, stopping when it is empty:

```
while (!stack.isEmpty ()) {
    Node node = (Node) stack.pop ();
    System.out.print (node + " ");
}
```

The output is 3 2 1. In other words, we just used a stack to print the elements of a list backwards! Granted, it's not the standard format for printing a list, but using a stack it was remarkably easy to do.

You should compare this code to the implementations of printBackward in the previous chapter. There is a natural parallel between the recursive version of printBackward and the stack algorithm here. The difference is that printBackward uses the run-time stack to keep track of the nodes while it traverses the list, and then prints them on the way back from the recursion. The stack algorithm does the same thing, just using a Stack object instead of the run-time stack.

15.4   Wrapper classes

For every primitive type in Java, there is a built-in object type called a **wrapper class**. For example, the wrapper class for int is called Integer; for double it is called Double.

Wrapper classes are useful for several reasons:

- You can instantiate wrapper classes and create objects that contain primitive values. In other words, you can wrap a primitive value up in an object, which is useful if you want to invoke a method that requires an object type.

- Each wrapper class contains special values (like the minimum and maximum values for the type), and methods that are useful for converting between types.

15.5   Creating wrapper objects

The most straightforward way to create a wrapper object is to use its constructor:

```
Integer i = new Integer (17);
Double d = new Double (3.14159);
Character c = new Character ('b');
```

Technically `String` is not a wrapper class, because there is no corresponding primitive type, but the syntax for creating a `String` object is the same:

```
String s = new String ("fred");
```

On the other hand, no one ever uses the constructor for `String` objects, because you can get the same effect with a simple `String` value:

```
String s = "fred";
```

15.6   Creating more wrapper objects

Some of the wrapper classes have a second constructor that takes a `String` as an argument and tries to convert to the appropriate type. For example:

```
Integer i = new Integer ("17");
Double d = new Double ("3.14159");
```

The type conversion process is not very robust. For example, if the `Strings` are not in the right format, they will cause a `NumberFormatException`. Any non-numeric character in the `String`, including a space, will cause the conversion to fail.

```
Integer i = new Integer ("17.1");       // WRONG!!
Double d = new Double ("3.1459 ");      // WRONG!!
```

It is usually a good idea to check the format of the `String` before you try to convert it.

15.7   Getting the values out

Java knows how to print wrapper objects, so the easiest way to extract a value is just to print the object:

```
Integer i = new Integer (17);
Double d = new Double (3.14159);
System.out.println (i);
System.out.println (d);
```

Alternatively, you can use the `toString` method to convert the contents of the wrapper object to a String

```
String istring = i.toString();
String dstring = d.toString();
```

Finally, if you just want to extract the primitive value from the object, there is an object method in each wrapper class that does the job:

```
int iprim = i.intValue ();
double dprim = d.doubleValue ();
```

There are also methods for converting wrapper objects into different primitive types. You should check out the documentation for each wrapper class to see what is available.

15.8   Useful methods in the wrapper classes

As I mentioned, the wrapper classes contain useful methods that pertain to each type. For example, the `Character` class contains lots of methods for converting characters to upper and lower case, and for checking whether a character is a number, letter, or symbol.

The `String` class also contains methods for converting to upper and lower case. Keep in mind, though, that they are functions, not modifiers (see Section 7.9).

As another example, the `Integer` class contains methods for interpreting and printing integers in different bases. If you have a `String` that contains a number in base 6, you can convert to base 10 using `parseInt`.

```
String base6 = "12345";
int base10 = Integer.parseInt (base6, 6);
System.out.println (base10);
```

Since `parseInt` is a class method, you invoke it by naming the class and the method in dot notation.

Base 6 might not be all that useful, but hexadecimal (base 16) and octal (base 8) are common for computer science related things.

15.9   Postfix expressions

In most programming languages, mathematical expressions are written with the operator between the two operands, as in 1+2. This format is called **infix**. An alternative format used by some calculators is called **postfix**. In postfix, the operator follows the operands, as in 1 2+.

The reason postfix is sometimes useful is that there is a natural way to evaluate a postfix expression using a stack.

- Starting at the beginning of the expression, get one term (operator or operand) at a time.

- – If the term is an operand, push it on the stack.

- – If the term is an operator, pop two operands off the stack, perform the operation on them, and push the result back on the stack.

- When we get to the end of the expression, there should be exactly one operand left on the stack. That operand is the result.

As an exercise, apply this algorithm to the expression 1 2 + 3 *.

This example demonstrates one of the advantages of postfix: there is no need to use parentheses to control the order of operations. To get the same result in infix, we would have to write (1 + 2) * 3. As an exercise, write a postfix expression that is equivalent to 1 + 2 * 3.

15.10   Parsing

In order to implement the algorithm from the previous section, we need to be able to traverse a string and break it into operands and operators. This process is an example of **parsing**, and the results—the individual chunks of the string—are called **tokens**.

Java provides a built-in class called a `StringTokenizer` that parses strings and breaks them into tokens. To use it, you have to import it from `java.util`.

In its simplest form, the `StringTokenizer` uses spaces to mark the boundaries between tokens. A character that marks a boundary is called a **delimiter**.

We can create a `StringTokenizer` in the usual way, passing as an argument the string we want to parse.

```
StringTokenizer st = new StringTokenizer ("Here are four tokens.");
```

The following loop is a standard idiom for extracting the tokens from a `StringTokenizer`.

```
while (st.hasMoreTokens ()) {
    System.out.println (st.nextToken());
}
```

The output is

```
Here
are
four
tokens.
```

For parsing expressions, we have the option of specifying additional characters that will be used as delimiters:

```
StringTokenizer st = new StringTokenizer ("11 22+33*", " +-*/");
```

The second argument is a `String` that contains all the characters that will be used as delimiters. Now the output is:

11
22
33

This succeeds at extracting all the operands but we have lost the operators. Fortunately, there is one more option for StringTokenizers.

```
StringTokenizer st = new StringTokenizer ("11 22+33*", " +-*/", true);
```

The third argument says, "Yes, we would like to treat the delimiters as tokens." Now the output is

11

22
+
33
*

This is just the stream of tokens we would like for evaluating this expression.

15.11   Implementing ADTs

One of the fundamental goals of an ADT is to separate the interests of the provider, who writes the code that implements the ADT, and the client, who uses the ADT. The provider only has to worry about whether the implementation is correct—in accord with the specification of the ADT—and not how it will be used.

Conversely, the client *assumes* that the implementation of the ADT is correct and doesn't worry about the details. When you are using one of Java's built-in classes, you have the luxury of thinking exclusively as a client.

When you implement an ADT, on the other hand, you also have to write client code to test it. In that case, you sometimes have to think carefully about which role you are playing at a given instant.

In the next few sections we will switch gears and look at one way of implementing the Stack ADT, using an array. Start thinking like a provider.

15.12   Array implementation of the Stack ADT

The instance variables for this implementation are an array of Objects, which will contain the items on the stack, and an integer index which will keep track of the next available space in the array. Initially, the array is empty and the index is 0.

To add an element to the stack (push), we'll copy a reference to it onto the stack and increment the index. To remove an element (pop) we have to decrement the index first and then copy the element out.

Here is the class definition:

```
public class Stack {
    Object[] array;
    int index;

    public Stack () {
        this.array = new Object[128];
        this.index = 0;
    }
}
```

As usual, once we have chosen the instance variables, it is a mechanical process to write a constructor. For now, the default size is 128 items. Later we will consider better ways of handling this.

Checking for an empty stack is trivial.

```
public boolean isEmpty () {
    return index == 0;
}
```

It is important to remember, though, that the number of elements in the stack is not the same as the size of the array. Initially the size is 128, but the number of elements is 0.

The implementations of push and pop follow naturally from the specification.

```
public void push (Object item) {
    array[index] = item;
    index++;
}

public Object pop () {
    index--;
    return array[index];
}
```

To test these methods, we can take advantage of the client code we used to exercise the built-in Stack. All we have to do is comment out the line import java.util.Stack. Then, instead of using the stack implementation from java.util the program will use the implementation we just wrote.

If everything goes according to plan, the program should work without any additional changes. Again, one of the strengths of using an ADT is that you can change implementations without changing client code.

15.13   Resizing arrays

A weakness of this implementation is that it chooses an arbitrary size for the array when the Stack is created. If the user pushes more than 128 items onto the stack, it will cause an ArrayIndexOutOfBounds exception.

An alternative is to let the client code specify the size of the array. This alleviates the problem, but it requires the client to know ahead of time how many items are needed, and that is not always possible.

A better solution is to check whether the array is full and make it bigger when necessary. Since we have no idea how big the array needs to be, it is a reasonable strategy to start with a small size and double it each time it overflows.

Here's the improved version of push:

```
public void push (Object item) {
    if (full ()) resize ();

    // at this point we can prove that index < array.length

    array[index] = item;
    index++;
}
```

Before putting the new item in the array, we check if the array is full. If so, we invoke resize. After the if statement, we know that either (1) there was room in the array, or (2) the array has been resized and there is room. If full and resize are correct, then we can prove that index < array.length, and therefore the next statement cannot cause an exception.

Now all we have to do is implement full and resize.

```
private boolean full () {
    return index == array.length;
}

private void resize () {
    Object[] newArray = new Object[array.length * 2];

    // we assume that the old array is full
    for (int i=0; i<array.length; i++) {
        newArray[i] = array[i];
    }
    array = newArray;
}
```

Both methods are declared private, which means that they cannot be invoked from another class, only from within this one. This is acceptable, since there is no reason for client code to use these functions, and desirable, since it enforces the boundary between the provider code and the client.

The implementation of full is trivial; it just checks whether the index has gone beyond the range of valid indices.

The implementation of resize is straightforward, with the caveat that it assumes that the old array is full. In other words, that assumption is a precondition of this method. It is easy to see that this precondition is satisfied, since the only way `resize` is invoked is if `full` returns true, which can only happen if `index == array.length`.

At the end of `resize`, we replace the old array with the new (causing the old to be garbage collected). The new `array.length` is twice as big as the old, and `index` hasn't changed, so now it must be true that `index < array.length`. This assertion is a **postcondition** of `resize`: something that must be true when the method is complete (as long as its preconditions were satisfied).

Preconditions, postconditions, and invariants are useful tools for analyzing programs and demonstrating their correctness. In this example I have demonstrated a programming style that facilitates program analysis and a style of documentation that helps demonstrate correctness.

15.14   Glossary

abstract data type (ADT): A data type (usually a collection of objects) that is defined by a set of operations, but that can be implemented in a variety of ways.

client: A program that uses an ADT (or the person who wrote the program).

provider: The code that implements an ADT (or the person who wrote it).

wrapper class: One of the Java classes, like `Double` and `Integer` that provide objects to contain primitive types, and methods that operate on primitives.

private: A Java keyword that indicates that a method or instance variable cannot be accessed from outside the current class definition.

infix: A way of writing mathematical expressions with the operators between the operands.

postfix: A way of writing mathematical expressions with the operators after the operands.

parse: To read a string of characters or tokens and analyze their grammatical structure.

token: A set of characters that are treated as a unit for purposes of parsing, like the words in a natural language.

delimiter: A character that is used to separate tokens, like the punctuation in a natural language.

predicate: A mathematical statement that is either true or false.

postcondition: A predicate that must be true at the end of a method (provided that the preconditions were true at the beginning).

15.15   Exercises

Exercise 15.1   Write a method named `reverse` that takes an array of integers, traverses the array pushing each item onto a stack, and then pops the items off the stack, putting them back into the array in the reverse of their original order.

The point of this exercise is to practice the mechanisms for creating wrapper objects, pushing and popping objects, and typecasting generic Objects to a specific type.

Exercise 15.2   This exercise is based on the solution to Exercise 14.1. Start by making a copy of your implementation of `IntList` called `LinkedList`.

   a. Transform the linked list implementation into a generic list by making the cargo an `Object` instead of an integer. Modify the test code accordingly and run the program.

   b. Write a `LinkedList` method called `split` that takes a `String`, breaks it up into words (using spaces as delimiters), and returns a list of `Strings`, with one word per list node. Your implementation should be efficient, meaning that it takes time proportional to the number of words in the string.

   c. Write a `LinkedList` method named `join` that returns a String that contains the String representation of each of the objects in the list, in the order they appear, with spaces in between.

   d. Write a `toString` method for `LinkedList`.

Exercise 15.3   Write an implementation of the Stack ADT using your `LinkedList` implementation as the underlying data structure. There are two general approaches to this: the Stack might contain a LinkedList as an instance variable, or the Stack class might extend the LinkedList class. Choose whichever sounds better to you, or, if you are feeling ambitious, implement both and compare them.

Exercise 15.4   Write a program called `Balance.java` that reads a file and checks that the parentheses () and brackets [] and squiggly-braces {} are balanced and nested correctly.

HINT: See Section C for code that reads lines from a file.

Exercise 15.5   Write a method called `evalPostfix` that takes a String containing a postfix expression and returns a double that contains the result. You can use a String-Tokenizer to parse the String and a Stack of Doubles to evaluate the expression.

Exercise 15.6   Write a program that prompts the user for a mathematical expression in postfix and that evaluates the expression and prints the result. The following steps are my suggestion for a program development plan.

   a. Write a program that prompts the user for input and prints the input string, over and over, until the user types "quit". See Section C for information about getting input from the keyboard. You can use the following code as a starter:

```
public static void inputLoop () throws IOException {
    BufferedReader stdin =
        new BufferedReader (new InputStreamReader (System.in));
```

```
        while (true) {
            System.out.print ("=>");          // print a prompt
            String s = stdin.readLine();      // get input
            if (s == null) break;
            // check if s is "quit"
            // print s
        }
    }
```

b. Identify helper methods you think will be useful, and write and debug them in isolation. Suggestions: `isOperator`, `isOperand`, `parseExpression`, `performOperation`.

c. We know we want to push `int` values onto the stack and pop them off, which means we will have to use a wrapper class. Make sure you know how to do that, and test those operations in isolation. Maybe make them helper methods.

d. Write a version of `evaluate` that only handles one kind of operator (like addition). Test it in isolation.

e. Connect your evaluator to your input/output loop.

f. Add the other operations.

g. Once you have code that works, you might want to evaluate the structural design. How should you divide the code into classes? What instance variables should the classes have? What parameters should be passed around?

h. In addition to making the design elegant, you should also make the code bulletproof, meaning that is should not cause an exception under any circumstances, even if the user types something weird.

Chapter 16

Queues and Priority Queues

This chapter presents two ADTs: Queues and Priority Queues. In real life a **queue** is a line of customers waiting for service of some kind. In most cases, the first customer in line is the next customer to be served. There are exceptions, though. For example, at airports customers whose flight is leaving imminently are sometimes taken from the middle of the queue. Also, at supermarkets a polite customer might let someone with only a few items go first.

The rule that determines who goes next is called a **queueing discipline**. The simplest queueing discipline is called **FIFO**, for "first-in-first-out." The most general queueing discipline is **priority queueing**, in which each customer is assigned a priority, and the customer with the highest priority goes first, regardless of the order of arrival. The reason I say this is the most general discipline is that the priority can be based on anything: what time a flight leaves, how many groceries the customer has, or how important the customer is. Of course, not all queueing disciplines are "fair," but fairness is in the eye of the beholder.

The Queue ADT and the Priority Queue ADT have the same set of operations and their interfaces are the same. The difference is in the semantics of the operations: a Queue uses the FIFO policy, and a Priority Queue (as the name suggests) uses the priority queueing policy.

As with most ADTs, there are a number of ways to implement queues. Since a queue is a collection of items, we can use any of the basic mechanisms for storing collections, including arrays and lists. Our choice among them will be based in part on their performance— how long it takes to perform the operations we want to perform— and partly on ease of implementation.

16.1   The queue ADT

The queue ADT is defined by the following operations:

constructor: Create a new, empty queue.

add: Add a new item to the queue.

remove: Remove and return an item from the queue. The item that is returned is the first one that was added.

isEmpty: Check whether the queue is empty.

Here is an implementation of a generic Queue, based on the built-in class `java.util.LinkedList`:

```
public class Queue {
    private LinkedList list;

    public Queue () {
        list = new LinkedList ();
    }

    public boolean isEmpty () {
        return list.isEmpty ();
    }

    public void add (Object obj) {
        list.addLast (obj);
    }

    public Object remove () {
        return list.removeFirst ();
    }
}
```

A queue object contains a single instance variable, which is the list that implements it. For each of the other methods, all we have to do is invoke one of the methods from the `LinkedList` class.

We can write the same implementation a bit more concisely by taking advantage of inheritance:

```
public class Queue extends LinkedList {

    public Object remove () {
        return removeFirst ();
    }
}
```

Ok, it's a lot more concise! Because `Queue` extends `LinkedList`, we inherit the constructor, `isEmpty` and `add`. We also inherit `remove`, but the version of `remove` we get from the `LinkedList` class doesn't do what we want; it removes the *last* element in the list, not the first. We fix that by providing a new version of `remove`, which **overrides** the version we inherited.

The choice between these implementations depends on several factors. Inheritance can make an implementation more concise, as long as there are methods in the parent class that are useful. But it can also make an implementation more difficult to read and debug, because the methods for the new class are not in one place. Also, it can lead to unexpected behavior, because the new class inherits *all* the methods from the parent class, not just the ones you need. That means that the second version of Queue provides methods like removeLast and clear that are not part of the Queue ADT. The first implementation is safer; by declaring a private instance variable, it prevents clients from invoking methods on the LinkedList.

16.2   Veneer

By using a LinkedList to implement a Queue, we were able to take advantage of existing code; the code we wrote just translates LinkedList methods into Queue methods. An implementation like this is called a **veneer**. In real life, veneer is a thin coating of good quality wood used in furniture-making to hide lower quality wood underneath. Computer scientists use this metaphor to describe a small piece of code that hides the details of an implementation and provides a simpler, or more standard, interface.

The Queue example demonstrates one of the nice things about a veneer, which is that it is easy to implement, and one of the dangers of using a veneer, which is the **performance hazard**!

Normally when we invoke a method we are not concerned with the details of its implementation. But there is one "detail" we might want to know—the performance characteristics of the method. How long does it take, as a function of the number of items in the list?

To answer that question, we have to know more about the implementation. If we assume that LinkedList is really implemented as a linked list, then the implementation of removeFirst probably looks something like this:

```
public Object removeFirst () {
    Object result = head;
    if (head != null) {
        head = head.next;
    }
    return result.cargo;
}
```

We assume that head refers to the first node in the list, and that each node contains cargo and a reference to the next node in the list.

There are no loops or function calls here, so the run time of this method is pretty much the same every time. Such a method is called a **constant time** operation. In reality, the method might be slightly faster when the list is empty, since it skips the body of the conditional, but that difference is not significant.

The performance of addLast is very different. Here is a hypothetical implementation:

```
public void addLast (Object obj) {
    // special case: empty list
    if (head == null) {
        head = new Node (obj, null);
        return;
    }
    Node last;
    for (last = head; last.next != null; last = last.next) {
        // traverse the list to find the last node
    }
    last.next = new Node (obj, null);
}
```

The first conditional handles the special case of adding a new node to an empty list. In this case, again, the run time does not depend on the length of the list. In the general case, though, we have to traverse the list to find the last element so we can make it refer to the new node.

This traversal takes time proportional to the length of the list. Since the run time is a linear function of the length, we would say that this method is **linear time**. Compared to constant time, that's very bad.

16.3   Linked Queue

We would like an implementation of the Queue ADT that can perform all operations in constant time. One way to accomplish that is to implement a **linked queue**, which is similar to a linked list in the sense that it is made up of zero or more linked Node objects. The difference is that the queue maintains a reference to both the first and the last node, as shown in the figure.

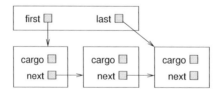

Here's what a linked Queue implementation looks like:

```
public class Queue {
    public Node first, last;

    public Queue () {
        first = null;
        last = null;
    }

    public boolean isEmpty () {
```

```
        return first == null;
    }
}
```

So far it is straightforward. In an empty queue, both `first` and `last` are null. To check whether a list is empty, we only have to check one of them.

`add` is a little more complicated because we have to deal with several special cases.

```
public void add (Object obj) {
    Node node = new Node (obj, null);
    if (last != null) {
        last.next = node;
    }
    last = node;
    if (first == null) {
        first = last;
    }
}
```

The first condition checks to make sure that `last` refers to a node; if it does then we have to make it refer to the new node.

The second condition deals with the special case where the list was initially empty. In this case both `first` and `last` refer to the new node.

`remove` also deals with several special cases.

```
public Object remove () {
    Node result = first;
    if (first != null) {
        first = first.next;
    }
    if (first == null) {
        last = null;
    }
    return result;
}
```

The first condition checks whether there were any nodes in the queue. If so, we have to copy the `next` node into `first`. The second condition deals with the special case that the list is now empty, in which case we have to make `last` null.

As an exercise, draw diagrams showing these operations in both the normal case and in the special cases, and convince yourself that they are correct.

Clearly, this implementation is more complicated than the veneer implementation, and it is more difficult to demonstrate that it is correct. The advantage is that we have achieved the goal: `add` and `remove` are constant time operations.

16.4   Circular buffer

Another common implementation of a queue is a **circular buffer**. "Buffer" is a general name for a temporary storage location, although it often refers to an array, as it does in this case. What it means to say a buffer is "circular" should become clear in a minute.

The implementation of a circular buffer is similar to the array implementation of a stack in Section 15.12. The queue items are stored in an array, and we use indices to keep track of where we are in the array. In the stack implementation, there was a single index that pointed to the next available space. In the queue implementation, there are two indices: `first` points to the space in the array that contains the first customer in line and `next` points to the next available space.

The following figure shows a queue with two items (represented by dots).

There are two ways to think of the variables `first` and `last`. Literally, they are integers, and their values are shown in boxes on the right. Abstractly, though, they are indices of the array, and so they are often drawn as arrows pointing to locations in the array. The arrow representation is convenient, but you should remember that the indices are not references; they are just integers.

Here is an incomplete array implementation of a queue:

```
public class Queue {
    public Object[] array;
    public int first, next;

    public Queue () {
        array = new Object[128];
        first = 0;
        next = 0;
    }

    public boolean isEmpty () {
        return first == next;
    }
```

The instance variables and the constructor are straightforward, although again we have the problem that we have to choose an arbitrary size for the array.

Later we will solve that problem, as we did with the stack, by resizing the array if it gets full.

The implementation of isEmpty is a little surprising. You might have thought that first == 0 would indicate an empty queue, but that neglects the fact that the head of the queue is not necessarily at the beginning of the array. Instead, we know that the queue is empty if head equals next, in which case there are no items left. Once we see the implementation of add and remove, that condition will make more sense.

```
public void add (Object item) {
    array[next] = item;
    next++;
}

public Object remove () {
    Object result = array[first];
    first++;
    return result;
}
```

add looks very much like push in Section 15.12; it puts the new item in the next available space and then increments the index.

remove is similar. It takes the first item from the queue and then increments first so it refers to the new head of the queue. The following figure shows what the queue looks like after both items have been removed.

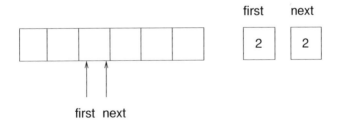

It is always true that next points to an available space. If first catches up with next and points to the same space, then first is referring to an "empty" location, and the queue is empty. I put "empty" in quotation marks because it is possible that the location that first points to actually contains a value (we do nothing to ensure that empty locations contain null); on the other hand, since we know the queue is empty, we will never read this location, so we can think of it, abstractly, as empty.

Exercise 16.1 Modify remove so that it returns null if the queue is empty.

The next problem with this implementation is that eventually it will run out of space. When we add an item we increment next and when we remove an item we increment `first`, but we never decrement either. What happens when we get to the end of the array?

The following figure shows the queue after we add four more items:

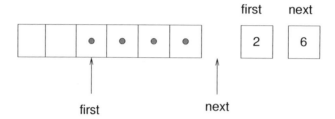

The array is now full. There is no "next available space," so there is nowhere for `next` to point. One possibility is that we could resize the array, as we did with the stack implementation. But in that case the array would keep getting bigger regardless of how many items were actually in queue. A better solution is to wrap around to the beginning of the array and reuse the spaces there. This "wrap around" is the reason this implementation is called a circular buffer.

One way to wrap the index around is to add a special case whenever we increment an index:

```
next++;
if (next == array.length) next = 0;
```

A fancy alternative is to use the modulus operator:

```
next = (next + 1) % array.length;
```

Either way, we have one last problem to solve. How do we know if the queue is *really* full, meaning that we cannot add another item? The following figure shows what the queue looks like when it is "full."

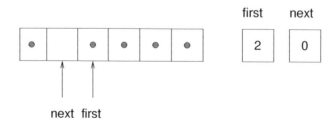

There is still one empty space in the array, but the queue is full because if we add another item, then we have to increment `next` such that `next == first`, and in that case it would appear that the queue was empty!

To avoid that, we sacrifice one space in the array. So how can we tell if the queue is full?

```
if ((next + 1) % array.length == first)
```

And what should we do if the array is full? In that case resizing the array is probably the only option.

Exercise 16.2   Write an implementation of a queue using a circular buffer that resizes itself when necessary.

16.5   Priority queue

The Priority Queue ADT has the same interface as the Queue ADT, but different semantics. The interface is:

constructor: Create a new, empty queue.

add: Add a new item to the queue.

remove: Remove and return an item from the queue. The item that is returned is the one with the highest priority.

isEmpty: Check whether the queue is empty.

The semantic difference is that the item that is removed from the queue is not necessarily the first one that was added. Rather, it is whatever item in the queue has the highest priority. What the priorities are, and how they compare to each other, are not specified by the Priority Queue implementation. It depends on what the items are that are in the queue.

For example, if the items in the queue have names, we might choose them in alphabetical order. If they are bowling scores, we might choose from highest to lowest, but if they are golf scores, we would go from lowest to highest.

So we face a new problem. We would like an implementation of Priority Queue that is generic—it should work with any kind of object—but at the same time the code that implements Priority Queue needs to have the ability to compare the objects it contains.

We have seen a way to implement generic data structures using Objects, but that does not solve this problem, because there is no way to compare Objects unless we know what type they are.

The answer lies in a Java feature called a **metaclass**.

16.6   Metaclass

A metaclass is a set of classes that provide a common set of methods. The metaclass definition specifies the requirements a class must satisfy to be a member of the set.

Often metaclasses have names that end in "able" to indicate the fundamental capability the metaclass requires. For example, any class that provides a method named `draw` can be a member of the metaclass named `Drawable`. Any class that contains a method named `start` can be a member of the metaclass `Runnable`.

Java provides a built-in metaclass that we can use in an implementation of a Priority Queue. It is called `Comparable`, and it means what it says. Any class that belongs to the `Comparable` metaclass has to provide a method named `compareTo` that compares two objects and returns a value indicating whether one is larger or smaller than the other, or whether they are the same.

Many of the built-in Java classes are members of the `Comparable` metaclass, including numeric wrapper classes like `Integer` and `Double`.

In the next section I will show how to write an ADT that manipulates a metaclass. Then we will see how to write a new class that belongs to an existing metaclass. In the next chapter we will see how to define a new metaclass.

16.7   Array implementation of Priority Queue

In the implementation of the Priority Queue, every time we specify the type of the items in the queue, we specify the metaclass `Comparable`. For example, the instance variables are an array of `Comparable`s and an integer:

```
public class PriorityQueue {
    private Comparable[] array;
    private int index;
}
```

As usual, `index` is the index of the next available location in the array. The instance variables are declared `private` so that other classes cannot have direct access to them.

The constructor and `isEmpty` are similar to what we have seen before. The initial size of the array is arbitrary.

```
    public PriorityQueue () {
        array = new Comparable [16];
        index = 0;
    }

    public boolean isEmpty () {
        return index == 0;
    }
```

`add` is similar to `push`:

```
    public void add (Comparable item) {
        if (index == array.length) {
            resize ();
        }
```

```
        array[index] = item;
        index++;
    }
```

The only substantial method in the class is `remove`, which has to traverse the array to find and remove the largest item:

```
    public Comparable remove () {
        if (index == 0) return null;

        int maxIndex = 0;

        // find the index of the item with the highest priority
        for (int i=1; i<index; i++) {
            if (array[i].compareTo (array[maxIndex]) > 0) {
                maxIndex = i;
            }
        }
        Comparable result = array[maxIndex];

        // move the last item into the empty slot
        index--;
        array[maxIndex] = array[index];
        return result;
    }
```

As we traverse the array, `maxIndex` keeps track of the index of the largest element we have seen so far. What it means to be the "largest" is determined by `compareTo`. In this case the `compareTo` method is provided by the `Integer` class, and it does what we expect—larger (more positive) numbers win.

16.8   A Priority Queue client

The implementation of Priority Queue is written entirely in terms of `Comparable` objects, but there is no such thing as a `Comparable` object! Go ahead, try to create one:

```
    Comparable comp = new Comparable ();        // ERROR
```

You'll get a compile-time message that says something like "java.lang.Comparable is an interface. It can't be instantiated." In Java, metaclasses are called **interfaces**. I have avoided this word so far because it also means several other things, but now you have to know.

Why can't metaclasses be instantiated? Because a metaclass only specifies requirements (you must have a `compareTo` method); it does not provide an implementation.

To create a `Comparable` object, you have to create one of the objects that belongs to the `Comparable` set, like `Integer`. Then you can use that object anywhere a `Comparable` is called for.

```
PriorityQueue pq = new PriorityQueue ();
Integer item = new Integer (17);
pq.add (item);
```

This code creates a new, empty Priority Queue and a new Integer object. Then it adds the Integer into the queue. add is expecting a Comparable as a parameter, so it is perfectly happy to take an Integer. If we try to pass a Rectangle, which does not belong to Comparable, we get a compile-time message like, "Incompatible type for method. Explicit cast needed to convert java.awt.Rectangle to java.lang.Comparable."

That's the compiler telling us that if we want to make that conversion, we have to do it explicitly. We might try to do what it says:

```
Rectangle rect = new Rectangle ();
pq.add ((Comparable) rect);
```

But in that case we get a run-time error, a ClassCastException. When the Rectangle tries to pass as a Comparable, the run-time system checks whether it satisfies the requirements, and rejects it. So that's what we get for following the compiler's advice.

To get items out of the queue, we have to reverse the process:

```
while (!pq.isEmpty ()) {
    item = (Integer) pq.remove ();
    System.out.println (item);
}
```

This loop removes all the items from the queue and prints them. It assumes that the items in the queue are Integers. If they were not, we would get a ClassCastException.

16.9 The Golfer class

Finally, let's look at how we can make a new class that belongs to Comparable. As an example of something with an unusual definition of "highest" priority, we'll use golfers:

```
public class Golfer implements Comparable {
    String name;
    int score;

    public Golfer (String name, int score) {
        this.name = name;
        this.score = score;
    }
}
```

The class definition and the constructor are pretty much the same as always; the difference is that we have to declare that Golfer implements Comparable. In this case the keyword `implements` means that `Golfer` implements the interface specified by `Comparable`.

If we try to compile `Golfer.java` at this point, we get something like "class Golfer must be declared abstract. It does not define int compareTo(java.lang.Object) from interface java.lang.Comparable." In other words, to be a `Comparable`, `Golfer` has to provide a method named `compareTo`. So let's write one:

```
public int compareTo (Object obj) {
    Golfer that = (Golfer) obj;

    int a = this.score;
    int b = that.score;

    // for golfers, low is good!
    if (a<b) return 1;
    if (a>b) return -1;
    return 0;
}
```

Two things here are a little surprising. First, the parameter is an `Object`. That's because in general the caller doesn't know what type the objects are that are being compared. For example, in `PriorityQueue.java` when we invoke `compareTo`, we pass a `Comparable` as a parameter. We don't have to know whether it is an `Integer` or a `Golfer` or whatever.

Inside `compareTo` we have to convert the parameter from an `Object` to a `Golfer`. As usual, there is a risk when we do this kind of cast: if we cast to the wrong type we get an exception.

Finally, we can create some golfers:

```
Golfer tiger = new Golfer ("Tiger Woods", 61);
Golfer phil = new Golfer ("Phil Mickelson", 72);
Golfer hal = new Golfer ("Hal Sutton", 69);
```

And put them in the queue:

```
pq.add (tiger);
pq.add (phil);
pq.add (hal);
```

When we pull them out:

```
while (!pq.isEmpty ()) {
    golfer = (Golfer) pq.remove ();
    System.out.println (golfer);
}
```

They appear in descending order (for golfers):

```
Tiger Woods      61
Hal Sutton       69
Phil Mickelson   72
```

When we switched from `Integers` to `Golfers`, we didn't have to make any
changes in `PriorityQueue.java` at all. So we succeeded in maintaining a barrier
between `PriorityQueue` and the classes that use it, allowing us to reuse the code
without modification. Furthermore, we were able to give the client code control
over the definition of `compareTo`, making this implementation of `PriorityQueue`
more versatile.

16.10   Glossary

queue: An ordered set of objects waiting for a service of some kind.

queueing discipline: The rules that determine which member of a queue is
removed next.

FIFO: "first in, first out," a queueing discipline in which the first member to
arrive is the first to be removed.

priority queue: A queueing discipline in which each member has a priority
determined by external factors. The member with the highest priority is
the first to be removed.

Priority Queue: An ADT that defines the operations one might perform on
a priority queue.

veneer: A class definition that implements an ADT with method definitions
that are invocations of other methods, sometimes with simple transforma-
tions. The veneer does no significant work, but it improves or standardizes
the interface seen by the client.

performance hazard: A danger associated with a veneer that some of the
methods might be implemented inefficiently in a way that is not apparent
to the client.

constant time: An operation whose run time does not depend on the size of
the data structure.

linear time: An operation whose run time is a linear function of the size of
the data structure.

linked queue: An implementation of a queue using a linked list and references
to the first and last nodes.

circular buffer: An implementation of a queue using an array and indices of
the first element and the next available space.

metaclass: A set of classes. The metaclass specification lists the requirements
a class must satisfy to be included in the set.

interface: The Java word for a metaclass. Not to be confused with the more
broad meaning of the word interface.

16.11   Exercises

Exercise 16.3   This question is based on Exercise 9.3.

Write a `compareTo` method for the `Rational` class that would allow `Rational` to implement `Comparable`. Hint: don't forget that the parameter is an `Object`.

Exercise 16.4   Write a class definition for `SortedList`, which extends `LinkedList`. A SortedList is similar to a LinkedList; the difference is that the elements have to be Comparable, and the list is sorted in decreasing order.

Write an object method for `SortedList` called `add` that takes a Comparable as a parameter and that adds the new object into the list, at the appropriate place so that the list stays sorted.

If you want, you can write a helper method in the `Node` class.

Exercise 16.5   Write an object method for the `LinkedList` class named `maximum` that can be invoked on a `LinkedList` object, and that returns the largest cargo object in the list, or null if the list is empty.

You can assume that every cargo element belongs to a class that belongs to the meta-class `Comparable`, and that any two elements can be compared to each other.

Exercise 16.6   Write an implementation of a Priority Queue using a linked list. There are three ways you might proceed:

- A Priority Queue might contain a LinkedList object as an instance variable.
- A Priority Queue might contain a reference to the first Node object in a linked list.
- A Priority Queue might extend (inherit from) the existing LinkedList class.

Think about the pros and cons of each and choose one. Also, you can choose whether to keep the list sorted (slow add, fast remove) or unsorted (slow remove, fast add).

Exercise 16.7   An event queue is a data structure that keeps track of a set of events, where each event has a time associated with it. The ADT is:

constructor: make a new, empty event queue

add: put a new event in the queue. The parameters are the event, which is an Object, and the time the event occurs, which is a `Date` object. The event Object must not be null.

nextTime: return the `Date` at which the next event occurs, where the "next" event is the one in the queue with the earliest time. Do not remove the event from the queue. Return null if the queue is empty.

nextEvent: return the next event (an `Object`) from the queue and remove it from the queue. Return null if the queue is empty.

The `Date` class is defined in `java.util` and it implements `Comparable`. According to the documentation, its `compareTo` method returns "the value 0 if the argument Date is equal to this Date; a value less than 0 if this Date is before the Date argument; and a value greater than 0 if this Date is after the Date argument."

Write an implementation of an event queue using the PriorityQueue ADT. You should not make any assumptions about how the PriorityQueue is implemented.

HINT: create a class named `Event` that contains a `Date` and an event `Object`, and that implements `Comparable` appropriately.

Chapter 17

Trees

17.1 A tree node

Like lists, trees are made up of nodes. A common kind of tree is a **binary tree**, in which each node contains a reference to two other nodes (possibly null). The class definition looks like this:

```
public class Tree {
    Object cargo;
    Tree left, right;
}
```

Like list nodes, tree nodes contain cargo: in this case a generic Object. The other instance variables are named `left` and `right`, in accordance with a standard way to represent trees graphically:

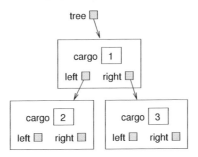

The top of the tree (the node referred to by `tree`) is called the **root**. In keeping with the tree metaphor, the other nodes are called branches and the nodes at the tips with null references are called **leaves**. It may seem odd that we draw the picture with the root at the top and the leaves at the bottom, but that is not the strangest thing.

To make things worse, computer scientists mix in yet another metaphor: the family tree. The top node is sometimes called a **parent** and the nodes it refers to are its **children**. Nodes with the same parent are called **siblings**, and so on.

Finally, there is also a geometric vocabulary for taking about trees. I already mentioned left and right, but there is also "up" (toward the parent/root) and down (toward the children/leaves). Also, all the nodes that are the same distance from the root comprise a **level** of the tree.

I don't know why we need three metaphors for talking about trees, but there it is.

17.2   Building trees

The process of assembling tree nodes is similar to the process of assembling lists. We have a constructor for tree nodes that initializes the instance variables.

```
public Tree (Object cargo, Tree left, Tree right) {
    this.cargo = cargo;
    this.left = left;
    this.right = right;
}
```

We allocate the child nodes first:

```
Tree left = new Tree (new Integer(2), null, null);
Tree right = new Tree (new Integer(3), null, null);
```

We can create the parent node and link it to the children at the same time:

```
Tree tree = new Tree (new Integer(1), left, right);
```

This code produces the state shown in the previous figure.

17.3   Traversing trees

The most natural way to traverse a tree is recursively. For example, to add up all the integers in a tree, we could write this class method:

```
public static int total (Tree tree) {
    if (tree == null) return 0;
    Integer cargo = (Integer) tree.cargo;
    return cargo.intValue() + total (tree.left) + total (tree.right);
}
```

This is a class method because we would like to use null to represent the empty tree, and make the empty tree the base case of the recursion. If the tree is empty, the method returns 0. Otherwise it makes two recursive calls to find the total value of its two children. Finally, it adds in its own cargo and returns the total.

Although this method works, there is some difficulty fitting it into an object-oriented design. It should not appear in the Tree class because it requires the cargo to be `Integer` objects. If we make that assumption in `Tree.java` then we lose the advantages of a generic data structure.

On the other hand, this code accesses the instance variables of the `Tree` nodes, so it "knows" more than it should about the implementation of the tree. If we change that implementation later this code will break.

Later in this chapter we will develop ways to solve this problem, allowing client code to traverse trees containing any kinds of objects without breaking the abstraction barrier between the client code and the implementation. Before we get there, let's look at an application of trees.

17.4 Expression trees

A tree is a natural way to represent the structure of a mathematical expression. Unlike other notations, it can represent the computation unambiguously. For example, the infix expression 1 + 2 * 3 is ambiguous unless we know that the multiplication happens before the addition.

The following figure represents the same computation:

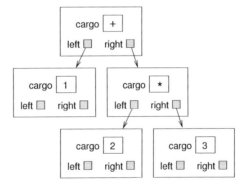

The nodes can be operands like 1 and 2 or operators like + and *. Operands are leaf nodes; operator nodes contain references to their operands (all of these operators are **binary**, meaning they have exactly two operands).

Looking at this figure, there is no question what the order of operations is: the multiplication happens first in order to compute the first operand of the addition.

Expression trees like this have many uses. The example we are going to look at is translation from one format (postfix) to another (infix). Similar trees are used inside compilers to parse, optimize and translate programs.

17.5 Traversal

I already pointed out that recursion provides a natural way to traverse a tree.
We can print the contents of an expression tree like this:

```
public static void print (Tree tree) {
    if (tree == null) return;
    System.out.print (tree + " ");
    print (tree.left);
    print (tree.right);
}
```

In other words, to print a tree, first print the contents of the root, then print the
entire left subtree, then print the entire right subtree. This way of traversing
a tree is called a **preorder**, because the contents of the root appear before the
contents of the children.

For the example expression the output is + 1 * 2 3. This is different from
both postfix and infix; it is a new notation called **prefix**, in which the operators
appear before their operands.

You might suspect that if we traverse the tree in a different order we get the
expression in a different notation. For example, if we print the subtrees first,
and then the root node:

```
public static void printPostorder (Tree tree) {
    if (tree == null) return;
    printPostorder (tree.left);
    printPostorder (tree.right);
    System.out.print (tree + " ");
}
```

We get the expression in postfix (1 2 3 * +)! As the name of the method
implies, this order of traversal is called **postorder**. Finally, to traverse a tree
inorder, we print the left tree, then the root, then the right tree:

```
public static void printInorder (Tree tree) {
    if (tree == null) return;
    printInorder (tree.left);
    System.out.print (tree + " ");
    printInorder (tree.right);
}
```

The result is 1 + 2 * 3, which is the expression in infix.

To be fair, I have to point out that I omitted an important complication. Sometimes when we write an expression in infix we have to use parentheses to preserve
the order of operations. So an inorder traversal is not quite sufficient to generate
an infix expression.

Nevertheless, with a few improvements, the expression tree and the three recursive traversals provide a general way to translate expressions from one format
to another.

17.6   Encapsulation

As I mentioned before, there is a problem with the way we have been traversing trees: it breaks down the barrier between the client code (the application that uses the tree) and the provider code (the Tree implementation). Ideally, tree code should be general; it shouldn't know anything about expression trees. And the code that generates and traverses the expression tree shouldn't know about the implementation of the trees. This design criterion is called **object encapsulation** to distinguish it from the encapsulation we saw in Section 6.6, which we might call **method encapsulation**.

In the current version, the Tree code knows too much about the client. Instead, the Tree class should provide the general capability of traversing a tree in various ways. As it traverses, it should perform operations on each node that are specified by the client.

To facilitate this separation of interests, we will create a new metaclass, called Visitable. The items stored in a tree will be required to be visitable, which means that they define a method named visit that does whatever the client wants done to each node. That way the Tree can perform the traversal and the client can perform the node operations.

Here are the steps we have to perform to wedge a metaclass between a client and a provider:

1. Define a metaclass that specifies the methods the provider code will need to invoke on its components.

2. Write the provider code in terms of the new metaclass, as opposed to generic Objects.

3. Define a class that belongs to the metaclass and that implements the required methods as appropriate for the client.

4. Write the client code to use the new class.

The next few sections demonstrate these steps.

17.7   Defining a metaclass

There are actually two ways to implement a metaclass in Java, an an **interface** or as an **abstract class**. The differences between them aren't important for now, so we'll start by defining an interface.

An interface definition looks a lot like a class definition, with two differences:

- The keyword class is replaced with interface, and

- The method definitions have no bodies.

An interface definition specifies the methods a class has to implement in order to be in the metaclass. The specification includes the name, parameter types, and return type of each method.

The definition of `Visitable` is

```
public interface Visitable {
    public void visit ();
}
```

That's it! The definition of `visit` looks like any other method definition, except that it has no body. This definition specifies that any class that implements `Visitable` has to have a method named `visit` that takes no parameters and that returns `void`.

Like other class definitions, interface definitions go in a file with the same name as the class (in this case `Visitable.java`).

17.8   Implementing a metaclass

If we are using an expression tree to generate infix, then "visiting" a node means printing its contents. Since the contents of an expression tree are tokens, we'll create a new class called `Token` that implements `Visitable`

```
public class Token implements Visitable {
    String str;

    public Token (String str) {
        this.str = str;
    }

    public void visit () {
        System.out.print (str + " ");
    }
}
```

When we compile this class definition (which is in a file named `Token.java`), the compiler checks whether the methods provided satisfy the requirements specified by the metaclass. If not, it will produce an error message. For example, if we misspell the name of the method that is supposed to be `visit`, we might get something like, "class Token must be declared abstract. It does not define void visit() from interface Visitable." This is one of many error messages where the solution suggested by the compiler is wrong. When it says the class "must be declared abstract," what it means is that you have to fix the class so that it implements the interface properly. Sometimes I think the people who write these messages should be beaten.

The next step is to modify the parser to put `Token` objects into the tree instead of `Strings`. Here is a small example:

```
String expr = "1 2 3 * +";
StringTokenizer st = new StringTokenizer (expr, " +-*/", true);
String token = st.nextToken();
Tree tree = new Tree (new Token (token), null, null));
```

This code takes the first token in the string and wraps it in a `Token` object, then puts the `Token` into a tree node. If the `Tree` requires the cargo to be `Visitable`, it will convert the `Token` to be a `Visitable` object. When we remove the `Visitable` from the tree, we will have to cast it back into a `Token`.

Exercise 17.1   Write a version of `printPreorder` called `visitPreorder` that traverses the tree and invokes `visit` on each node in preorder.

The flow of execution for methods like `visitPreorder` is unusual. The client invokes a method provided by the Tree implementation, and then the tree implementation invokes a method provided by the client. This pattern is called a **callback**; it is a good way to make provider code more general without breaking down the abstraction barrier.

17.9   The Vector class

The `Vector` is a built-in Java class in the `java.util` package. It is an implementation of an array of `Objects`, with the added feature that it can resize itself automatically, so we don't have to.

Before using the `Vector` class, you should understand a few concepts. Every `Vector` has a capacity, which is the amount of space that has been allocated to store values, and a size, which is the number of values that are actually in the vector.

The following figure is a simple diagram of a `Vector` that contains three elements, but it has a capacity of seven.

There are two sets of methods for accessing the elements of a vector. They provide different semantics and different error-checking capabilities, and they are easy to get confused.

The simpler accessors methods are `get` and `set`, which provide semantics similar to the array index operator `[]`. `get` takes an integer index and returns the element at the indicated position. `set` takes an index and an element, and stores the new element at the indicated position, replacing the existing element.

`get` and `set` do not change the size of the vector (number of elements). It is the responsibility of the client code to make sure that the vector has sufficient size before invoking `set` or `get`. The `size` method returns the number of elements in the Vector. If you try to access an element that does not exist (in this case the elements with indices 3 through 6), you will get an `ArrayIndexOutOfBounds` exception.

The other set of methods includes several versions of `add` and `remove`. These methods change the size of the Vector and, if necessary, the capacity. One version of `add` takes an element as a parameter and adds it to the end of the Vector. This method is safe in the sense that it will not cause an exception.

Another version of `add` takes an index and an element and, like `set`, it puts the new element at the given position. The difference is that `add` doesn't replace the existing element; it increases the size of the Vector and shifts elements to the right to make room for the new one. Thus, the invocation `v.add (0, elt)` add the new element at the beginning of the Vector. Unfortunately, this method is neither safe nor efficient; it can cause an `ArrayIndexOutOfBounds` exception and, in most implementations, it is linear time (proportional to the size of the Vector).

Most of the time the client doesn't have to worry about capacity. Whenever the size of the `Vector` changes, the capacity is updated automatically. For performance reasons, some applications take control of this function, which is why there are additional methods for increasing and decreasing capacity.

Because the client code has no access to the implementation of a vector, it is not clear how we should traverse one. Of course, one possibility is to use a loop variable as an index into the vector:

```
for (int i=0; i<v.size(); i++) {
    System.out.println (v.get(i));
}
```

There's nothing wrong with that, but there is another way that serves to demonstrate the `Iterator` class. Vectors provide a method named `iterator` that returns an `Iterator` object that makes it possible to traverse the vector.

17.10   The `Iterator` class

`Iterator` is an interface in the `java.util` package. It specifies three methods:

`hasNext`: Does this iteration have more elements?

`next`: Return the next element, or throw an exception if there is none.

`remove`: Remove the most recent element from the data structure we are traversing.

The following example uses an iterator to traverse and print the elements of a vector.

```
Iterator it = vector.it ();
while (it.hasNext ()) {
    System.out.println (it.next ());
}
```

Once the Iterator is created, it is a separate object from the original Vector. Subsequent changes in the Vector are not reflected in the Iterator. In fact, if you modify the Vector after creating an Iterator, the Iterator becomes invalid. If you access the Iterator again, it will cause a ConcurrentModification exception.

In a previous section we used the Visitable metaclass to allow a client to traverse a data structure without knowing the details of its implementation. Iterators provide another way to do the same thing. In the first case, the provider performs the iteration and invokes client code to "visit" each element. In the second case the provider gives the client an object that it can use to select elements one at a time (albeit in an order controlled by the provider).

Exercise 17.2   Write a class named PreIterator that implements the Iterator interface, and write a method named preorderIterator for the Tree class that returns a PreIterator that selects the elements of the Tree in preorder.

HINT: The easiest way to build an Iterator is to put elements into a Vector in the order you want and then invoke iterator on the Vector.

17.11   Glossary

binary tree: A tree in which each node refers to 0, 1, or 2 dependent nodes.

root: The top-most node in a tree, to which no other nodes refer.

leaf: A bottom-most node in a tree, which refers to no other nodes.

parent: The node that refers to a given node.

child: One of the nodes referred to by a node.

level: A set of nodes equidistant from the root.

prefix notation: A way of writing a mathematical expression with each operator appearing before its operands.

preorder: A way to traverse a tree, visiting each node before its children.

postorder: A way to traverse a tree, visiting the children of each node before the node itself.

inorder: A way to traverse a tree, visiting the left subtree, then the root, then the right subtree.

class variable: A static variable declared outside of any method. It is accessible from any method.

binary operator: An operator that takes two operands.

object encapsulation: The design goal of keeping the implementations of two objects as separate as possible. Neither class should have to know the details of the implementation of the other.

method encapsulation: The design goal of keeping the interface of a method separate from the details of its implementation.

callback: A flow of execution where provider code invokes a method provided by the client.

17.12   Exercises

Exercise 17.3

   a. What is the value of the postfix expression 1 2 + 3 *?

   b. What is the postfix expression that is equivalent to the infix expression 1 + 2 * 3?

   c. What is the value of the postfix expression 17 1 - 5 /, assuming that / performs integer division?

Exercise 17.4   The height of a tree is the longest path from the root to any leaf. Height can be defined recursively as follows:

- The height of a null tree is 0.
- The height of a non-null tree is 1 + max (leftHeight, rightHeight), where leftHeight is the height of the left child and rightHeight is the height of the right child.

Write a method named `height` that calculates the height of the Tree provided as a parameter.

Exercise 17.5   Imagine we define a Tree that contains Comparable objects as cargo:

```
public class ComparableTree {
    Comparable cargo;
    Tree left, right;
}
```

Write a Tree class method named `findMax` that returns the largest cargo in the tree, where "largest" is defined by `compareTo`.

Exercise 17.6   A binary search tree is a special kind of tree where, for every node N:

all the cargo in the left subtree of N < the cargo in node N

and

the cargo in node N < all the cargo in the right subtree of N

Using the following class definition, write an object method called `contains` that takes an `Object` as an argument and that returns true if the object appears in the tree or false otherwise. You can assume that the target object and all the objects in the tree are `Comparable`.

```
public class SearchTree {
    Comparable cargo;
    SearchTree left, right;
}
```

Exercise 17.7   In mathematics, a **set** is a collection of elements that contains no duplicates. The interface `java.util.Set` is intended to model a mathematical set. The methods it requires are `add`, `contains`, `containsAll`, `remove`, `size`, and `iterator`.

Write a class called `TreeSet` that extends `SearchTree` and that implements `Set`. To keep things simple, you can assume that `null` does not appear in the tree or as an argument to any of the methods.

Exercise 17.8   Write a method called `union` that takes two Sets as parameters and returns a new `TreeSet` that contains all the elements that appear in either Set.

You can add this method to your implementation of `TreeSet`, or create a new class that extends `java.util.TreeSet` and provides `union`.

Exercise 17.9   Write a method called `intersection` that takes two Sets as parameters and returns a new `TreeSet` that contains all the elements that appear in both Sets.

`union` and `intersection` are generic in the sense that the parameters can be any type in the metaclass `Set`. The two parameters don't even have to be the same type.

Exercise 17.10   One of the reasons the `Comparable` interface is useful is that it allows an object type to specify whatever ordering is appropriate. For types like `Integer` and `Double`, the appropriate ordering is obvious, but there are lots of examples where the ordering depends on what the objects are supposed to represent. In golf, for example, a low score is better than a high score; if we compare two `Golfer` objects, the one with the lower score wins.

    a. Write a definition of a Golfer class that contains a name and an integer score as instance variables. The class should implement `Comparable` and provide a `compareTo` method that gives higher priority to the lower score.

    b. Write a program that reads a file containing the names and scores of a set of golfers. It should create Golfer objects, put them in a Priority Queue and then take them out and print them. They should appear in descending order of priority, which is increasing order by score.

```
Tiger Woods      61
Hal Sutton       69
Phil Mickelson   72
Allen Downey     158
```

HINT: See Section C for code that reads lines from a file.

Exercise 17.11   Write an implementation of a Stack using a Vector. Think about whether it is better to push new elements onto the beginning or the end of the Vector.

Chapter 18

Heap

18.1 Array implementation of a tree

What does it mean to "implement" a tree? So far we have only seen one implementation of a tree, a linked data structure similar to a linked list. But there are other structures we would like to identify as trees. Anything that can perform the basic set of tree operations should be recognized as a tree.

So what are the tree operations? In other words, how do we define the Tree ADT?

constructor: Build an empty tree.

getLeft: Return the left child of this node.

getRight: Return the left child of this node.

getParent: Return the parent of this node.

getCargo: Return the cargo object from this node.

setCargo: Assign a cargo object to this node (and create the node, if necessary).

In the linked implementation, the empty tree is represented by the special value null. getLeft and getRight are performed by accessing the instance variables of the node, as are getCargo and setCargo. We have not implemented getParent yet (you might think about how to do it).

There is another implementation of trees that uses arrays and indices instead of objects and references. To see how it works, we will start by looking at a hybrid implementation that uses both arrays and objects.

This figure shows a tree like the ones we have been looking at, although it is laid out at an angle. At the right there is an array of references that refer to the cargo in the nodes.

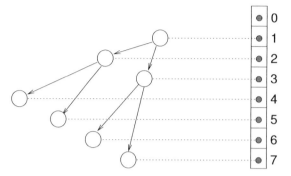

Each node in the tree has a unique index. Furthermore, the indices have been assigned to the nodes according to a deliberate pattern, in order to achieve the following results:

1. The left child of the node with index i has index $2i$.

2. The right child of the node with index i has index $2i + 1$.

3. The parent of the node with index i has index $i/2$ (rounded down).

Using these formulas, we can implement getLeft, getRight and getParent just by doing arithmetic; we don't have to use the references at all!

Since we don't use the references, we can get rid of them, which means that what used to be a tree node is now just cargo and nothing else. That means we can implement the tree as an array of cargo objects; we don't need tree nodes.

Here's what one implementation looks like:

```
public class ArrayTree {
    Object[] array;
    int size;

    public ArrayTree () {
        array = new Object [128];
    }
```

No surprises so far. The only instance variable is the array of Objects that contains the tree's cargo. The constructor initializes the array with an arbitrary initial capacity; the result is an empty tree.

Here is the simplest implementation of getCargo and setCargo.

```
    public Object getCargo (int i) {
        return array[i];
    }

    public void setCargo (int i, Object obj) {
        array[i] = obj;
    }
```

These methods don't do any error-checking, so if the parameter is wrong, they might generate an `ArrayIndexOutOfBounds` exception.

The implementation of `getLeft`, `getRight` and `getParent` is just arithmetic:

```
public int getLeft (int i)  { return 2*i; }
public int getRight (int i) { return 2*i + 1; }
public int parent (int i)   { return i/2; }
```

Finally we are ready to build a tree. In another class (the client), we would write

```
ArrayTree tree = new ArrayTree ();
tree.setCargo (1, "cargo for root");
```

The constructor builds an empty tree. Invoking `setCargo` puts the string `"cargo for root"` into the root node.

To add children to the root nodes:

```
tree.setCargo (tree.getLeft(1), "cargo for left");
tree.setCargo (tree.getRight(1), "cargo for right");
```

In the tree class we could provide a method that prints the contents of the tree in preorder.

```
public void print (int i) {
    Object cargo = tree.getCargo (i);
    if (cargo == null) return;
    System.out.println (cargo);
    print (getRight (i));
    print (getLeft (i));
}
```

To invoke this method, we have to pass the index of the root as a parameter.

```
tree.print (1);
```

The output is

```
cargo for root
cargo for left
cargo for right
```

This implementation provides the basic operations that define a tree. As I pointed out, the linked implementation of a tree provides the same operations, but the syntax is different.

In some ways, the array implementation is a bit awkward. For one thing, we assume that `null` cargo indicates a non-existent node, but that means that we can't put a `null` object in the tree as cargo.

Another problem is that subtrees aren't represented as objects; they are represented by indices into the array. To pass a tree node as a parameter, we have to pass a reference to the tree object and an index into the array. Finally, some operations that are easy in the linked implementation, like replacing an entire subtree, are harder in the array implementation.

On the other hand, this implementation saves space, since there are no links between the nodes, and there are several operations that are easier and faster in the array implementation. It turns out that these operations are just the ones we want to implement a Heap.

A Heap is an implementation of the Priority Queue ADT that is based on the array implementation of a Tree. It turns out to be more efficient than the other implementations we have seen.

To prove this claim, we will proceed in a few steps. First, we need to develop ways of comparing the performance of various implementations. Next, we will look at the operations Heaps perform. Finally, we will compare the Heap implementation of a Priority Queue to the others (arrays and lists) and see why the Heap is considered particularly efficient.

18.2   Performance analysis

When we compare algorithms, we would like to have a way to tell when one is faster than another, or takes less space, or uses less of some other resource. It is hard to answer those questions in detail, because the time and space used by an algorithm depend on the implementation of the algorithm, the particular problem being solved, and the hardware the program runs on.

The objective of this section is to develop a way of talking about performance that is independent of all of those things, and only depends on the algorithm itself. To start, we will focus on run time; later we will talk about other resources.

Our decisions are guided by a series of constraints:

1. First, the performance of an algorithm depends on the hardware it runs on, so we usually don't talk about run time in absolute terms like seconds. Instead, we usually count the number of abstract operations the algorithm performs.

2. Second, performance often depends on the particular problem we are trying to solve – some problems are easier than others. To compare algorithms, we usually focus on either the worst-case scenario or an average (or common) case.

3. Third, performance depends on the size of the problem (usually, but not always, the number of elements in a collection). We address this dependence explicitly by expressing run time as a function of problem size.

4. Finally, performance depends on details of the implementation like object allocation overhead and method invocation overhead. We usually ignore these details because they don't affect the rate at which the number of abstract operations increases with problem size.

To make this process more concrete, consider two algorithms we have already seen for sorting an array of integers. The first is **selection sort**, which we saw in Section 12.3. Here is the pseudocode we used there.

```
selectionsort (array) {
    for (int i=0; i<array.length; i++) {
        // find the lowest item at or to the right of i
        // swap the ith item and the lowest item
    }
}
```

To perform the operations specified in the pseudocode, we wrote helper methods named findLowest and swap. In pseudocode, findLowest looks like this

```
// find the index of the lowest item between
// i and the end of the array

findLowest (array, i) {
    // lowest contains the index of the lowest item so far
    lowest = i;
    for (int j=i+1; j<array.length; j++) {
        // compare the jth item to the lowest item so far
        // if the jth item is lower, replace lowest with j
    }
    return lowest;
}
```

And swap looks like this:

```
swap (i, j) {
    // store a reference to the ith card in temp
    // make the ith element of the array refer to the jth card
    // make the jth element of the array refer to temp
}
```

To analyze the performance of this algorithm, the first step is to decide what operations to count. Obviously, the program does a lot of things: it increments i, compares it to the length of the deck, it searches for the largest element of the array, etc. It is not obvious what the right thing is to count.

It turns out that a good choice is the number of times we compare two items. Many other choices would yield the same result in the end, but this is easy to do and we will find that it allows us to compare the sorting algorithms most easily.

The next step is to define the "problem size." In this case it is natural to choose the size of the array, which we'll call n.

Finally, we would like to derive an expression that tells us how many abstract operations (in this case, comparisons) we have to do, as a function of n.

We start by analyzing the helper methods. swap copies several references, but it doesn't perform any comparisons, so we ignore the time spent performing swaps. findLowest starts at i and traverses the array, comparing each item to lowest. The number of items we look at is $n - i$, so the total number of comparisons is $n - i - 1$.

Next we consider how many times findLowest gets invoked and what the value of i is each time. The last time it is invoked, i is $n - 2$ so the number of comparisons is 1. The previous iteration performs 2 comparisons, and so on. During the first iteration, i is 0 and the number of comparisons is $n - 1$.

So the total number of comparisons is $1 + 2 + \cdots + n - 1$. This sum is equal to $n^2/2 - n/2$. To describe this algorithm, we would typically ignore the lower order term $(n/2)$ and say that the total amount of work is proportional to n^2. Since the leading order term is quadratic, we might also say that this algorithm is **quadratic time**.

18.3   Analysis of mergesort

In Section 12.6 I claimed that mergesort takes time that is proportional to $n \log n$, but I didn't explain how or why. Now I will.

Again, we start by looking at pseudocode for the algorithm. For mergesort, it's

```
mergeSort (array) {
  // find the midpoint of the array
  // divide the array into two halves
  // sort the halves recursively
  // merge the two halves and return the result
}
```

At each level of the recursion, we split the array in half, make two recursive calls, and then merge the halves. Graphically, the process looks like this:

	# arrays	items per array	# merges	comparisons per merge	total work
	1	n	1	n–1	~n
	2	n/2	2	n/2–1	~n
⋮	⋮	⋮	⋮	⋮	⋮
	n/2	2	n/2	2–1	~n
	n	1	0	0	

Each line in the diagram is a level of the recursion. At the top, a single array divides into two halves. At the bottom, n arrays with one element each are merged into $n/2$ arrays with 2 elements each.

The first two columns of the table show the number of arrays at each level and the number of items in each array. The third column shows the number of merges that take place at each level of recursion. The next column is the one that takes the most thought: it shows the number of comparisons each merge performs.

If you look at the pseudocode (or your implementation) of merge, you should convince yourself that in the worst case it takes $m - 1$ comparisons, where m is the total number items being merged.

The next step is to multiply the number of merges at each level by the amount of work (comparisons) per merge. The result is the total work at each level. At this point we take advantage of a small trick. We know that in the end we are only interested in the leading-order term in the result, so we can go ahead and ignore the -1 term in the comparisons per merge. If we do that, then the total work at each level is simply n.

Next we need to know the number of levels as a function of n. Well, we start with an array of n items and divide it in half until it gets to 1. That's the same as starting at 1 and multiplying by 2 until we get to n. In other words, we want to know how many times we have to multiply 2 by itself before we get to n. The answer is that the number of levels, l, is the logarithm, base 2, of n.

Finally, we multiply the amount of work per level, n, by the number of levels, $\log_2 n$ to get $n \log_2 n$, as promised. There isn't a good name for this functional form; most of the time people just say, "en log en."

It might not be obvious at first that $n \log_2 n$ is better than n^2, but for large values of n, it is. As an exercise, write a program that prints $n \log_2 n$ and n^2 for a range of values of n.

18.4   Overhead

Performance analysis takes a lot of handwaving. First we ignored most of the operations the program performs and counted only comparisons. Then we decided to consider only worst case performance. During the analysis we took the liberty of rounding a few things off, and when we finished, we casually discarded the lower-order terms.

When we interpret the results of this analysis, we have to keep all this handwaving in mind. Because mergesort is $n \log_2 n$, we consider it a better algorithm than selection sort, but that doesn't mean that mergesort is *always* faster. It just means that eventually, if we sort bigger and bigger arrays, mergesort will win.

How long that takes depends on the details of the implementation, including the additional work, besides the comparisons we counted, that each algorithm performs. This extra work is sometimes called **overhead**. It doesn't affect the performance analysis, but it does affect the run time of the algorithm.

For example, our implementation of mergesort actually allocates subarrays before making the recursive calls and then lets them get garbage collected after they are merged. Looking again at the diagram of mergesort, we can see that the total amount of space that gets allocated is proportional to $n \log_2 n$, and the total number of objects that get allocated is about $2n$. All that allocating takes time.

Even so, it is most often true that a bad implementation of a good algorithm is better than a good implementation of a bad algorithm. The reason is that for large values of n the good algorithm is better and for small values of n it doesn't matter because both algorithms are good enough.

As an exercise, write a program that prints values of $1000n \log_2 n$ and n^2 for a range of values of n. For what value of n are they equal?

18.5   Priority Queue implementations

In Chapter 16 we looked at an implementation of a Priority Queue based on an array. The items in the array are unsorted, so it is easy to add a new item (at the end), but harder to remove an item, because we have to search for the item with the highest priority.

An alternative is an implementation based on a sorted list. In this case when we add a new item we traverse the list and put the new item in the right spot. This implementation takes advantage of a property of lists, which is that it is easy to add a new node into the middle. Similarly, removing the item with the highest priority is easy, provided that we keep it at the beginning of the list.

Performance analysis of these operations is straightforward. Adding an item to the end of an array or removing a node from the beginning of a list takes the same amount of time regardless of the number of items. So both operations are constant time.

Any time we traverse an array or list, performing a constant-time operation on each element, the run time is proportional to the number of items. Thus, removing something from the array and adding something to the list are both linear time.

So how long does it take to add and then remove n items from a Priority Queue? For the array implementation, n adds takes time proportional to n, but the removals take longer. The first removal has to traverse all n items; the second has to traverse $n - 1$, and so on, until the last removal, which only has to look at 1 item. Thus, the total time is $1 + 2 + \cdots + n$, which is $n^2/2 + n/2$. So the total for the adds and the removals is the sum of a linear function and a quadratic function, which we would characterize as quadratic.

The analysis of the list implementation is similar. The first add doesn't require any traversal, but after that we have to traverse at least part of the list each time we add a new item. In general we don't know how much of the list we will have to traverse, since it depends on the data and what order they are added, but we can assume that on average we have to traverse half of the list. Unfortunately, even traversing half of the list is a linear operation.

So, once again, to add and remove n items takes time proportional to n^2. Thus, based on this analysis we cannot say which implementation is better; the array and list are both quadratic time implementations.

If we implement a Priority Queue using a heap, we can perform both adds and removals in time proportional to $logn$. Thus the total time for n items is $n \log n$, which is better than n^2. That's why, at the beginning of the chapter, I said that a heap is a particularly efficient implementation of a Priority Queue.

18.6   Definition of a Heap

A heap is a special kind of tree. It has two properties that are not generally true for other trees:

completeness: The tree is complete, which means that nodes are added from top to bottom, left to right, without leaving any spaces.

heapness: The item in the tree with the highest priority is at the top of the tree, and the same is true for every subtree.

Both of these properties call for a little explaining. This figure shows a number of trees that are considered complete or not complete:

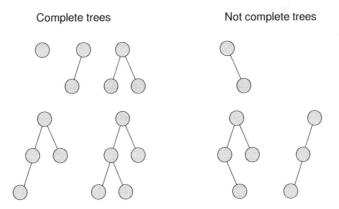

An empty tree is also considered complete. We can define completeness more rigorously by comparing the height of the subtrees. Recall that the **height** of a tree is the number of levels.

Starting at the root, if the tree is complete, then the height of the left subtree and the height of the right subtree should be equal, or the left subtree may be taller by one. In any other case, the tree cannot be complete. Furthermore, if the tree is complete, then the height relationship between the subtrees has to be true for every node in the tree.

The **heap property** is similarly recursive. In order for a tree to be a heap, the largest value in the tree has to be at the root, *and* the same has to be true for each subtree. As another exercise, write a method that checks whether a tree has the heap property.

Exercise 18.1   Write a method that takes a Tree as a parameter and checks whether it is complete.

HINT: You can use the `height` method from Exercise 17.4.

Exercise 18.2   Write a method that takes a Tree as a parameter and checks whether it has the heap property.

18.7   Heap `remove`

It might seem odd that we are going to remove things from the heap before we add any, but I think removal is easier to explain.

At first glance, we might think that removing an item from the heap is a constant time operation, since the item with the highest priority is always at the root. The problem is that once we remove the root node, we are left with something that is no longer a heap. Before we can return the result, we have to restore the heap property. We call this operation `reheapify`.

The situation is shown in the following figure:

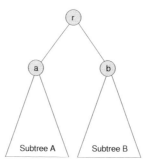

The root node has priority r and two subtrees, A and B. The value at the root of Subtree A is a and the value at the root of Subtree B is b.

We assume that before we remove r from the tree, the tree is a heap. That implies that r is the largest value in the heap and that a and b are the largest values in their respective subtrees.

Once we remove r, we have to make the resulting tree a heap again. In other words we need to make sure it has the properties of completeness and heapness.

The best way to ensure completeness is to remove the bottom-most, right-most node, which we'll call c and put its value at the root. In a general tree implementation, we would have to traverse the tree to find this node, but in the array implementation, we can find it in constant time because it is always the last (non-null) element of the array.

Of course, the chances are that the last value is not the highest, so putting it at the root breaks the heapness property. Fortunately it is easy to restore. We know that the largest value in the heap is either a or b. Therefore we can select whichever is larger and swap it with the value at the root.

Arbitrarily, let's say that b is larger. Since we know it is the highest value left in the heap, we can put it at the root and put c at the top of Subtree B. Now the situation looks like this:

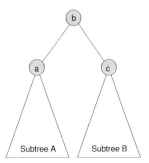

Again, c is the value we copied from the last element in the array and b is the highest value left in the heap. Since we haven't changed Subtree A at all, we know that it is still a heap. The only problem is that we don't know if Subtree B is a heap, since we just stuck a (probably low) value at its root.

Wouldn't it be nice if we had a method that could reheapify Subtree B? Wait... we do!

18.8   Heap add

Adding a new item in a heap is a similar operation, except that instead of trickling a value down from the top, we trickle it up from the bottom.

Again, to guarantee completeness, we add the new element at the bottom-most, rightmost position in the tree, which is the next available space in the array.

Then to restore the heap property, we compare the new value with its neighbors. The situation looks like this:

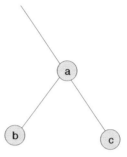

The new value is c. We can restore the heap property of this subtree by comparing c to a. If c is smaller, then the heap property is satisfied. If c is larger, then we swap c and a. The swap satisfies the heap property because we know that c must also be bigger than b, because c > a and a > b.

Now that the subtree is reheapified, we can work our way up the tree until we reach the root.

18.9   Performance of heaps

For both add and remove, we perform a constant time operation to do the actual addion and removal, but then we have to reheapify the tree. In one case we start at the root and work our way down, comparing items and then recursively reheapifying one of the subtrees. In the other case we start at a leaf and work our way up, again comparing elements at each level of the tree.

As usual, there are several operations we might want to count, like comparisons and swaps. Either choice would work; the real issue is the number of levels of the tree we examine and how much work we do at each level. In both cases we keep examining levels of the tree until we restore the heap property, which means we might only visit one, or in the worst case we might have to visit them all. Let's consider the worst case.

At each level, we perform only constant time operations like comparisons and swaps. So the total amount of work is proportional to the number of levels in the tree, a.k.a. the height.

So we might say that these operations are linear with respect to the height of the tree, but the "problem size" we are interested in is not height, it's the number of items in the heap.

As a function of n, the height of the tree is $log_2 n$. This is not true for all trees, but it is true for complete trees. To see why, think of the number of nodes on each level of the tree. The first level contains 1, the second contains 2, the third contains 4, and so on. The ith level contains 2^i nodes, and the total number in all levels up to i is $2^i - 1$. In other words, $2^h = n$, which means that $h = log_2 n$.

Thus, both add and remove take **logarithmic** time. To add and remove n items takes time proportional to $n \log_2 n$.

18.10   Heapsort

The result of the previous section suggests yet another algorithm for sorting. Given n items, we add them into a Heap and then remove them. Because of the Heap semantics, they come out in order. We have already shown that this algorithm, which is called **heapsort**, takes time proportional to $n \log_2 n$, which is better than selection sort and the same as mergesort.

As the value of n gets large, we expect heapsort to be faster than selection sort, but performance analysis gives us no way to know whether it will be faster than mergesort. We would say that the two algorithms have the same **order of growth** because their runtimes grow with the same functional form. Another way to say the same thing is that they belong to the same **complexity class**.

Complexity classes are sometimes written in "big-O notation". For example, $\mathcal{O}(n^2)$, pronounced "oh of en squared" is the set of all functions that grow no faster than n^2 for large values of n. To say that an algorithm is $\mathcal{O}(n^2)$ is the same as saying that it is quadratic. The other complexity classes we have seen, in decreasing order of performance, are:

$\mathcal{O}(1)$	constant time
$\mathcal{O}(\log n)$	logarithmic
$\mathcal{O}(n)$	linear
$\mathcal{O}(n \log n)$	"en log en"
$\mathcal{O}(n^2)$	quadratic
$\mathcal{O}(2^n)$	exponential

So far none of the algorithms we have looked at are **exponential**. For large values of n, these algorithms quickly become impractical. Nevertheless, the phrase "exponential growth" appears frequently in even non-technical language. It is frequently misused so I wanted to include its technical meaning.

People often use "exponential" to describe any curve that is increasing and accelerating (that is, one that has positive slope and curvature). Of course, there are many other curves that fit this description, including quadratic functions (and higher-order polynomials) and even functions as undramatic as $n \log n$. Most of these curves do not have the (often detrimental) explosive behavior of exponentials.

18.11   Glossary

selection sort: The simple sorting algorithm in Section 12.3.

mergesort: A better sorting algorithm from Section 12.6.

heapsort: Yet another sorting algorithm.

complexity class: A set of algorithms whose performance (usually run time) has the same order of growth.

order of growth: A set of functions with the same leading-order term, and therefore the same qualitative behavior for large values of n.

overhead: Additional time or resources consumed by a program performing operations other than the abstract operations considered in performance analysis.

18.12   Exercises

Exercise 18.3

a. Draw the Heap represented by the following array.

b. Show what the array would look like after the value 68 is added to the Heap.

Exercise 18.4   Assume that there are n elements in a Heap. To find the median value of the elements, we could remove $n/2 - 1$ elements and then return the value of the $n/2$-eth element. Then we would have to put $n/2$ elements back into the Heap. What would be the order of growth of this algorithm?

Exercise 18.5   How many times will the following loop execute? Express your answer as a function of n:

```
while (n > 1) {
    n = n / 2;
}
```

Exercise 18.6   How many recursive calls will zippo make? Express your answer as a function of x or n or both.

```
public static double zippo (double x, int n) {
    if (n == 0) return 1.0;
    return x * zippo (x, n-1);
}
```

Exercise 18.7   Write an implementation of a Heap based on the array implementation of a tree. The run time of the add and remove operations should be proportional to $\log n$, where n is the number of elements in the Heap.

Chapter 19

Maps

19.1 Arrays, Vectors and Maps

Arrays are a generally useful data structure, but they suffer from two important limitations:

- The size of the array does not depend on the number of items in it. If the array is too big, it wastes space. If it is too small it might cause an error, or we might have to write code to resize it.

- Although the array can contain any type of item, the indices of the array have to be integers. We cannot, for example, use a String to specify an element of an array.

In Section 17.9 we saw how the built-in `Vector` class solves the first problem. As the client code adds items the Vector expands automatically. It is also possible to shrink a Vector so that the capacity is the same as the current size.

But `Vectors` don't help with the second problem. The indices are still integers. That's where the Map ADT comes in. A Map is similar to a Vector; the difference is that it can use any object type as an index. These generalized indices are called **keys**.

Just as you use an index to access a value in a Vector, you use a key to access a value in a Map. Each key is associated with a value, which is why Maps are sometimes called **associative arrays**. The association of a particular key with a particular value is called an **entry**.

A common example of a map is a dictionary, which maps words (the keys) onto their definitions (the values). Because of this example Maps are also sometimes called Dictionaries. And, just for completeness, Maps are also sometimes called Tables.

19.2   The Map ADT

Like the other ADTs we have looked at, Maps are defined by the set of operations they support:

constructor: Make a new, empty map.

put: Create an entry that associates a value with a key.

get: For a given key, find the corresponding value.

containsKey: Return true if there is an entry in the Map with the given Key.

keySet : Returns a Set that contains all the keys in the Map.

19.3   The built-in HashMap

Java provides an implementation of the Map ADT called java.util.HashMap. Later in the chapter we'll see why it is called HashMap.

To demonstrate the use of a HashMap we'll write a short program that traverses a String and counts the number of times each word appears.

We'll create a new class called WordCount that will build the Map and then print its contents. Each WordCount object contains a HashMap as an instance variable:

```
public class WordCount {
    HashMap map;

    public WordCount () {
        map = new HashMap ();
    }
}
```

The only public methods for WordCount are processLine, which takes a String and adds its words to the Map, and print, which prints the results at the end.

processLine breaks the String into words using a StringTokenizer and passes each word to processWord.

```
    public void processLine (String s) {
        StringTokenizer st = new StringTokenizer (s, " ,.");
        while (st.hasMoreTokens()) {
            String word = st.nextToken();
            processWord (word.toLowerCase ());
        }
    }
```

The interesting work is in processWord.

```
    public void processWord (String word) {
        if (map.containsKey (word)) {
            Integer i = (Integer) map.get (word);
            Integer j = new Integer (i.intValue() + 1);
            map.put (word, j);
        } else {
            map.put (word, new Integer (1));
        }
    }
```

If the word is already in the map, we get its counter, increment it, and put the new value. Otherwise, we just put a new entry in the map with the counter set to 1.

To print the entries in the map, we need to be able to traverse the keys in the map. Fortunately, HashMap provides a method, keySet, that returns a Set object, and Set provides a method iterator that returns (you guessed it) an Iterator.

Here's how to use keySet to print the contents of the HashMap:

```
public void print () {
    Set set = map.keySet();
    Iterator it = set.iterator();
    while (it.hasNext ()) {
        String key = (String) it.next ();
        Integer value = (Integer) map.get (key);
        System.out.println ("{ " + key + ", " + value + " }");
    }
}
```

Each of the elements of the Iterator is an Object, but since we know they are keys, we typecast them to be Strings. When we get the values from the Map, they are also Objects, but we know they are counters, so we typecast them to be Integers.

Finally, to count the words in a string:

```
        WordCount wc = new WordCount ();
        wc.processLine ("you spin me right round baby " +
                        "right round like a record baby " +
                        "right round round round");
        wc.print ();
```

The output is

```
{ you, 1 }
{ round, 5 }
{ right, 3 }
{ me, 1 }
{ like, 1 }
{ baby, 2 }
{ spin, 1 }
```

```
{ record, 1 }
{ a, 1 }
```

The elements of the Iterator are not in any particular order. The only guarantee is that all the keys in the map will appear.

19.4   A Vector implementation

An easy way to implement the Map ADT is to use a `Vector` of entries, where each Entry is an object that contains a key and a value. A class definition for Entry might look like this:

```
class Entry {
    Object key, value;

    public Entry (Object key, Object value) {
        this.key = key;
        this.value = value;
    }

    public String toString () {
        return "{ " + key + ", " + value + " }";
    }
}
```

Then the implementation of Map looks like this:

```
public class MyMap {
    Vector entries;

    public Map () {
        entries = new Vector ();
    }
}
```

To put a new entry in the map, we just add a new `Entry` to the `Vector`:

```
    public void put (Object key, Object value) {
        entries.add (new Entry (key, value));
    }
```

Then to look up a key in the Map we have to traverse the Vector and find an Entry with a matching key:

```
    public Object get (Object key) {
        Iterator it = entries.iterator ();
        while (it.hasNext ()) {
            Entry entry = (Entry) it.next ();
            if (key.equals (entry.key)) {
                return entry.value;
            }
        }
```

```
        return null;
    }
```

The idiom to traverse a `Vector` is the one we saw in Section 17.10. When we compare keys, we use deep equality (the `equals` method) rather than shallow equality (the `==` operator). This allows the key class to specify the definition of equality. In the example, the keys are Strings, so `get` will use the `equals` method in the `String` class.

For most of the built-in classes, the `equals` method implements deep equality. For some classes, though, it is not easy to define what that means. For example, see the documentation of `equals` for `Doubles`.

Because `equals` is an object method, this implementation of `get` does not work if a key is `null`. In order to handle `null` keys, we would have to add a special case to `get` or write a class method that compares keys and handles `null` parameters safely. But we will skip this detail.

Now that we have `get`, we can write a version of `put` that is more complete. If there is already an entry in the map with the given key, `put` is supposed to update it (give it a new value), and return the old value (or `null` if there was none). Here is an implementation that provides this feature:

```
public Object put (Object key, Object value) {
    Object result = get (key);
    if (result == null) {
        Entry entry = new Entry (key, value);
        entries.add (entry);
    } else {
        update (key, value);
    }
    return result;
}

private void update (Object key, Object value) {
    Iterator it = entries.iterator ();
    while (it.hasNext ()) {
        Entry entry = (Entry) it.next ();
        if (key.equals (entry.key)) {
            entry.value = value;
            break;
        }
    }
}
```

The `update` method is not part of the Map ADT, so it is declared `private`. It traverses the vector until it finds the right `Entry` and then it updates the `value` field. Notice that we don't modify the `Vector` itself, just one of the objects it contains.

The only methods we haven't implemented are `containsKey` and `keySet`. The `containsKey` method is almost identical to `get` except that it returns `true` or false instead of an object reference or null.

Exercise 19.1   Implement keySet by building and returning a TreeSet object. Use your implementation of TreeSet from Exercise 17.7 or the built-in implementation java.util.TreeSet.

19.5   The List metaclass

The java.util package defines a metaclass called List that specifies the set of operations a class has to implement in order to be considered (very abstractly) a list. This does not mean, of course, that every class that implements List has to be a linked list.

Not surprisingly, the built-in LinkedList class is a member of the List metaclass. Surprisingly, so is Vector.

The methods in the List definition include add, get and iterator. In fact, all the methods from the Vector class that we used to implement Map are defined in the List metaclass. That means that instead of a Vector, we could have used any List class. In our implementation of Map we can replace Vector with LinkedList, and the program still works!

This kind of type generality can be useful for tuning the performance of a program. You can write the program in terms of a metaclass like List and then test the program with several different implementations to see which yields the best performance.

19.6   HashMap implementation

The reason that the built-in implementation of the Map ADT is called HashMap is that it uses a particularly efficient implementation of a Map called a hash table.

In order to understand the hash table implementation, and why it is considered efficient, we'll start by analyzing the performance of the List implementation.

Looking at the implementation of put, we see that there are two cases. If the key is not already in the map, then we only have to create a new entry and add it to the List. Both of these are constant-time operations.

In the other case, we have to traverse the List to find the existing entry. That's a linear time operation. For the same reason, get and containsKey are also linear.

Although linear operations are often good enough, we can do better. It turns out that there is a way to implement the Map ADT so that both put and get are constant time operations!

The key is to realize that traversing a list takes time proportional to the length of the list. If we can put an upper bound on the length of the list, then we can put an upper bound on the traverse time, and anything with a fixed upper bound is considered constant time.

But how can we limit the length of the lists without limiting the number of items in the map? By increasing the number of lists. Instead of one long list, we'll keep many short lists.

As long as we know which list to search, we can put a bound on the amount of searching.

19.7 Hash Functions

And that's where hash functions come in. We need some way to look at a key and know, without searching, which list it will be in. We'll assume that the lists are in an array (or `Vector`) so we can refer to them by index.

The solution is to come up with some mapping—almost any mapping—between the key values and the indices of the lists. For every possible key there has to be a single index, but there might be many keys that map to the same index.

For example, imagine an array of 8 Lists and a map made up of keys that are `Integers` and values that are `Strings`. It might be tempting to use the `intValue` of the `Integers` as indices, since they are the right type, but there are a whole lot of integers that do not fall between 0 and 7, which are the only legal indices.

The modulus operator provides a simple (in terms of code) and efficient (in terms of run time) way to map *all* the integers into the range $(0, 7)$. The expression

```
key.intValue() % 8
```

is guaranteed to produce a value in the range from -7 to 7 (including both). If you take its absolute value (using `Math.abs`) you will get a legal index.

For other types, we can play similar games. For example, to convert a `Character` to an integer, we can use the built-in method `Character.getNumericValue` and for `Doubles` there is `intValue`.

For `Strings` we could get the numeric value of each character and add them up, or instead we might use a **shifted sum**. To calculate a shifted sum, you alternate between adding new values to the accumulator and shifting the accumulator to the left. By "shift to the left" I mean "multiply by a constant."

To see how this works, take the list of numbers $1, 2, 3, 4, 5, 6$ and compute their shifted sum as follows. First, initialize the accumulator to 0. Then,

1. Multiply the accumulator by 10.

2. Add the next element of the list to the accumulator.

3. Repeat until the list is finished.

As an exercise, write a method that calculates the shifted sum of the numeric values of the characters in a `String` using a multiplier of 16.

For each type, we can come up with a function that takes values of that type and generates a corresponding integer value. These functions are called **hash functions**, because they often involve making a hash of the components of the object. The integer value for each object is called its **hash code**.

There is one other way we might generate a hash code for Java objects. Every Java object provides a method called `hashCode` that returns an integer that corresponds to that object. For the built-in types, the `hashCode` method is implemented so that if two objects contain the same data (deep equality), they will have the same hash code. The documentation of these methods explains what the hash function is. You should check them out.

For user-defined types, it is up to the implementor to provide an appropriate hash function. The default hash function, provided in the `Object` class, often uses the location of the object to generate a hash code, so its notion of "sameness" is shallow equality. Most often when we are searching a Map for a key, shallow equality is not what we want.

Regardless of how the hash code is generated, the last step is to use modulus and absolute value functions to map the hash code into the range of legal indices.

19.8   Resizing a hash map

Let's review. A hash table consists of an array (or Vector) of `Lists`, where each `List` contains a small number of entries. To add a new entry to a map, we calculate the hash code of the new key and add the entry to the corresponding `List`.

To look up a key, we hash it again and search the corresponding list. If the lengths of the lists are bounded then the search time is bounded.

So how do we keep the lists short? Well, one goal is to keep them as balanced as possible, so that there are no very long lists at the same time that others are empty. This is not easy to do perfectly—it depends on how well we chose the hash function—but we can usually do a pretty good job.

Even with perfect balance, the average list length grows linearly with the number of entries, and we have to put a stop to that.

The solution is to keep track of the average number of entries per list, which is called the **load factor**; if the load factor gets too high, we have to resize the hash table.

To resize, we create a new hash table, usually twice as big as the original, take all the entries out of the old one, hash them again, and put them in the new hash table. Usually we can get away with using the same hash function; we just use a different value for the modulus operator.

19.9   Performance of resizing

How long does it take to resize the hash table? Clearly it is linear with the number of entries. That means that *most* of the time put takes constant time, but every once in a while —when we resize—it takes linear time.

At first that sounds bad. Doesn't that undermine my claim that we can perform put in constant time? Well, frankly, yes. But with a little wheedling, we can fix it.

Since some put operations take longer than others, let's figure out the *average* time for a put operation. The average is going to be c, the constant time for a simple put, plus an additional term of p, the percentage of the time I have to resize, times kn, the cost of resizing.

$$t(n) = c + p \cdot kn \tag{19.1}$$

We don't know what c and k are, but we can figure out what p is. Imagine that we have just resized the hash map by doubling its size. If there are n entries, then we can add an addition n entries before we have to resize again. So the percentage of the time we have to resize is $1/n$.

Plugging into the equation, we get

$$t(n) = c + 1/n \cdot kn = c + k \tag{19.2}$$

In other words, $t(n)$ is constant time!

19.10   Glossary

map: An ADT that defines operations on a collection of entries.

entry: An element in a map that contains a key and a value.

key: An index, of any type, used to look up values in a map.

value: An element, of any type, stored in a map.

dictionary: Another name for a map.

associative array: Another name for a dictionary.

hash map: A particularly efficient implementation of a map.

hash function: A function that maps values of a certain type onto integers.

hash code: The integer value that corresponds to a given value.

shifted sum: A simple hash function often used for compounds objects like Strings.

load factor: The number of entries in a hashmap divided by the number of lists in the hashmap; i.e. the average number of entries per list.

19.11   Exercises

Exercise 19.2

  a. Compute the shifted sum of the numbers 1, 2, 3, 4, 5, 6 using a multiplier of 10.

  b. Compute the shifted sum of the numbers 11, 12, 13, 14, 15, 16 using a multiplier of 100.

  c. Compute the shifted sum of the numbers 11, 12, 13, 14, 15, 16 using a multiplier of 10.

Exercise 19.3   Imagine you have a hash table that contains 100 lists. If you are asked to get the value associated with a certain key, and the hash code for that key is 654321, what is the index of the list where the key will be (if it is in the map)?

Exercise 19.4   If there are 100 lists and there are 89 entries in the map and the longest list contains 3 entries, and the median list length is 1 and 19% of the lists are empty, what is the load factor?

Exercise 19.5   Imagine that there are a large number of people at a party. You would like to know whether any two of them have the same birthday. First, you design a new kind of Java object that represents birthdays with two instance variables: month, which is an integer between 1 and 12, and day, which is an integer between 1 and 31.

Next, you create an array of Birthday objects that contains one object for each person at the party, and you get someone to help type in all the birthdays.

  a. Write an equals method for Birthday so that Birthdays with the same month and day are equal.

  b. Write a method called hasDuplicate that takes an array of Birthdays and returns true if there are two or more people with the same birthday. Your algorithm should only traverse the array of Birthdays once.

  c. Write a method called randomBirthdays that takes an integer n and returns an array with n random Birthday objects. To keep things simple, you can pretend that all months have 30 days.

  d. Generate 100 random arrays of 10 Birthdays each, and see how many of them contain duplicates.

  e. If there are 20 people at a party, what is the probability that two or more of them have the same birthday?

Exercise 19.6   A Map is said to be **invertible** if each key and each value appears only once. In a HashMap, it is always true that each key appears only once, but it is possible for the same value to appear many times. Therefore, some HashMaps are invertible and some are not.

Write a method called isInvertible that takes a HashMap and returns true if the map is invertible and false otherwise.

Exercise 19.7

The goal of this exercise is to find the 20 most common words in this book. Type in the code from the book that uses the built-in HashMap to count word frequencies. Download the text of the book from http://thinkapjava.com/thinkapjava.txt.

The plain text version of the book is generated automatically by a program called detex that tries to strip out all the typesetting commands, but it leaves behind assorted junk. Think about how your program should handle punctuation and any other wierdness that appears in the file.

Write programs to answer the following questions:

a. How many words are there in the book?

b. How many *different* words are there in the book? For purposes of comparison, there are (very roughly) 500,000 words in English, of which (very roughly) 50,000 are in current use. What percentage of this vast lexicon did I find fit to use?

c. How many times does the word "encapsulation" appear?

d. What are the 20 most common words in the book? HINT: there is another data structure that might help with this part of the exercise.

Exercise 19.8   Write a method for the LinkedList class that checks whether the list contains a loop. You should not assume that the length field is correct. Your method should be linear in the number of nodes.

Exercise 19.9   Write a hash table implementation of the Map ADT (as defined in Section 19.2). Test it by using it with any of the programs you have written so far. Hints:

a. Start with the Vector implementation in the book and make sure it works with existing programs.

b. Modify the implementation to use either an array of LinkedLists or a Vector of LinkedLists, whichever you prefer.

Exercise 19.10   Write an implementation of the Set interface using a HashMap.

Exercise 19.11

The java.util package provides two implementations of the Map interface, called HashMap and TreeMap. HashMap is based on a hash table like the one described in this chapter. TreeMap is based on a red-black tree, which is similar to the search tree in Exercise 17.6.

Although these implementations provide the same interface, we expect them to achieve different performance. As the number of entries, n, increases, we expect add and contains to take constant time for the hash table implementation, and logarithmic time for the tree implementation.

Perform an experiment to confirm (or refute!) these performance predictions. Write a program that adds n entries to a HashMap or TreeMap, then invokes contains on each of the keys. Record the runtime of the program for a range of values of n and make a plot of runtime versus n. Is the performance behavior in line with our expectations.

Chapter 20

Huffman code

20.1 Variable-length codes

If you are familiar with Morse code, you know that it is a system for encoding the letters of the alphabet as a series of dots and dashes. For example, the famous signal ...---... represents the letters SOS, which comprise an internationally-recognized call for help. This table shows the rest of the codes:

A	.-	N	-.	1	.----	.	.-.-.-
B	-...	O	---	2	..---	,	--..--
C	-.-.	P	.--.	3	...--	?	..--..
D	-..	Q	--.-	4	....-	(	-.--.
E	.	R	.-.	5	.....	)	-.--.-
F	..-.	S	...	6	-....	-	-....-
G	--.	T	-	7	--...	"	.-..-.
H	....	U	..-	8	---..	_	..--.-
I	..	V	...-	9	----.	'	.----.
J	.---	W	.--	0	-----	:	---...
K	-.-	X	-..-	/	-..-.	;	-.-.-.
L	.-..	Y	-.--	+	.-.-.	$	...-..-
M	--	Z	--..	=	-...-		

Notice that some codes are longer than others. By design, the most common letters have the shortest codes. Since there are a limited number of short codes, that means that less common letters and symbols have longer codes. A typical message will have more short codes than long ones, which minimizes the average transmission time per letter.

Codes like this are called variable-length codes. In this chapter, we will look at an algorithm for generating a variable-length code called a **Huffman code**. It is an interesting algorithm in its own right, but it also makes a useful exercise because its implementation uses many of the data structures we have been studying.

Here is an outline of the next few sections:

- First, we will use a sample of English text to generate a frequency table. A frequency table is like a histogram; it counts the number of times each letter appears in the sample text.

- The heart of a Huffman code is the Huffman tree. We will use the frequency table to build the Huffman tree, and then use the tree to encode and decode sequences.

- Finally, we will traverse the Huffman tree and built a code table, which contains the sequence of dots and dashes for each letter.

20.2   The frequency table

Since the goal is to give short codes to common letters, we have to know how often each letter occurs. In Edgar Allen Poe's short story "The Gold Bug," one of the characters uses letter frequencies to crack a cypher. He explains,

> "Now, in English, the letter which most frequently occurs is e. Afterwards, the succession runs thus: a o i d h n r s t u y c f g l m w b k p q x z. E however predominates so remarkably that an individual sentence of any length is rarely seen, in which it is not the prevailing character."

So our first mission is to see whether Poe got it right. To check, I chose as my sample the text of "The Gold Bug" itself, which I downloaded from one of the Web sites that take advantage of its entry into the public domain.

Exercise 20.12   Write a class called `FreqTab` that counts the number of times each letter appears in a sample text. Download the text of your favorite public-domain short story, and analyse the frequency of the letters.

I found it most convenient to make `FreqTab` extend `HashMap`. Then I wrote a method called `increment` that takes a letter as a parameter and either adds or updates an entry in the HashMap for each letter.

You can use `keySet` to get the entries from the HashMap, and print a list of letters with their frequencies. Unfortunately, they will not appear in any particular order. The next exercise solves that problem.

Exercise 20.13   Write a class called `Pair` that represents a letter-frequency pair. Pair objects should contain a letter and a frequency as instance variables. `Pair` should implement `Comparable`, where the Pair with the higher frequency wins.

Now sort the letter-frequency pairs from the HashMap by traversing the set of keys, building `Pair` objects, adding the Pairs to a PriorityQueue, removing the Pairs from the PriorityQueue, and printing them in descending order by frequency.

How good was Poe's guess about the most frequent letters?

20.3   The Huffman Tree

The next step is to assemble the Huffman tree. Each node of the tree contains a letter and its frequency, and pointers to the left and right nodes.

To assemble the Huffman tree, we start by creating a set of singleton trees, one for each entry in the frequency table. Then we build the tree from the bottom up, starting with the least-frequent letters and iteratively joining subtrees until we have a single tree that contains all the letters.

Here is the algorithm in more detail.

1. For each entry in the frequency table, create a singleton Huffman tree and add it to a PriorityQueue. When we remove a tree from the PriorityQueue, we get the one with the lowest frequency.

2. Remove two trees from the PriorityQueue and join them by creating a new parent node that refers to the removed nodes. The frequency of the parent node is the sum of the frequencies of the children.

3. If the PriorityQueue is empty, we are done. Otherwise, put the new tree into the PriorityQueue and go to Step 2.

An example will make this clearer. To keep things managable, we will use a sample text that only contains the letters adenrst:

> Eastern Tennessee anteaters ensnare and eat red ants, detest ant antennae (a tart taste) and dread Antarean anteater-eaters. Rare Andean deer eat tender sea reeds, aster seeds and rats' ears. Dessert? Rats' asses.

This eloquent treatise on the eating habits of various fauna yields the following frequency table:

e	40
a	32
t	24
s	22
n	20
r	19
d	13

So after Step 1, the PriorityQueue looks like this:

In Step 2, we remove the two trees with the lowest frequency (r and d) and join them by creating a parent node with frequency 32. The letter value for the internal nodes is irrelevant, so it is omitted from the figures. When we put the new tree back in the PriorityQueue, the result looks like this:

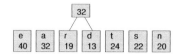

Now we repeat the process, combining s and n:

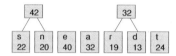

After the next interation, we have the following collection of trees. By the way, a collection of trees is called a **forest**.

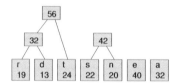

After two more iterations, there is only one tree left:

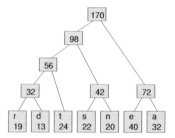

This is the Huffman tree for the sample text. Actually, it is not the only one, because each time we join two trees, we choose arbitrarily which goes on the left and which on the right, and when there is a tie in the PriorityQueue, the choice is arbitrary. So there may be many possible trees for a given sample.

So how to we get a code from the Huffman tree? The code for each letter is determined by the path from the root of the tree to the leaf that contains the letter. For example, the path from the root to s is left-right-left. If we represent a left with . and a right with – (another arbitrary choice) we get the following code table.

```
e        -.
a        --
t        ..-
s        .-.
n        .--
r        ....
d        ...-
```

Notice that we have achieved the goal: the most frequent letters have the shortest codes.

Exercise 20.14   By hand, figure out a Huffman tree for the following frequency table:

e	93
s	71
r	57
t	53
n	49
i	44
d	43
o	37

20.4   The super method

One way to implement `HuffTree` is to extend `Pair` from Exercise 20.13.

```
public class HuffTree extends Pair implements Comparable {
    HuffTree left, right;

    public HuffTree (int freq, String letter,
                     HuffTree left, HuffTree right) {
        this.freq = freq;
        this.letter = letter;
        this.left = left;
        this.right = right;
    }
}
```

`HuffTree` implements `Comparable` so we can put HuffTrees into a PriorityQueue. In order to implement `Comparable`, we have to provide a `compareTo` method. We could write one from scratch, but it is easier to take advantage of the version of `compareTo` in the `Pair` class.

Unfortunately, the existing method doesn't do exactly what we want. For Pairs, we give priority to the higher frequency. For HuffTrees, we want to give priority to the lower frequency. Of course, we could write a new version of `compareTo`, but that would override the version in the parent class, and we would like to be able to invoke the version in the parent class.

Apparently we are not the first people to encounter this little **Catch 22**, because the nice people who invented Java have provided a solution. The keyword `super` allows us to invoke a method that has been overridden. It's called `super` because parent classes are sometimes called **superclasses**.

Here's an example from my implementation of `HuffTree`:

```
public int compareTo (Object obj) {
    return -super.compareTo (obj);
}
```

When `compareTo` is invoked on a `HuffTree`, it turns around and invokes the overridden version of `compareTo`, and then negates the result, which has the effect of reversing the order of priority.

When a child class (also called a **subclass**) overrides a constructor, it can invoke the parent's constructor using `super`:

```
public HuffTree (int freq, String letter,
                 HuffTree left, HuffTree right) {
    super (freq, letter);
    this.left = left;
    this.right = right;
}
```

In this example, the parent's constructor initializes `freq` and `letter`, and then the child's constructor initializes `left` and `right`.

Although this feature is useful, it is also error prone. There are some odd restrictions—the parent's constructor has to be invoked first, before the other instance variables are initialized—and there are some gotchas you don't even want to know about. In general, this mechanism is like a first aid kit. If you get into real trouble, it can help you out. But you know what's even better? Don't get into trouble. In this case, it is simpler to initialize all four instance variables in the child's constructor.

Exercise 20.15   Type in the `HuffTree` class definition from this section and add a class method called `build` that takes a `FreqTab` and returns a `HuffTree`. Use the algorithm in Section 20.3.

20.5   Decoding

When we receive an encoded message, we use the Huffman tree to decode it. Here is the algorithm:

1. Start at the root of the HuffTree.

2. If the next symbol is ., go to the left child; otherwise, go to the right child.

3. If you are at a leaf node, get the letter from the node and append it to the result. Go back to the root.

4. Go to Step 2.

Consider the code ..--.--, as an example. Starting at the top of the tree, we go left-left-right and get to the letter t. Then we start at the root again, go right-left and get to the letter e. Back to the top, then right-right, and we get the letter a. If the code is well-formed, we should be at a leaf node when the code ends. In this case the message is my beverage of choice, tea.

Exercise 20.16   Use the example HuffTree to decode the following words:

   a. .-.--.--..---

   b. .-...--.-......-.

   c. ...--.-.....

   d. -.--.-...-

   Notice that until you start decoding, you can't tell how many letters there are or where the boundaries fall.

Exercise 20.17   Write a class definition for `Huffman`. The constructor should take a string that contains sample text, and it should build a frequency table and a Huffman tree.

Write a method called `decode` that takes a String of dots and dashes and that uses the Huffman tree to decode the String and return the result.

Note: even if you use the sample string in Section 20.2, you won't necessarily get the same HuffTree as in Section 20.3, so you (probably) won't be able to use your program to decode the examples in the previous exercise.

20.6   Encoding

In a sense, encoding a message is harder than decoding, because for a given letter we might have to search the tree to find the leaf node that contains the letter, and then figure out the path from the root to that node.

This process is much more efficient if we traverse the tree once, compute all the codes, and build a Map from letters to codes.

By now we have seen plenty of tree traversals, but this one is unusual because as we move around the tree, we want to keep track of the path we are on. At first, that might seem hard, but there is a natural way to perform this computation recursively. Here is the key observation: if the path from the root to a given node is represented by a string of dots and dashes called `path`, then the path to the left child of the node is `path + '-'` and the path to the right child is `path + '.'`.

Exercise 20.18

   a. Write a class definition for `CodeTab`, which extends `HashMap`.

   b. In the CodeTab definition, write a recursive method called `getCodes` that traverses a HuffTree in any order. When it reaches a leaf node, it should print the letter in the node and the code that represents the path from the root to the node.

c. Once getCodes is working, modify it so that when it reaches a leaf node, it makes an entry in the HashMap, with the letter as the key and the code as the value.

d. Write a constructor for CodeTab that takes a HuffTree as a parameter and that invokes getCodes to build the code table.

e. In the Huffman class, write a method called encode that traverses a string, looks up each character in the code table, and returns the encoding of the string. Test this method by passing the result to decode and see if you get the original string back.

20.7   Glossary

forest: A collection of trees (duh!).

Catch 22: A situation in which the apparent solution to a problem seems inevitably to preclude any solution to the problem. The term comes from Joseph Heller's book of the same title (and the excellent movie directed by Stanley Kubrick).

superclass: Another name for a parent class.

subclass: Another name for a child class.

super: A keyword that can be used to invoke an overridden method from a superclass.

Appendix A

Program development plan

If you are spending a lot of time debugging, it is probably because you do not have an effective **program development plan**.

A typical, bad program development plan goes something like this:

1. Write an entire method.

2. Write several more methods.

3. Try to compile the program.

4. Spend an hour finding syntax errors.

5. Spend an hour finding run time errors.

6. Spend three hours finding semantic errors.

The problem, of course, is the first two steps. If you write more than one method, or even an entire method, before you start the debugging process, you are likely to write more code than you can debug.

If you find yourself in this situation, the *only* solution is to remove code until you have a working program again, and then gradually build the program back up. Beginning programmers are often unwilling to do this, because their carefully crafted code is precious to them. To debug effectively, you have to be ruthless!

Here is a better program development plan:

1. Start with a working program that does something visible, like printing something.

2. Add a small number of lines of code at a time, and test the program after every change.

3. Repeat until the program does what it is supposed to do.

After every change, the program should produce some visible effect that demonstrates the new code. This approach to programming can save a lot of time. Because you only add a few lines of code at a time, it is easy to find syntax errors. Also, because each version of the program produces a visible result, you are constantly testing your mental model of how the program works. If your mental model is erroneous, you will be confronted with the conflict (and have a chance to correct it) before you have written a lot of erroneous code.

One problem with this approach is that it is often difficult to figure out a path from the starting place to a complete and correct program.

I will demonstrate by developing a method called `isIn` that takes a String and a character, and that returns a boolean: `true` if the character appears in the String and `false` otherwise.

1. The first step is to write the shortest possible method that will compile, run, and do something visible:

   ```
   public static boolean isIn (char c, String s) {
       System.out.println ("isIn");
       return false;
   }
   ```

   Of course, to test the method we have to invoke it. In `main`, or somewhere else in a working program, we need to create a simple test case.

   We'll start with a case where the character appears in the String (so we expect the result to be `true`).

   ```
   public static void main (String[] args) {
       boolean test = isIn ('n', "banana");
       System.out.println (test);
   }
   ```

   If everything goes according to plan, this code will compile, run, and print the word `isIn` and the value `false`. Of course, the answer isn't correct, but at this point we know that the method is getting invoked and returning a value.

   In my programming career, I have wasted way too much time debugging a method, only to discover that it was never getting invoked. If I had used this development plan, it never would have happened.

2. The next step is to check the parameters the method receives.

   ```
   public static boolean isIn (char c, String s) {
       System.out.println ("isIn looking for " + c);
       System.out.println ("in the String " + s);
       return false;
   }
   ```

The first print statement allows us to confirm that isIn is looking for the right letter. The second statement confirms that we are looking in the right place.

Now the output looks like this:

```
isIn looking for n
in the String banana
```

Printing the parameters might seem silly, since we know what they are supposed to be. The point is to confirm that they are what we think they are.

3. To traverse the String, we can take advantage of the code from Section 7.3. In general, it is a great idea to reuse code fragments rather than writing them from scratch.

```
public static boolean isIn (char c, String s) {
    System.out.println ("isIn looking for " + c);
    System.out.println ("in the String " + s);

    int index = 0;
    while (index < s.length()) {
        char letter = s.charAt (index);
        System.out.println (letter);
        index = index + 1;
    }
    return false;
}
```

Now when we run the program it prints the characters in the String one at a time. If all goes well, we can confirm that the loop examines all the letters in the String.

4. So far we haven't given much thought to what this method is going to do. At this point we probably need to figure out an algorithm. The simplest algorithm is a linear search, which traverses the vector and compares each element to the target word.

Happily, we have already written the code that traverses the vector. As usual, we'll proceed by adding just a few lines at a time:

```
public static boolean isIn (char c, String s) {
    System.out.println ("isIn looking for " + c);
    System.out.println ("in the String " + s);

    int index = 0;
    while (index < s.length()) {
        char letter = s.charAt (index);
        System.out.println (letter);
        if (letter == c) {
```

```
                System.out.println ("found it");
            }
            index = index + 1;
        }
        return false;
    }
```

As we traverse the String, we compare each letter to the target character. If we find it, we print something, so that when the new code executes it produces a visible effect.

5. At this point we are pretty close to working code. The next change is to return from the method if we find what we are looking for:

```
public static boolean isIn (char c, String s) {
    System.out.println ("isIn looking for " + c);
    System.out.println ("in the String " + s);

    int index = 0;
    while (index < s.length()) {
        char letter = s.charAt (index);
        System.out.println (letter);
        if (letter == c) {
            System.out.println ("found it");
            return true;
        }
        index = index + 1;
    }
    return false;
}
```

If we find the target character, we return `true`. If we get all the way through the loop without finding it, then the correct return value is `false`.

If we run the program at this point, we should get

```
isIn looking for n
in the String banana
b
a
n
found it
true
```

6. The next step is to make sure that the other test cases work correctly. First, we should confirm that the method returns `false` if the character is not in the String. Then we should check some of the typical troublemakers, like an empty String, `""`, or a String with a single character.

As always, this kind of testing can help find bugs if there are any, but it can't tell you if the method is correct.

7. The penultimate step is to remove or comment out the print statements.

```java
public static boolean isIn (char c, String s) {
    int index = 0;
    while (index < s.length()) {
        char letter = s.charAt (index);
        if (letter == c) {
    return true;
        }
        index = index + 1;
    }
    return false;
}
```

Commenting out the print statements is a good idea if you think you might have to revisit this method later. But if this is the final version of the method, and you are convinced that it is correct, you should remove them.

Removing the comments allows you to see the code most clearly, which can help you spot any remaining problems.

If there is anything about the code that is not obvious, you should add comments to explain it. Resist the temptation to translate the code line by line. For example, no one needs this:

```java
// if letter equals c, return true
if (letter == c) {
    return true;
}
```

You should use comments to explain non-obvious code, to warn about conditions that could cause errors, and to document any assumptions that are built into the code. Also, before each method, it is a good idea to write an abstract description of what the method does.

8. The final step is to examine the code and see if you can convince yourself that it is correct. At this point we know that the method is syntactically correct, because it compiles. To check for run time errors, you should find every statement that can cause an error and figure out what conditions cause the error.

In this method, the only statement that can cause a run-time error is `s.charAt (index)`. This statement will fail if s is null or if the index is out of bounds. Since we get s as a parameter, we can't be sure that it is not null; all we can do is check. In general, it is a good idea for methods to make sure their parameters are legal. The structure of the while loop ensures that index is always between 0 and s.length-1. If we check all the problem conditions, or prove that they cannot happen, then we can prove that this method will not cause a run time error.

We haven't proven yet that the method is semantically correct, but by proceeding incrementally, we have avoided many possible errors. For example, we already know that the method is getting parameters correctly and that the loop traverses the entire String. We also know that it is comparing characters successfully, and returning `true` if it finds the target. Finally, we know that if the loop exits, the target is not in the String.

Short of a formal proof, that is probably the best we can do.

Appendix B

Debugging

There are a few different kinds of errors that can occur in a program, and it is useful to distinguish between them in order to track them down more quickly.

- Compile-time errors are produced by the compiler and usually indicate that there is something wrong with the syntax of the program. Example: omitting the semi-colon at the end of a statement.

- Run-time errors are produced by the run-time system if something goes wrong while the program is running. Most run-time errors are Exceptions. Example: an infinite recursion eventually causes a StackOverflowException.

- Semantic errors are problems with a program that compiles and runs, but doesn't do the right thing. Example: an expression may not be evaluated in the order you expect, yielding an unexpected result.

The first step in debugging is to figure out which kind of error you are dealing with. Although the following sections are organized by error type, there are some techniques that are applicable in more than one situation.

B.1 Compile-time errors

The best kind of debugging is the kind you don't have to do, because you avoid making errors in the first place. In the previous section, I suggested a program development plan that minimizes the number of errors you will make and makes it easy to find them when you do. The key is to start with a working program and add small amounts of code at a time. That way, when there is an error, you will have a pretty good idea where it is.

Nevertheless, you might find yourself in one of the following situations. For each situation, I make some suggestions about how to proceed.

The compiler is spewing error messages.

If the compiler reports 100 error messages, that doesn't mean there are 100 errors in your program. When the compiler encounters an error, it often gets thrown off track for a while. It tries to recover and pick up again after the first error, but sometimes it fails, and it reports spurious errors.

In general, only the first error message is reliable. I suggest that you only fix one error at a time, and then recompile the program. You may find that one semi-colon "fixes" 100 errors. Of course, if you see several legitimate error messages, you might as well fix more than one bug per compilation attempt.

I'm getting a weird compiler message and it won't go away.

First of all, read the error message carefully. It is written in terse jargon, but often there is a kernel of information there that is carefully hidden.

If nothing else, the message will tell you where in the program the problem occurred. Actually, it tells you where the compiler was when it noticed a problem, which is not necessarily where the error is. Use the information the compiler gives you as a guideline, but if you don't see an error where the compiler is pointing, broaden the search.

Generally the error will be prior to the location of the error message, but there are cases where it will be somewhere else entirely. For example, if you get an error message at a method invocation, the actual error may be in the method definition.

If you are building the program incrementally, you should have a good idea about where the error is. It will be in the last line you added.

If you are copying code from a book, start by comparing your code to the book's code very carefully. Check every character. At the same time, remember that the book might be wrong, so if you see something that looks like a syntax error, it might be.

If you don't find the error quickly, take a breath and look more broadly at the entire program. Now is a good time to go through the whole program and make sure it is indented properly. I won't say that good indentation makes it easy to find syntax errors, but bad indentation sure makes it harder.

Now, start examining the code for the common syntax errors.

1. Check that all parentheses and brackets are balanced and properly nested. All method definitions should be nested within a class definition. All program statements should be within a method definition.

2. Remember that upper case letters are not the same as lower case letters.

3. Check for semi-colons at the end of statements (and no semi-colons after squiggly-braces).

4. Make sure that any strings in the code have matching quotation marks. Make sure that you use double-quotes for Strings and single quotes for characters.

5. For each assignment statement, make sure that the type on the left is the same as the type on the right. Make sure that the expression on the left is a variable name or something else that you can assign a value to (like an element of an array).

6. For each method invocation, make sure that the arguments you provide are in the right order, and have right type, and that the object you are invoking the method on is the right type.

7. If you are invoking a fruitful method, make sure you are doing something with the result. If you are invoking a void method, make sure you are not *trying* to do something with the result.

8. If you are invoking an object method, make sure you are invoking it on an object with the right type. If you are invoking a class method from outside the class where it is defined, make sure you specify the class name.

9. Inside an object method you can refer to the instance variables without specifying an object. If you try that in a class method, you will get a confusing message like, "Static reference to non-static variable."

If nothing works, move on to the next section...

I can't get my program to compile no matter what I do.

If the compiler says there is an error and you don't see it, that might be because you and the compiler are not looking at the same code. Check your development environment to make sure the program you are editing is the program the compiler is compiling. If you are not sure, try putting an obvious and deliberate syntax error right at the beginning of the program. Now compile again. If the compiler doesn't find the new error, there is probably something wrong with the way you set up the project.

Otherwise, if you have examined the code thoroughly, it is time for desperate measures. You should start over with a program that you can compile and then gradually add your code back.

- Make a copy of the file you are working on. If you are working on Fred.java, make a copy called Fred.java.old.

- Delete about half the code from Fred.java. Try compiling again.
  - If the program compiles now, then you know the error is in the other half. Bring back about half of the code you deleted and repeat.
  - If the program still doesn't compile, the error must be in this half. Delete about half of the code and repeat.

- Once you have found and fixed the error, start bringing back the code you deleted, a little bit at a time.

This process is called "debugging by bisection." As an alternative, you can comment out chunks of code instead of deleting them. For really sticky syntax problems, though, I think deleting is more reliable—you don't have to worry about the syntax of the comments, and by making the program smaller you make it more readable.

I did what the compiler told me to do, but it still doesn't work.

Some compiler messages come with tidbits of advice, like "class Golfer must be declared abstract. It does not define int compareTo(java.lang.Object) from interface java.lang.Comparable." It sounds like the compiler is telling you to declare Golfer as an abstract class, and if you are reading this book, you probably don't know what that is or how to do it.

Fortunately, the compiler is wrong. The solution in this case is to make sure `Golfer` has a method called `compareTo` that takes an `Object` as a parameter.

In general, don't let the compiler lead you by the nose. Error messages give you evidence that something is wrong, but they can be misleading, and their "advice" is often wrong.

B.2   Run-time errors

My program hangs.

If a program stops and seems to be doing nothing, we say it is "hanging." Often that means that it is caught in an infinite loop or an infinite recursion.

- If there is a particular loop that you suspect is the problem, add a print statement immediately before the loop that says "entering the loop" and another immediately after that says "exiting the loop."

    Run the program. If you get the first message and not the second, you've got an infinite loop. Go to the section titled "Infinite loop."

- Most of the time an infinite recursion will cause the program to run for a while and then produce a StackOverflowException. If that happens, go to the section titled "Infinite recursion."

    If you are not getting a StackOverflowException, but you suspect there is a problem with a recursive method, you can still use the techniques in the infinite recursion section.

- If neither of those things works, start testing other loops and other recursive methods.

- If none of these suggestions helps, then it is possible that you don't understand the flow of execution in your program. Go to the section titled "Flow of execution."

Infinite loop

If you think you have an infinite loop and think you know what loop is causing the problem, add a print statement at the end of the loop that prints the values of the variables in the condition, and the value of the condition.

For example,

```
while (x > 0 && y < 0) {
    // do something to x
    // do something to y

    System.out.println ("x: " + x);
    System.out.println ("y: " + y);
    System.out.println ("condition: " + (x > 0 && y < 0));
}
```

Now when you run the program you will see three lines of output for each time through the loop. The last time through the loop, the condition should be false. If the loop keeps going, you will be able to see the values of x and y and you might figure out why they are not being updated correctly.

Infinite recursion

Most of the time an infinite recursion will cause the program to run for a while and then produce a StackOverflowException.

If you know that a method is causing an infinite recursion, start by checking to make sure that there is a base case. In other words, there should be some condition that will cause the method to return without making a recursive invocation. If not, then you need to rethink the algorithm and identify a base case.

If there is a base case, but the program doesn't seem to be reaching it, add a print statement at the beginning of the method that prints the parameters. Now when you run the program you will see a few lines of output every time the method is invoked, and you will see the parameters. If the parameters are not moving toward the base case, you will get some ideas about why not.

Flow of execution

If you are not sure how the flow of execution is moving through your program, add print statements to the beginning of each method with a message like "entering method foo," where foo is the name of the method.

Now when you run the program it will print a trace of each method as it is invoked.

It is often useful to print the parameters each method receives when it is invoked. When you run the program, check whether the parameters are reasonable, and check for one of the classic errors—providing parameters in the wrong order.

When I run the program I get an Exception.

If something goes wrong during run time, the Java run-time system prints a message that includes the name of the exception, the line of the program where the problem occurred, and a stack trace.

The stack trace includes the method that is currently running, and then the method that invoked it, and then the method that invoked *that*, and so on. In other words, it traces the stack of method invocations that got you to where you are.

The first step is to examine the place in the program where the error occurred and see if you can figure out what happened.

NullPointerException: You tried to access an instance variable or invoke a method on an object that is currently `null`. You should figure out what variable is `null` and then figure out how it got to be that way.

Remember that when you declare a variable with an object type, it is initially `null`, until you assign a value to it. For example, this code causes a NullPointerException:

```
Point blank;
System.out.println (blank.x);
```

ArrayIndexOutOfBoundsException: The index you are using to access an array is either negative or greater than `array.length-1`. If you can find the site where the problem is, add a print statement immediately before it to print the value of the index and the length of the array. Is the array the right size? Is the index the right value?

Now work your way backwards through the program and see where the array and the index come from. Find the nearest assignment statement and see if it is doing the right thing.

If either one is a parameter, go to the place where the method is invoked and see where the values are coming from.

StackOverFlowException: See "Infinite recursion."

I added so many print statements I get inundated with output.

One of the problems with using print statements for debugging is that you can end up buried in output. There are two ways to proceed: either simplify the output or simplify the program.

To simplify the output, you can remove or comment out print statements that aren't helping, or combine them, or format the output so it is easier to understand. As you develop a program, you will conceive ways to visualize the execution of the program, and develop code that generates concise, informative visualizations.

To simplify the program, there are several things you can do. First, scale down the problem the program is working on. For example, if you are sorting an array, sort a *small* array. If the program takes input from the user, give it the simplest input that causes the error.

Second, clean up the program. Remove dead code and reorganize the program to make it as easy to read as possible. For example, if you suspect that the error is in a deeply-nested part of the program, try rewriting that part with simpler structure. If you suspect a large method, try splitting it into smaller methods and testing them separately.

Often the process of finding the minimal test case leads you to the bug. For example, if you find that a program works when the array has an even number of elements, but not when it has an odd number, that gives you a clue about what is going on.

Similarly, rewriting a piece of code can help you find subtle bugs. If you make a change that you think doesn't affect the program, and it does, that can tip you off.

B.3 Semantic errors

My program doesn't work.

In some ways semantic errors are the hardest, because the compiler and the run-time system provide no information about what is wrong. Only you know what the program was supposed to do, and only you know that it isn't doing it.

The first step is to make a connection between the program text and the behavior you are seeing. You need a hypothesis about what the program is actually doing. One of the things that makes this hard is that computers run so fast. You will often wish that you could slow the program down to human speed, but there is no straightforward way to do that, and even if there were, it is not really a good way to debug.

Here are some questions to ask yourself:

- Is there something the program was supposed to do, but doesn't seem to be happening? Find the section of the code that performs that function and make sure it is executing when you think it should. Add a print statement to the beginning of the suspect methods.

- Is something happening that shouldn't? Find code in your program that performs that function and see if it is executing when it shouldn't.

- Is a section of code producing an effect that is not what you expected? Make sure that you understand the code in question, especially if it involves invocations to built-in Java methods. Read the documentation for the methods you invoke. Try out the methods by invoking the methods directly with simple test cases, and check the results.

In order to program, you need to have a mental model of how programs work. If your program that doesn't do what you expect, very often the problem is not in the program; it's in your mental model.

The best way to correct your mental model is to break the program into its components (usually the classes and methods) and test each component independently. Once you find the discrepancy between your model and reality, you can solve the problem.

Of course, you should be building and testing components as you develop the program. If you encounter a problem, there should be only a small amount of new code that is not known to be correct.

Here are some common semantic errors that you might want to check for:

- If you use the assignment operator, =, instead of the equality operator, ==, in the condition of an if, while or for statement, you might get an expression that is syntactically legal, but it doesn't do what you expect.

- When you apply the equality operator, ==, to an object, it checks shallow equality. If you meant to check deep equality, you should use the equals method (or define one, for user-defined objects).

- Some Java libraries expect user-defined objects to define methods like equals. If you don't define them yourself, you will inherit the default behavior from the parent class, which may not be what you want.

- Inheritance can lead to subtle semantic errors, because you may be executing inherited code without realizing it. To make sure you understand the flow of execution in your program, see the section titled "Flow of Execution."

I've got a big hairy expression and it doesn't do what I expect.

Writing complex expressions is fine as long as they are readable, but they can be hard to debug. It is often a good idea to break a complex expression into a series of assignments to temporary variables.

For example:

```
rect.setLocation (rect.getLocation().translate
                    (-rect.getWidth(), -rect.getHeight()));
```

Can be rewritten as

```
int dx = -rect.getWidth();
int dy = -rect.getHeight();
Point location = rect.getLocation();
Point newLocation = location.translate (dx, dy);
rect.setLocation (newLocation);
```

The explicit version is easier to read, because the variable names provide additional documentation, and easier to debug, because we can check the types of the intermediate variables and display their values.

Another problem that can occur with big expressions is that the order of evaluation may not be what you expect. For example, if you are translating the expression $\frac{x}{2\pi}$ into Java, you might write

```
double y = x / 2 * Math.PI;
```

That is not correct, because multiplication and division have the same precedence, and are evaluated from left to right. So this expression computes $x\pi/2$.

A good way to debug expressions is to add parentheses to make the order of evaluation explicit.

```
double y = x / (2 * Math.PI);
```

Any time you are not sure of the order of evaluation, use parentheses. Not only will the program be correct (in the sense of doing what you intend); it will also be more readable for other people who haven't memorized the rules of precedence.

I've got a method that doesn't return what I expect.

If you have a return statement with a complex expression, you don't have a chance to print the return value before returning. Again, you can use a temporary variable. For example, instead of

```
public Rectangle intersection (Rectangle a, Rectangle b) {
    return new Rectangle (
        Math.min (a.x, b.x),
        Math.min (a.y, b.y),
        Math.max (a.x+a.width, b.x+b.width)-Math.min (a.x, b.x)
        Math.max (a.y+a.height, b.y+b.height)-Math.min (a.y, b.y) );
}
```

You could write

```
public Rectangle intersection (Rectangle a, Rectangle b) {
    int x1 = Math.min (a.x, b.x);
    int y2 = Math.min (a.y, b.y);
    int x2 = Math.max (a.x+a.width, b.x+b.width);
    int y2 = Math.max (a.y+a.height, b.y+b.height);
    Rectangle rect = new Rectangle (x1, y1, x2-x1, y2-y1);
    return rect;
}
```

Now you have the opportunity to display any of the intermediate variables before returning.

My print statement isn't doing anything

If you use the `println` method, the output gets displayed immediately, but if you use `print` (at least in some environments) the output gets stored without being displayed until the next newline character gets output. If the program terminates without producing a newline, you may never see the stored output.

If you suspect that this is happening to you, try changing some or all of the `print` statements to `println`.

I'm really, really stuck and I need help

First of all, try getting away from the computer for a few minutes. Computers emit waves that affect the brain, causing the following symptoms:

- Frustration and/or rage.

- Superstitious beliefs ("the computer hates me") and magical thinking ("the program only works when I wear my hat backwards").

- Random walk programming (the attempt to program by writing every possible program and choosing the one that does the right thing).

If you find yourself suffering from any of these symptoms, get up and go for a walk. When you are calm, think about the program. What is it doing? What are some possible causes of that behavior? When was the last time you had a working program, and what did you do next?

Sometimes it just takes time to find a bug. I often find bugs when I am away from the computer and I let my mind wander. Some of the best places to find bugs are trains, showers, and in bed, just before you fall asleep.

No, I really need help.

It happens. Even the best programmers occasionally get stuck. Sometimes you work on a program so long that you can't see the error. A fresh pair of eyes is just the thing.

Before you bring someone else in, make sure you have exhausted the techniques described here. You program should be as simple as possible, and you should be working on the smallest input that causes the error. You should have print statements in the appropriate places (and the output they produce should be comprehensible). You should understand the problem well enough to describe it concisely.

When you bring someone in to help, be sure to give them the information they need.

- What kind of bug is it? Compile-time, run-time, or semantic?

- If the bug occurs at compile-time or run-time, what is the error message, and what part of the program does it indicate?

- What was the last thing you did before this error occurred? What were the last lines of code that you wrote, or what is the new test case that fails?

- What have you tried so far, and what have you learned?

Often you will find that by the time you have explained the problem to someone else, you will see the answer. This phenomenon is so pervasive that some people recommend a debugging technique called "rubber ducking." Here's how it works:

1. Buy a standard-issue rubber duck.

2. When you are really stuck on a problem, put the rubber duck on the desk in front of you and say, "Rubber duck, I am stuck on a problem. Here's what's happening..."

3. Explain the problem to the rubber duck.

4. See the solution.

5. Thank the rubber duck.

I found the bug!

Most often, when you find a bug, it is obvious how to fix it. But not always. Sometimes what seems to be a bug is really an indication that you don't really understand the program, or there is an error in your algorithm. In these cases, you might have to rethink the algorithm, or adjust your mental model of the program. Take some time away from the computer to think about the program, work through some test cases by hand, or draw diagrams to represent the computation.

When you fix a bug, don't just dive in and start making new errors. Take a second to think about what kind of bug it was, why you made the error in the first place, how the error manifested itself, and what you could have done to find it faster. Next time you see something similar, you will be able to find the bug more quickly.

Appendix C

Input and Output in Java

System objects

`System` is the name of the built-in class that contains methods and objects used to get input from the keyboard, print text on the screen, and do file input/output (I/0).

`System.out` is the name of the object we use to to display text on the screen. When you invoke `print` and `println`, you invoke them on the object named `System.out`.

Interestingly, you can print `System.out`:

`System.out.println (System.out);`

The output is:

`java.io.PrintStream@80cc0e5`

As usual, when Java prints an object, it prints the type of the object, which is `PrintStream`, the package in which that type is defined, `java.io`, and a unique identifier for the object. On my machine the identifier is 80cc0e5, but if you run the same code, you will probably get something different.

There is also an object named `System.in` that has type `BufferedInputStream`. `System.in` makes it possible to get input from the keyboard. Unfortunately, it does not make it easy to get input from the keyboard.

Keyboard input

First, you have to use `System.in` to create a new `InputStreamReader`.

`    InputStreamReader in = new InputStreamReader (System.in);`

Then you use `in` to create a new `BufferedReader`:

`    BufferedReader keyboard = new BufferedReader (in);`

The point of all this manipulation is that there is a method you can invoke on a BufferedReader, called readLine, that gets input from the keyboard and converts it into a String. For example:

```
String s = keyboard.readLine ();
System.out.println (s);
```

reads a line from the keyboard and prints the result.

There is only one problem. There are things that can go wrong when you invoke readLine, and they might cause an IOException. There is a rule in Java that if a method might cause an exception, it should say so. The syntax looks like this:

```
public static void main (String[] args) throws IOException {
    // body of main
}
```

This indicates that main might "throw" an IOException. You can think of throwing an exception as similar to throwing a tantrum.

File input

Reading input from a file is equally stupid. Here is an example:

```
public static void main (String[] args)
    throws FileNotFoundException, IOException {

    processFile ("/usr/dict/words");
}

public static void processFile (String filename)
    throws FileNotFoundException, IOException {

    FileReader fileReader = new FileReader (filename);
    BufferedReader in = new BufferedReader (fileReader);

    while (true) {
        String s = in.readLine();
        if (s == null) break;
        System.out.println (s);
    }
}
```

This program reads each line of the named file (/usr/dict/words) into a String and then prints the line. Again, the declaration throws FileNotFoundException, IOException is required by the compiler. The object types FileReader and BufferedReader are part of the insanely complicated class hierarchy Java uses to do incredibly common, simple things. Other than that, there is not much value in the details of how this code fragment works.

Appendix D

Graphics

D.1   Slates and Graphics objects

There are a number of ways to create graphics in Java, some more complicated
than others. To keep things simple, I have created a object type called Slate
that represents a surface you can draw on. When you create a Slate, a new
blank window appears. The Slate contains a Graphics object, which you use
to draw on the slate.

The methods that pertain to Graphics objects are defined in the built-in
Graphics class. The methods that pertain to Slates are defined in the Slate
class, which is shown in Section D.6.

Use the new operator to create a new Slate object:

```
Slate slate = new Slate (500, 500);
```

The parameters are the width and height of the window. The return value gets
assigned to a variable named slate. There is no conflict between the name
of the class (with an upper-case "S") and the name of the variable (with a
lower-case "s").

The next method we need is getSlateGraphics, which returns a Graphics
object. You can think of a Graphics object as a piece of chalk.

```
Graphics g = slate.getSlateGraphics ();
```

Using the name g is conventional, but we could have called it anything.

D.2   Invoking methods on a Graphics object

In order to draw things on the screen, you invoke methods on the graphics
object.

```
g.setColor (Color.black);
```

setColor changes the current color, in this case to black. Everything that gets drawn will be black, until we use setColor again.

Color.black is a special value provided by the Color class, just as Math.PI is a special value provided by the Math class. Color, you will be happy to hear, provides a palette of other colors, including:

```
black     blue     cyan   darkGray   gray    lightGray
magenta   orange   pink   red        white   yellow
```

To draw on the Slate, we can invoke draw methods on the Graphics object. For example:

```
g.drawOval (x, y, width, height);
```

drawOval takes four integers as arguments. These arguments specify a **bounding box**, which is the rectangle in which the oval will be drawn (as shown in the figure). The bounding box itself is not drawn; only the oval is. The bounding box is like a guideline. Bounding boxes are always oriented horizontally or vertically; they are never at a funny angle.

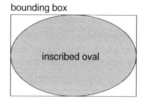

If you think about it, there are lots of ways to specify the location and size of a rectangle. You could give the location of the center or any of the corners, along with the height and width. Or, you could give the location of opposing corners. The choice is arbitrary, but in any case it will require the same number of parameters: four.

By convention, the usual way to specify a bounding box is to give the location of the *upper-left* corner and the width and height. The usual way to specify a location is to use a **coordinate system**.

D.3   Coordinates

You are probably familiar with Cartesian coordinates in two dimensions, in which each location is identified by an x-coordinate (distance along the x-axis) and a y-coordinate. By convention, Cartesian coordinates increase to the right and up, as shown in the figure.

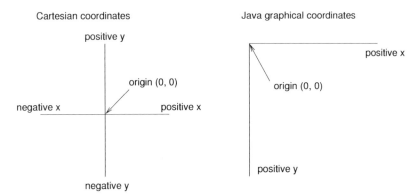

Annoyingly, it is conventional for computer graphics systems to use a variation on Cartesian coordinates in which the origin is in the upper-left corner of the screen or window, and the direction of the positive y-axis is *down*. Java follows this convention.

The unit of measure is called a **pixel**; a typical screen is about 1000 pixels wide. Coordinates are always integers. If you want to use a floating-point value as a coordinate, you have to round it off to an integer (See Section 3.2).

D.4 A lame Mickey Mouse

Let's say we want to draw a picture of Mickey Mouse. We can use the oval we just drew as the face, and then add ears. Before we do that it is a good idea to break the program up into two methods. `main` will create the `Slate` and `Graphics` objects and then invoke `draw`, which does the actual drawing.

When we are done invoking `draw` methods, we have to invoke `slate.repaint` to make the changes appear on the screen.

```java
public static void main (String[] args) {
  int width = 500;
  int height = 500;

  Slate slate = Slate.makeSlate (width, height);
  Graphics g = Slate.getGraphics (slate);

  g.setColor (Color.black);
  draw (g, 0, 0, width, height);
  slate.repaint ();
}

public static void draw
            (Graphics g, int x, int y, int width, int height) {
  g.drawOval (x, y, width, height);
```

```
    g.drawOval (x, y, width/2, height/2);
    g.drawOval (x+width/2, y, width/2, height/2);
}
```

The parameters for `draw` are the `Graphics` object and a bounding box. `draw` invokes `drawOval` three times, to draw Mickey's face and two ears. The following figure shows the bounding boxes for the ears.

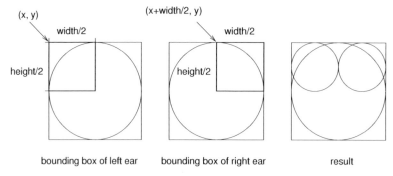

bounding box of left ear   bounding box of right ear   result

As shown in the figure, the coordinates of the upper-left corner of the bounding box for the left ear are (x, y). The coordinates for the right ear are (x+width/2, y). In both cases, the width and height of the ears are half the width and height of the original bounding box.

Notice that the coordinates of the ear boxes are all relative to the location (x and y) and size (width and height) of the original bounding box. As a result, we can use `draw` to draw a Mickey Mouse (albeit a lame one) anywhere on the screen in any size.

Exercise D.1   Modify the arguments passed to `draw` so that Mickey is one half the height and width of the screen, and centered.

D.5   Other drawing commands

Another drawing command with the same parameters as `drawOval` is

```
    drawRect (int x, int y, int width, int height)
```

Here I am using a standard format for documenting the name and parameters of methods. This information is sometimes called the method's **interface** or **prototype**. Looking at this prototype, you can tell what types the parameters are and (based on their names) infer what they do. Here's another example:

```
drawLine (int x1, int y1, int x2, int y2)
```

The use of parameter names x1, x2, y1 and y2 suggests that `drawLine` draws a line from the point (x1, y1) to the point (x2, y2).

One other command you might want to try is

```
drawRoundRect (int x, int y, int width, int height,
        int arcWidth, int arcHeight)
```

The first four parameters specify the bounding box of the rectangle; the remaining two parameters indicate how rounded the corners should be, specifying the horizontal and vertical diameter of the arcs at the corners.

There are also "fill" versions of these commands, that not only draw the outline of a shape, but also fill it in. The interfaces are identical; only the names have been changed:

```
fillOval (int x, int y, int width, int height)
fillRect (int x, int y, int width, int height)
fillRoundRect (int x, int y, int width, int height,
        int arcWidth, int arcHeight)
```

There is no such thing as `fillLine`—it just doesn't make sense.

D.6   The Slate Class

```
import java.awt.*;

class Example {

    // demonstrate simple use of the Slate class

    public static void main (String[] args) {
        int width = 500;
        int height = 500;

        Slate slate = new Slate (width, height);
        Graphics g = slate.getSlateGraphics ();

        g.setColor (Color.blue);

        draw (g, 0, 0, width, height);
        slate.repaint ();

        anim (slate);
    }

    // draw demonstrates a recursive pattern

    public static void draw (Graphics g, int x, int y, int width, int height
        if (height < 3) return;

        g.drawOval (x, y, width, height);

        draw (g, x, y+height/2, width/2, height/2);
```

```
        draw (g, x+width/2, y+height/2, width/2, height/2);
    }

    // anim demonstrates a simple animation

    public static void anim (Slate slate) {
        Graphics g = slate.image.getGraphics ();
        g.setColor (Color.red);

        for (int i=-100; i<500; i+=10) {
            g.drawOval (i, 100, 100, 100);
            slate.repaint ();
            try {
                Thread.sleep(10);
            } catch (InterruptedException e) {}
        }
    }
}

class Slate extends Frame {

    // image is a buffer: when Slate users draw things, they
    // draw on the buffer.  When the Slate gets painted, we
    // copy the image onto the screen.
    Image image;

    public Slate (int width, int height) {
        setBounds (100, 100, width, height);
        setBackground (Color.white);
        setVisible (true);
        image = createImage (width, height);
    }

    // when a Slate user asks for a Graphics object, we give
    // them one from the off-screen buffer.

    public Graphics getSlateGraphics () {
        return image.getGraphics ();
    }

    // normally update erases the screen and invokes paint, but
    // since we are overwriting the whole screen anyway, it is
    // slightly faster to override update and avoid clearing the
    // screen

    public void update (Graphics g) {
        paint (g);
```

```
    }

    // paint copies the off-screen buffer onto the screen

    public void paint (Graphics g) {
        if (image == null) return;
        g.drawImage (image, 0, 0, null);
    }
}
```

Exercise D.2

The purpose of this assignment is to practice using methods as a way of organizing and encapsulating complex tasks.

WARNING: It is very important that you take this assignment one step at a time, and get each step working correctly before you proceed. More importantly, make sure you understand each step before you proceed.

   a. Create a new program named `Snowperson.java`, Type in the code or get it from
      . Run it. A new window should appear with a bunch of blue circles and a bunch
      of red circles. This window is the Slate.

      Unlike the other programs we ran, there is no console window. However, if
      you add a `print` or `println` statement, the console window will appear. For
      graphical applications, the console is useful for debugging.

      I found that I could not close the Slate window by clicking on it, which is
      probably good, because it will remind you to quit from the interpreter every
      time you run the program.

   b. Look over the source code as it currently exists and make sure you understand
      all the code in `draw`. The method named `anim` is there for your entertainment,
      but we will not be using it for this assignment. You should remove it.

   c. The `Slate` class appears immediately after the `cs151` class. You might want to
      check it out, although a lot of it will not make sense at this point.

   d. Fiddle with the statements in `draw` and see what effect your changes have. Try
      out the various drawing commands. For more information about them, see
      `http://java.sun.com/products/jdk/1.1/docs/api/java.awt.Graphics.html`

   e. Change the width or height of the `Slate` and run the program again. You should
      see that the image adjusts its size and proportions to fit the size of the window.
      You are going to write drawing programs that do the same thing. The idea is to
      use variables and parameters to make programs more general; in this case the
      generality is that we can draw images that are any size or location.

Use a bounding box

The arguments that `draw` receives (not including the graphic object) make up a
bounding box. The bounding box specifies the invisible rectangle in which `draw`
should draw.

   a. Inside draw, create a new bounding box that is the same height as the `Slate`
      but only one-third of the width, and centered. When I say "create a bounding
      box" I mean define four local variables that will contain the location and size.
      You are going to pass this bounding box as an argument to `drawSnowperson`.

b. Create a new method named `drawSnowperson` that takes the same parameters as `draw`. To start, it should draw a single oval that fills the entire bounding box (in other words, it should have the same position and location as the bounding box).

c. Change the size of the `Slate` and run your program again. The size and proportion of the oval should adjust so that, no matter what the size the `Slate` is, the oval is the same height, one-third of the width, and centered.

Make a snowperson

a. Modify `drawSnowperson` so that it draws three ovals stacked on top of each other like a snowperson. The height and width of the snowperson should fill the bounding box, as in the figure on the quiz.

b. Change the size of the `Slate` and run your program again. Again, the snowperson should adjust so that the snowperson always touches the top and bottom of the screen, and the three ovals touch, and the proportion of the three ovals stays the same.

c. At this point, show your program to me so that I can make sure you understand the basic ideas behind this assignment. You should definitely not continue work on this assignment until I have seen your program.

Draw the snowperson *American Gothic*

a. Modify `draw` so that it draws two snowpeople side by side. One of them should be the same height as the window; the other should be 90% of the window height. (Snowpeople exhibit a sexual dimorphism in which females are roughly 10% smaller than males.)

Their widths should be proportional to their heights, and their bounding boxes should be adjacent (which means that the drawn ovals probably will not quite touch). The pair should be centered, meaning that there is the same amount of space on each side.

With a corn-cob pipe...

a. Write a method called `drawFace` that takes the same number and type of parameters as `drawSnowperson`, and that draws a simple face within the given bounding box. Two eyes will suffice, but you can get as elaborate as you like.

Again, as you resize the window, the proportions of the face should not change, and all the features should fit within the oval (with the possible exception of ears).

b. Modify `drawSnowperson` so that it invokes `drawFace` in order to fill in the top oval (the face). The bounding box you pass to `drawFace` should be the same as the bounding box that created the face oval.

Give the Snowpeople T-shirts

a. Add a new method called `drawShirt` that takes the usual parameters and that draws some sort of T-shirt logo within the bounding box. You can use any of the drawing commands, although you might want to avoid `drawString` because it is not easy to guarantee that the string will fit within the bounding box.

    b. Modify `drawSnowperson` so that it invokes `drawShirt` in order to emblazon something on the chest (middle oval) of each snowperson.

Make Mrs. Snowperson pregnant

    a. I realize that this is a little risqué, but there is a point. Modify `draw` so that after drawing Mrs. Snowperson, it draws a baby snowperson inside her abdomen oval.

       Notice that adding something to `draw` affects just one snowperson. Adding something to `drawSnowperson` affects all snowpeople.

Note: The next part of the assignment will not make sense until after class on Friday, so I recommend stopping here (if you get this far in lab).

Make all snowpeople pregnant

Ok, now let's imagine that instead of making a particular snowperson pregnant, we want to make all snowpeople pregnant. Instead of adding a line to `draw`, we would add a line to `drawSnowperson`. What would that line do? It would invoke drawSnowperson! Can you do that? Can you invoke a method from within itself? Well, yes, you can, but you have to be careful.

SO DON'T DO THIS YET!!!

Think for a minute. What if we draw a big snowperson, and then put a small snowperson in the abdomen oval. Then we have to put an even smaller snowperson in the small abdomen oval, and so on and so on. The problem is, it would never stop. We would be drawing smaller and smaller snowpeople until doomsday!

One solution is to pick a minimum snowperson size, and say that below that size, we refuse to draw any more snowpeople.

    a. Add a line at the beginning of drawSnowperson that checks the height of the bounding box and returns immediately if it is less than 10.

```
if (height < 10) return;
```

    b. Now that you have that line, it is safe to add code at the end of the method so that after drawing the ovals, and the face, and the t-shirt, it invokes drawSnowperson to put a small snowperson in the abdomen.

Exercise D.3

    a. Create a new program named `Moire.java`.

    b. Add the following code to your project, and replace the contents of `draw` with a single line that invokes `moire`.

```
public static void moire
        (Graphics g, int x, int y, int width, int height) {
    int i = 1;
    while (i<width) {
        g.drawOval (0, 0, i, i);
        i = i + 2;
    }
}
```

c. Look at the code before you run it and draw a sketch of what you expect it to do. Now run it. Did you get what you expected? For a partial explanation of what is going on, see the following:

http://math.hws.edu/xJava/other/Moire1.html
http://tqd.advanced.org/3543/moirelesson.html

d. Modify the program so that the space between the circles is larger or smaller. See what happens to the image.

e. Modify the program so that the circles are drawn in the center of the screen and concentric, as in the following figure. Unlike in the figure, the distance between the circles should be small enough that the Moiré interference is apparent.

concentric circles   radial Moire pattern

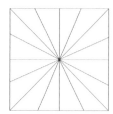

f. Write a method named `radial` that draws a radial set of line segments as shown in the figure, but they should be close enough together to create a Moiré pattern.

g. Just about any kind of graphical pattern can generate Moiré-like interference patterns. Play around and see what you can create.

25, 29, 33

Index

Made in the USA
Lexington, KY
09 October 2013